Living Powers:
The Arts in Education

In Memory of

Louis Arnaud Reid (1895–1986)

+   +   +   +   +

So emotion and cognition are no longer divided in the holistic experience of art, but completely united in existential knowledge of art. It is this which makes experience of the art of such importance, in itself, for everyone throughout life and in education, where the very existence of the arts is more than ever threatened. Children are stuffed with 'cognitive' facts, and in these days particularly, facts of highly specialised knowledge the acquisition of which is supposed to qualify them for jobs. Bored with school and starved there of emotional satisfaction, they turn for it to the stereotypes of commercial entertainment and are stuffed instead with wholly false conceptions of the human condition. Back in school, there is a chance that the new 'information technology' could ease much drudgery of factual learning, releasing time and energy for more 'creative' insights into the understanding of both fact and value — including as a major field the arts. The crucial question for humane education is, 'Will it?'

Louis Arnaud Reid
in his *Language, Arts and Education*
Open Seminar at the University of Sussex
23 October 1984

Living Powers:
The Arts in Education

Edited by
Peter Abbs

 The Falmer Press

(A Member of the Taylor & Francis Group)
London, New York and Philadelphia

UK   The Falmer Press, Falmer House, Barcombe, Lewes, East Sussex, BN8 5DL

USA   The Falmer Press, Taylor & Francis Inc., 242 Cherry Street, Philadelphia, PA 19106-1906

First published 1987

Library of Congress Cataloging in Publication Data

Living powers.

  Bibliography: p.
  Includes index.
  1. Arts—Study and teaching (Elementary). 2. Education, Elementary—Curricula. I. Abbs, Peter, 1942–
LB1591.L58   1987   372.5′044   87-13651
ISBN 1-85000-167-7
ISBN 1-85000-168-5 (pbk.)

Jacket design by Caroline Archer

Typeset in 11/13 Bembo by
Imago Publishing Ltd, Thame, Oxon

Printed in Great Britain by Taylor & Francis (Printers) Ltd, Basingstoke

Contents

Contents

List of Plates and Illustrations

Preface

The illuminating chapters in this book bring together, for the first time, the histories of the several arts — literature, theatre, film, music and the visual arts — within the school curriculum. But this amounts to far more than an interesting academic exercise. The writers gathered together here are drawing attention to a scandal: that is the destruction of aesthetic education in our schools. They reveal that, at present, the arts are taught in isolation from each other. They are certainly not claiming that there ever was a Golden Age of art education from which we have now fallen; nonetheless, most of them feel that the time and resources for aesthetic pursuits are being reduced. Even when an arts subject remains on the time-table, its content is often subject to insidious change. The teaching of English, for example, is becoming constantly prised apart from any sense of *literature*, rooted in a common tradition. And the visual arts have recently been shifted away from aesthetic concerns towards the technical or instrumental crafts and the new technologies.

One of the key themes that emerges from this book is the idea that within the curriculum there is — or rather there ought to be — an *aesthetic field*, which requires a coherent defence. These writers conceive of the *aesthetic field* as a family of related disciplines, all of which are rooted in aesthetic response, and aesthetic expression. This is an emphasis with which I concur. The aesthetic dimension of human life extends across a wide-range of human activities; and we ought to regard it as an inalienable human potentiality, as fundamental as the capacity for language. If a society cannot provide a facilitating environment within which the aesthetic potential of all of its members can find appropriate expression, then that society has failed.

And our society is failing. In his illuminating contribution, Peter

Peter Fuller

Abbs stresses how the ideologies of 'progress' and of 'modernism' have conspired to destroy those conditions in which aesthetic life can flourish, not only in our schools, but on the wider cultural stage. The contributors to this volume are all concerned about these developments; they adopt a position which is culturally conservationist. They acknowledge that aesthetic education ought to involve fostering of intuition and imagination, cultivation of the disinterested skills of the particular arts, *and* a sense of continuity with tradition, and with nature (including our own human natures). Aesthetic experience begins in the sense-responses of each individual; but it radiates out beyond these to involve a community's most compelling symbols — what I would call its 'shared symbolic order'. Those who oppose the 'individual' to 'society' have misunderstood both terms. As DW Winnicott, the psycho-analyst, once put it, echoing TS Eliot, 'There can be no originality without tradition.'

I also welcome this book because it roundly rejects the idea that those of us who insist upon such emphases are necessarily aligned with the forces of political and cultural reaction. In the 1960s, one often heard the view that the fine arts, and indeed aesthetic values, were 'bourgeois' phenomenon, which ought to be eradicated. The left was exhorted to concern itself with critical sociology of art, and the mass media. This situation gave rise to an unholy alliance between the radical 'avant-garde', and corporate and institutional philistines. Together they loudly endorsed the elimination of aesthetic pursuits and practices from every avenue of educational and cultural life — even, as Peter Abbs rightly observes, within our national art institutions themselves. (In my own section of the aesthetic field, that of the visual arts, the 'avant garde' and the government are united in their desire to eliminate 'messy', traditional, *aesthetic* activities, like painting and sculpture, from higher education, and to see them replaced by 'vocational' pursuits based on photography, graphic design, and computers.) All this is rather like destroying the forests, and farm-lands, on the grounds that they once constituted the private preserve of feudal land-owners.

In an 'aesthetically healthy' society, a book like this would not be necessary. Aesthetic experience would, in the best sense, be taken for granted and enjoyed. The innate aesthetic potential of each child would receive the nurture and encouragement which it needed to grow. But today, the location in which cultural experience can take place is constantly shrinking. The urgent and, at times, embattled tone of some of the following chapters confirms that those of us who

xii

care about such things have no choice but to become more belligerent.

Just before he died, Herbert Marcuse also raised his voice against the Philistine consensus. He argued cogently that 'renunciation of the aesthetic form is abdication of responsibility. It deprives art of the very form in which it can create that other reality within the established one — the cosmos of hope.' He stressed that the 'social function' of art lay solely in its aesthetic dimension, insisting, 'The qualities of aesthetic form negate those of the repressive society — the qualities of its life, labor, and love.' If we relinquish the aesthetic dimension, we are indeed lost. And there is no better place to begin its defence than within the curriculum itself.

Peter Fuller
Bath, July 1986

Plate 1 Self portrait by Michael Biggins painted at the age of 14, ink on newspaper, in his art lesson

Introduction

The picture opposite is a self-portrait by Michael Biggins, painted when he was 14 on a sheet of newspaper in one of his art lessons. The boy, on conventional tests, had a low IQ and was considered by his own school as having little intelligence. Like so many others, the boy left school at the earliest possible opportunity to enter a life of economic insecurity and general anonymity. Discussing the self-portrait at an educational conference Sir Alec Clegg remarked: 'the picture comes from a child who is branded as an educational failure. We have no right to talk about this child in those terms. His fate is a failure for me and for the West Riding'.[1] As most teachers of the major art disciplines know, the fate of Michael Biggins is the fate of thousands of children in our culture whose essentially aesthetic mode of intelligence goes often unrecognized and, where recognized, undervalued and unfulfilled. This symposium is an attempt to argue the case for a coherent aesthetic curriculum for all children, a curriculum in which the Michael Biggins of tomorrow will develop their expressive gifts and, in so doing, contribute to the culture. In our view, it is all but impossible to over-state the urgency of this need or to exaggerate the plight of the arts in our school.

I have before me standard timetable of a second-year class in a highly-regarded comprehensive school in south east England. The timetable shows that the second year do no drama, no dance and no film; in other words, it shows that three of the six great expressive art forms are not even taught. However, there are slots for the other three arts and they are as follows: a double period for music, for the visual arts and for literature. This means that out of twenty-two hours a week, the arts are allocated about three-and-a-half hours![2] But even this is problematic for, from the point of view of our symposium, much of what is done in these art periods is not deeply aesthetic in nature. In the case of this particular school, the music, for example, consists largely in listening to records (from Beethoven to the Beach Boys) and singing (either folk or pop music or hymns). As Marion Metcalfe will show later in the book, this is a gross diminution of what music should be. In the visual arts for much of the time the work is more instrumental than aesthetic in character (designing advertisements, drawing three-dimensional objects with perspectival accuracy), while in English the teaching of literature amounts to little more than discursive discussion of the literal content of the particular work. In other words, much of the teaching in these three-and-a-half hours is virtually *outside* what in this volume we will call the *aesthetic field*. It would not seem an exaggeration to say that the children in their second year in this school experience, on average, no more than an hour or so of genuine aesthetic activity each week. It is of related significance that in their third year they will begin a curriculum in which the arts, with the exception of literature, will become options. Thus it is quite possible from the age of 13 for the pupils to have no further acquaintance with five of the six aesthetic disciplines and, indeed, for many of them in their former schooling never to have experienced drama, dance or film. If it was publicly proposed that mathematics or the sciences should become options in the curriculum from the third year onwards and didn't have to be present in the primary school, there would be a national outcry — and rightly so; but if the arts, representing a different but equivalent symbolic mode of enquiry and exploration, are ignored or marginalized, there is only silence or, at most, an occasional column in the *Guardian*.

Our symposium is a response to this educational scandal. Its intention is to make visible the need for a coherent aesthetic education for all children in all the aesthetic disciplines: drama, dance, film, music, art and literature. Our symposium is also a response to the general fragmentation among arts teachers. We want to see not only a programme for the arts, but also a body of arts teachers who actively feel they form a unified community with a common purpose and a common aesthetic. What we offer then is not only a critique of the existing curriculum but also of many existing assumptions and practice among art teachers themselves. The outer revolution, securing proper time and resources for an arts curriculum, depends on an inner revolution, a fundamental reappraisal of many current practices and working assumptions. What, then, are the essential changes in understanding we would like to bring about?

First of all, in line with the work of Malcolm Ross and the *Gulbenkian Report: The Arts in Schools*, we believe that the individual arts — literature, drama, dance, music, film and art — must be conceived as forming a single community in the curriculum. This does not necessarily mean that they should be integrated in their teaching, but that they should be understood as serving similar aesthetic processes and purposes. *They all belong together under the category of the aesthetic.* For decades the conceptual nature of their unity has been expressed with eloquence and concision in such major works as Suzanne Langer's *Feeling and Form*, in Herbert Read's *Education through Art* and in the many writings of Louis Arnaud Reid. In practice, however, the arts in the curriculum have remained divided and insulated from each other to the point of philistinism. Put simply, the teacher of dance is, say, often unaware of the tradition and practice of the visual arts or literature, the teacher of music unaware of film or of drama and so forth ... One of the major intentions of this volume is to bring together in one volume, for the first time, the different histories of the arts in the curriculum. Here the different 'stories' of the expressive disciplines come together to form a *composite account of all the arts in education.* The complex historic configuration opens up the way to an informed comprehensive understanding of all the arts. These historic reconstructions placed together strike us as one necessary precondition for collaborative work, for that living sense of intricate connection and relationship which makes for a sense of unity and of belonging.

However, our aim has been more ambitious than this. With an eye to the future we have also sought to reconstruct the arts as related aesthetic disciplines working a common aesthetic field. We hope that the notion of an aesthetic field defined at some length at the end of the first chapter offers a valuable paradigm for the teaching of all the arts. Such a notion, which seems to be emerging in dance and music quite independently of our symposium, allows for a complex dynamic movement between making, presenting, responding and evaluating within a framework where there is a recognition of the reciprocity in art-making between the individual and the community and between innovation and tradition. As these terms are all developed at some length towards the end of the opening chapter there is no need to elaborate them further here. The essential point is that we are all committed to the primacy of the aesthetic category — to that modality of knowing which works through feeling and sensing in contact with the particular arts medium and its various established traditions. We believe that the arts offer a unique way of integrating and refining human understanding and that no curriculum can be complete in which it does not have a major place. In many ways, we would like to

Peter Abbs

think our book follows in the wake of the influential *Gulbenkian Report: The Arts in Schools* and takes the argument of that report — *art as a way of knowing* — further forward.

In our search for philosophical clarity and practical renewal, we have also had to look critically at two great movements in the cultural life of our own century, namely modernism in art and progressivism in education. This is not an easy matter for both those movements have been vast in extent, multiple in meaning and labile in energy. Nevertheless, in our historical reconstructions the two movements often intersect and they remain crucial to any understanding of the teaching of the arts in our century. For all their original energy and shaping power, we believe that both these movements are exhausted. Now is the time to make fresh initiatives and to forge new connections with the past. There is a conservationism in this book which is not, at any point, to be confused with conservatism. Our conservationism seeks to establish radical connections with the living cultures of the past. It represents, in part, a return to sources and a recognition of the need in the teaching of the arts for a complex repertoire of conventions, techniques, allusions, references. Perhaps we feel that the great challenge *after* modernism and progressivism is to bring as much of the cultural past into the present to make it, in the fundamental act of aesthetic and imaginative creation, both contemporary and deep. In practice, this means that we are suspicious of endless innovation for its own sake; of art which is only a kind of 'self-expression', of art which claims to be 'relevant' merely because it is 'of the moment' or stridently ideological in content. We are suspicious of all practices which are reluctant to acknowledge any predecessors or any need for a cumulatively acquired and tested discourse. In spirit we are cultural ecologists. We want to conserve for the arts an intricate web of symbolic connections in which the present is seen in living relationship to a past and in which the individual is seen as part of the communal culture. Modernism, in particular, erased the sense of tradition; we wish to bring it back, not as an inert acquisition, but as one indispensable element in an intricate aesthetic field. Thus, in the teaching of the arts, modernism should be seen as only one of the traditions to be drawn upon and as a tradition which, anyway, often depends for its aesthetic vitality on those very traditions it claimed, rather arrogantly, to supercede. When we talk about tradition we refer to both artistic works and ways of working which are still potentially vibrant today as aesthetic experience and as artistic exemplars. It has nothing to do with prescriptive learning or with cerebral knowledge or 'elitism'.

4

Finally, we have to express one major debt and a great sense of loss. Professor Louis Arnaud Reid who was to have contributed to this volume died before its completion. In a letter dated 11 May 1985, he wrote to the editor: 'Generally, I think that ... the conception of this kind of book is needed with desperate urgency as a counter to the slide towards the dehumanization of human beings by their schooling.' In a footnote in the same letter, he wrote, in modest parenthesis: '(I've just remembered that my first book *Knowledge and Truth* had as the title of the last chapter: 'Non-propositional knowledge'.) (Macmillan 1923).' That title could well have stood as the sub-title to this work or, perhaps better, put into its more affirmative form, *art as aesthetic understanding*. We can only hope that Louis Arnaud Reid, had he lived to see the completion of this symposium would have been, at least, satisfied with the result. With a mixed sense of loss and gratitude we dedicate our book to his memory.

Peter Abbs
University of Sussex
Summer 1986

Notes

1 *The Guardian*, 5 January 1972.
2 This figure is a little lower than figures culled from more comprehensive though somewhat dated sources DES figures show that, leaving aside English, the arts used to have a general allocation of between 9 per cent and 11½ per cent of the secondary curriculum time. See *Statistics of Education* (1968). No current figures are available from the DES. The six schools used in the Schools Council Project *Arts and the Adolescent* (working paper 54, published in 1975) show an allocation of 13½ per cent of total time available.

Part I
Confronting the Crisis within the Arts

1   Towards a Coherent Arts Aesthetic

Peter Abbs

... aesthetics only appears obsolete today because a great dimension of human life and experience is catastrophically threatened.

(Peter Fuller)

Introduction

In this opening chapter I want to define and place in an historical context what I believe to be a slow but dramatic shift in our current understanding of the arts[1] and of our teaching of the arts in our schools. What, precisely, is this shift of understanding? Very briefly, one could characterize it as a kind of dynamic conservationism at work in all the arts. It reveals itself as a new concern with the possibilities of tradition, with the possibilities of form and convention, with the need for continuous and developing engagement by the pupil with the artistic medium, with the need for, at the same time, a critical vocabulary, an awareness of the terms of interpretive discourse. Instead of emphasizing, as has been the practice in arts education, 'self-expression', the new sensibility emphasizes *a transpersonal involvement in the whole aesthetic field of the particular art form*; instead of using art as a means to ideological discussion (now a widespread practice), art itself is seen as possessing a liberating energy, often not requiring sociological explication of any kind. The new sensibility insists on the metaphoric and sensuous meaning of art, on the primacy of its aesthetic form, a form which requires, above all, an aesthetic response. Precisely what we mean by the term aesthetic will be made clear later in the chapter.

Following the pattern set by our symposium I will first explore historically the reasons for this current movement — not, as yet, the dominant movement, perhaps — in the arts debate. This will involve me in a lengthy critical examination of modernism in the arts and of the progressive movement in education — for there can be little doubt that the practice of teaching the arts in our schools has its philosophical roots in those two vast, complex and seminal developments. My methods will be both descriptive and critical. I will try to demonstrate what the two movements actually claimed and then attempt to indicate the fallacies informing those claims, the consequences of which have led, in part, (for there are other political and social influences which are not so difficult to delineate) to the present impasse and disorientation. It is inevitable that in the space given I must dramatize my case; but I hope the constriction of words has merely forced me to concentrate on the essential problems, the truly fundamental issues. In the critical delineation of modernism I have confined much of my analysis to the visual arts, partly because of lack of space and partly because the visual arts reveal the spirit of modernism in its purest, or perhaps, most excessive form. After the critique of modernism and progressivism, I then move forwards to suggest better terms for understanding the arts in the curriculum. I offer a model of an aesthetic field in which all the arts can work, a field which allows for a continuous reciprocity of movement between tradition and innovation, between the individual and the community, and between the various stages of creation: from making to presenting, to responding and evaluating. In this way, I argue, it might be possible to bring all the arts, with all their obvious differences, into a philosophical unity which ensures a common kind of practice, the practice of aesthetic education.

Coming to Terms with Modernism and Progressivism

It is not easy to turn critically on modernism and progressivism for, in different ways, they have provided the very conditions for the development of the arts in the curriculum. In their origins these two related movements were so liberating, so culturally and imaginatively demanding, it is still difficult for many of us to formally recognize how in their later phases they became narrowing and imprisoning. This is because modernism was never an object of our attention so much as the mode of our own sensibility. We saw through its eyes, spoke through its mouth, conceived through its mind. Just as one of Moliere's characters suddenly realized that he had been speaking prose all his life, so we now realize that we were all modernists, even without knowing it. But the realization changes the phenomena for it brings a critical distance. Once — it was only yesterday — it seemed that the artist was inevitably at the vanguard of his civilization, an innovator, opening up the forms of the future, an original and iconoclastic energy; once, it seemed in the order of things that the arts in schools should deal with the contemporary, work only through process, remain 'relevant', be 'original', wholly 'expressive'. Today we are less than sure. We turn on modernism now and ask of it, subversive questions. Why, for example, should the art-maker be conceived as always at *the vanguard* of civilization? What is so valuable about endless experimentation? Why should innovation be valued almost as if it were a self-justifying aesthetic category? And, in the teaching of the arts, why should work, say, in drama or dance, be confined to 'process' or restricted to contemporary relevance? In other words, we turn on the iconoclasm of the modernist spirit iconoclastically. We ask subversive questions of the self-consciously subversive. We interrogate the dominant traditions of our century and find ourselves, with a painful unease, on the outside, looking for better connections, concepts, possibilities; seeking not revolution but conservation, deep reclamation rather than innovation, continuities rather than discontinuities.

After a mere eighty years through which art has hurtled through the following stations: expressionism, fauvism, dadaism, cubism, surrealism, constructivism, functionalism, action painting, primitivism, conceptualism, minimalism, kinetic art, op art, pop art, where is there left to 'advance' to? When after the 1960s and 1970s, after the electrocuting of fish in London galleries, after the covering of cliffs in polythene (see Plate 2), after strutting for miles with a plank on your head, after filling the Tate Gallery with twigs and bricks and sand, after hanging up stained nappies and displaying coca-cola bottles — what further possible innovation was left to the aspiring art-maker? Well, there *was* one gesture left, and there were artists and critics and gallery organizers ready to make and applaud it. Frank Kermode tells us in his essay *Modernisms* that: 'Peter Selz, the Curator of Painting and Sculpture at the Museum of Modern Art was delighted with the famous *Homage*, which destroyed itself successfully, though not quite in the manner planned by the artist, before a distinguished audience.'[2] But after that? What then? As the poet Leopardi said, *fashion is the mother of death*. Modernism had to end with its own destruction because it was informed with a false conception of historical time and of the nature of art. Its destruction was implicit in its own premises. It was, in a sense, doomed to go to the edge. And, then, to leap over.

Peter Abbs

Plate 2 CHRISTO, *1969. Canvas and cord cover part of* Little Bay in Australia. *Innovation without tradition can become quickly meaningless.*

There was a time when modernism threw a light on the world — a demanding, dazzling light — allowing us to see in a new way, to see from diverse perspectives, unexpected angles, original vantage points. Then it often shocked, but the effect of the shock was to liberate, to extend, to deepen. It disturbed into awareness. Later, it shocked only to bore and enervate. It numbed the mind until finally the aesthetic of modernism, driven by its own internal logic, led to a widespread cultural anaesthesia. We are now coming round. And still we find it difficult to believe that only ten years ago so much pretentious and hollow art-making lay at the centre of American and European culture and at the centre of its complex network of validating institutions, the public and private galleries, the art colleges, and the Arts Council. Coming round, in a numb state of disbelief, we find it hard to believe it really happened. Late modernism seems like a nightmare we cannot now acknowledge, a tale told by an idiot full of sound and fury signifying nothing. Yet it did, of course, take place. And in the waste-land of late modernism, in its plastic debris and dust, we must now find a better aesthetic for our society and our schools.

But as all things are defined in some way dialectically we can only establish a more comprehensive philosophy and practice of the arts, by beginning with a diagnosis of modernism in art and progressivism in education. What happened to modernism? What happened to the progressive movement? I would like now to take each in turn and then, by bringing them together, outline the elements of an alternative practice for our schools.

What was Modernism?

Modernism, as it pertains to the arts, is not easy to define; yet the term exists and refers to a certain disposition of mind which most of us can recognize (if not tabulate) and probably feel in some confused way a part of. As to its meaning, the word itself, perhaps, gives a major clue for 'modernism' derives from the Latin 'modo' meaning 'just now' or, as the Americans would have it, 'right now!'. From the outset modernism self-consciously proclaimed its own contemporaneity, wanting to establish an art for what it saw as its own historic time. Modernism, true to its own name, is marked by a highly conscious orientation to time, particularly to the present tense. In 1925 Ortega y Gasset, the Spanish philosopher, attempting to describe and evaluate the first phase of modernism wrote:

> The new art is a world-wide fact. For about twenty years now the most alert young people of two successive generations in Berlin, Paris, London, New York, Rome, Madrid have found themselves faced with an undeniable fact that they have no use for traditional art; moreover that they detest it.[3]

From the outset, then, modernism envisaged itself as an international movement, defined negatively by its opposition to traditional culture; consciously setting itself against the past and facing only the present and the future. Art-makers traditionally seen as the conservers of their culture were conceived as revolutionaries, not in the rearguard of civilization, but in its vanguard, speaking the language of 'now' and 'tomorrow'.

Nearly all definitions of modernism are emphatic about its iconoclastic spirit;[4] its insistence on disruption and discontinuity, on its conscious departure from inherited traditions and established conventions. Its aim was continuous experimentation. 'Make it new', urged Ezra Pound in the early years of modernism and the imperative, which now strikes us as a piece of advertising copy, informed the whole complex movement from TS Eliot's *Waste Land* and the Dadaist's placing of a moustache on the revered *Mona Lisa*, to the

Plate 3 A<small>LAN</small> <small>CHARLTON</small>, Corner Painting in Ten Parts *exhibited in the Hayward Gallery 1986. We do not engage aesthetically with such work. We merely conceive it in a minimal way.*

shuffle-novel and John Cage's composition 3½, (being three-and-a-half minutes of unplayed silence: end of piece). In the same spirit as Pound but in radically altered cultural circumstances Marshal McLuhan told the electronic children of the 1960s: 'If it works, it is obsolete'. The signpost of modernism pointed only one way: forwards. *FORWARDS!*

It is possible to see modernism as a continuous movement running through the length of our century but having, at least, two distinct phases. I will designate these two phases as early modernism and late modernism. Rather arbitrarily, I will suggest that the first phase ran from 1900 to 1940 (with the major impetus in the first twenty years) and that the second phase ran from 1940 to 1980 (with its final gaudy efflorescence and extinction taking place in the last twenty years). The classification is partly determined by the convention of decades. The dates have no definitive precision — for clearly the mood of modernism can be found in the last twenty years of the nineteenth century in the French symbolists and the English aesthetes and, equally as clearly, the cult of the modern has continued, in certain odd places, after 1980. Yet the dates are not wholly arbitrary. 1900 saw the publication of Freud's *The Interpretation of Dreams*, which was to have such a profound effect on the twentieth century sensibility; while 1940 marked the middle of the Second World War in which the survival of any kind of qualitative European culture seemed distinctly unlikely; and 1980 marked Roy Strong's explosively hostile review of Norbert Lynton's book *Modern Art*. This review, published in *The Listener*, must have been one of the first public attacks on the second phase of modernism, late modernism, by a well-known member of the art establishment. The allegations and the tone in which they are expressed mark sudden warfare, an irritable and sniping attack on the triumphant subverters. To demonstrate the point I must quote at some length:

> I'm resentful of its patronizing attitude to artists whom it banishes beyond the pale — Sutherland or Ivon Hitchens don't even figure; I'm irritated by its pretensions; I groan at its often unnecessary aggressiveness; and I'm often affronted by the downright poor workmanship and shoddy technique which its exponents sometimes outrageously flaunt. The public has been brainwashed by decades of the modern art machine, a complex mechanism whose interests lie in sustaining the myth of modern art. As a result, we are saddled with something which is the consequence of tremendous vested interests by both the people and the institutions whose existence would be undermined if they admitted it was now a myth. After all, if you are a director of a museum of modern art, it is unlikely that you would ever want to upset the notion. This is a problem that has never bedevilled the creation of art before in quite the same way. It will be interesting to know what, in a century's time, will be made of this huge monster made up of museums, critics, journals, salerooms and dealers dedicated to the instant recognition and propagation of modern art.[5]

In fact, Roy Strong's review was not a solitary expression of outrage; it can be seen as part of a growing literature of opposition — from artists, art-critics, and humanists; and most eloquently in the work of Peter Fuller.[6] But perhaps, around 1980, it became clear to an increasing number of individuals concerned with the arts, that modernism *was over*; that endless innovation had led only to cultural enervation; that the tasks ahead were other than those described by the avant-garde, by most of the cosmopolitan critics and most of the newly-established 'artists'. A conservationist attitude was necessary; an ecological spirit; a movement back to discover and attend to all that was in danger of being lost.

The notion of two phases of modernism is not particularly subtle but it may be sufficient for my purposes which is, dialectically, to suggest the framework for another way of looking and to consider its implications for the teaching of the arts. Frank Kermode, in his own urbane analysis of modernism, likewise divides it into two phases: the palaeo-modernist and the neo-modernist. While he appears to give them different dates from myself, he certainly places the work, for example, of Andy Warhol, John Cage, William Burroughs, Robbe-Grillet and Oldenburg in the neomodernist category and asserts the existence of a fundamental continuity:

> A point to remember, though, is that the development (of neo-modernism) can be seen as following from paleo-modernist premises without any violent revolutionary change.[7]

Herbert Read, who had such a formidable influence on both the visual arts and on the teaching of art in school, in a disillusioned paper entitled significantly 'The Limits of Permissiveness' written just before his death in 1968, likewise indicates a breakage of Modernism with the Second World War and the emergence of a counterfeit version of it in the decades following the war. This paper is a profoundly important document in any analysis of the failure of modernism.[8] Finally, in a moving testimony the painter Josef Herman also points to two phases of modernism. Herman writes:

> What we call modern art is the art of the first half of this century. This was a period of definite achievement equalling all true art of any period in the history of man. Picasso, Matisse, Derain, Rouault, Chagall and so on, were all men of undisputable genius. If we add to these the great names of Germany, Belgium, Russia, or Mexico we will understand how fertile the times were. The effect of their works was truly revolutionary in the sense that it affected our view of nature, of artistic creation and of man as a social being. But no revolution can go on forever. *After the Second world War a lesser breed of men took over. In the works of artists of the last two decades we can see the exhaustion of ideas which were once rich in content and formal invention.* We see something equal to a stagnation and a monotonous repetition. What still goes under the word 'invention' is most often little more than a mindless activity. No more great dreamers; no more great dreams.[9] (my emphasis)

Like the art critic Herbert Read, so the painter Josef Herman posits a break at the time of the Second World War and then a kind of weakened continuity. What I want to suggest is that the spirit of modernism continued but that in radically altered circumstances it carried different cultural meanings and had different, though still related, artistic results. The demand 'Make it new!' must have had a profoundly different meaning for a young highly educated elite at the end of the Victorian period than it did for those who were young sixty years later when the whole complex web of Victorian culture had all but disappeared. And, indeed, now twenty years after that, after a storm of institutionally prescribed innovation, the slogan 'Make it new!' can only take on an ironic and mocking significance which marks its end. I have indicated that a major clue to understanding modernism lies in a recognition of its preoccupation with *the moment* — with *modernity*, with *modernization*, with *modishness*. As I believe its central fallacy derives from an extreme preoccupation with historical time I want now to examine this concern more fully.

The Nature of Modernism

The most cursory glance at the many manifestos and justifications of modernism, in both its phases, discloses a uniform and unifying desire to disown the past in order to inaugurate the present. All modernist manifestos are manifestos of the present tense. And innovation is invariably announced and placed against a tradition, often *all past traditions*, which the innovation is seen to supercede. Under the supremacy of modernism, tradition became a negative term denoting aesthetic limitation and, often, psychological repression. As the scientists during the seventeenth century had turned their backs on medieval theology and Greek humanism, insisting on a new kind of empiricism and mechanism, so the modernists of the twentieth century disowned in their public manifestos the immediate practice of all their forerunners. Indeed, as we shall see, they developed a phantasy of time, projected it into the world and thought it true.

In an early defense of expressionism, published in Munich in 1916, Herman Bahr, in characteristic euphoric spirit, proclaimed:

The various sayings and proclamations of expressionism can only tell us that what the expressionist is looking for is without parallel in the past. A new form of Art is dawning. And he who beholds an Expressionist picture by Matisse or

Picasso, by Pechstein or Kokoschka, by Kandinsky or Marc, or by Italian or Bohemian Futurists, agrees; he finds them quite unprecedented.... All that has hitherto been the aim of painting, since painting first began, is now denied and something is striven for which has never yet been attempted.[10]

A New Form of Art is Dawning

There is the motif of modernism; a new art, *now*, for a new age, *now*. Expressionism is thus seen as being 'without parallel in the past', something 'quite unprecedented'. But, as we can now see in retrospect, the art-critic is imprisoned in his own formulations. He sees what he expects to find. Not wanting parallels, not wanting past examples, he cannot locate them. Yet it is not difficult to find continuities for twentieth century expressionism in Van Gogh, in Gauguin, in Caspar David Friedrich, in El Greco, even in the work of Grunwald and Hieronymous Bosch, in other words, back and back into the inherited culture.

A similar notion of the new, informed by the teleological system of Marxist belief, can be found in another typical utterance made in 1923 by Nicolas Tarabukin in an essay significantly entitled *From the Easel to the Machine*:

Contemporaneity makes completely new demands on the artist. It wants not museum 'pictures' and 'sculptures' from him but objects which are socially justified in form and purpose.... But the death of painting, the death of easel painting as a form, does not yet mean the death of art in general.... Unusually wide horizons are now opening out in front of visual art ... These new forms are called 'production skills'.[11]

Here, echoing the sentiments of Herman Bahr, 'the death of painting' is announced because *contemporaneity demands new 'production skills'*. The argument is not aesthetic but *historical*; some force at work in the historical moment is seen both to justify and determine what must happen in the arts. As I will show later there is a crucial fallacy in such a conception that led easily to other fallacies which culminated, all but inevitably, in the exile of art from its own realm, in the paradoxical loss of the aesthetic in the artistic artefacts of our own symbolically impoverished time. Contemporaneity may not be either the best or the most legitimate arbiter in the serious matter of

Plate 4   HERBERT READ with Portrait of Herbert Read. Herbert Read was the champion of both modernism in art and progressivism in education. In his writing the two movements come together.

art-making. The socially redundant may be exactly what the imagination needs! For why should art serve history — what the literary critic Terry Eagleton naively calls 'real history'[12] — when we do not know what history can possibly mean and when art has its own timeless category to serve? But all this is to anticipate. Here it is important to note *the insistence on time.*

Herbert Read, who until late in his life was to be such a generous and eclectic champion of all things culturally new and educationally progressive, wrote in 1933, in the appropriately titled book *Art Now* (often viewed as a key text in the modernist canon)[13]

> The aim of five centuries of European effort is openly abandoned.[14]

And then, elucidating the idea further, addressing the Communists in 1935, claimed:

> But everywhere the greatest obstacle to the new social reality is the existence of the cultural heritage of the past — the

religion, the philosophy, the literature and the art which makes up the whole complex ideology of the bourgeois mind.[15]

Herbert Read's speech then ended with three modernist slogans[16]:

REVOLUTIONARY ART IS CONSTRUCTIVE
REVOLUTIONARY ART IS INTERNATIONAL
REVOLUTIONARY ART IS REVOLUTIONARY

The speech also referred to Walter Gropius and applauded his conception of a new architecture which 'bodies itself forth, not in stylistic imitation or ornamental frippery, but in those simple and sharply modelled designs in which every part merges naturally into the comprehensive volume of the whole'. Thus, any conserving notion of ornamentation, any traditional notion of creative imitation is dismissed and a geometrical conception of art with no reference to the great historic past hailed as constructive, international and revolutionary; of the age and therefore artistically mandatory.

And so every movement entered, often briefly, and made its attack on tradition and arrogantly claimed its own unique rights, its own contemporaneity: *now, now, right now!* In an early manifesto for *Concrete poetry* it was stated:

> Assuming that the historical cycle of verse (as formal-rhythmical unity) is closed, concrete poetry begins by being aware of graphic state as structural agent ...[17]

It is the assumption that is so telling, for it is unquestioned assumptions that create the world-picture and time-picture in which people operate. The assumption is that all historical practices are over; in this case, the writing of verse. In the case of Robbe-Grillet, leading figure in the establishment of the *nouveau roman*, it is the traditional form of the novel. Robbe-Grillet writes: 'The new literature itself is ... going to represent in its fulfilment a revolution more total than those from which such movements as romanticism and naturalism were born'.[18] The aspiration which over time has, in turn become a tradition, a convention, a *modus operandi*, is *total revolution*. But what total revolution can you possibly have after total revolution?

The essential polarity between innovation and tradition is, perhaps, expressed most strongly (and most absurdly) by the painter George Mathieu:

> For the past ten years, painting ... has been freeing itself from the yoke of this burdensome inheritance. After twenty-

Plate 5 BRIDGET RILEY Current, 1964. How appropriate a symbol of late modernism the kinetic image, is creating an effect of endless movement based on the scientific principle of optics.

five centuries of a culture we have made our own, we are witnessing in certain aspects of lyrical non-configuration a new phenomenon in painting — and, one might add, in the arts in general — which calls into question the very foundations of 40,000 years of aesthetic activity.[19]

This extraordinary testimony expresses the extreme logic of modernism; the contemporary art-maker finally lifts himself up and regards himself infinitely superior to all established time, to the whole of recorded experience. However 'international', this must, surely, strike us as the supreme expression of temporal provincialism and cultural isolation? Yet the attitude not only exists but remains widespread, permeating the sensibility of all 'advanced' modernist cultures.

The Essential Fallacies of Modernism

In 1965 the literary critic Leslie Fiedler wrote:

> Surely there has never been a moment in which the most naive
> as well as the most sophisticated have been so acutely aware of
> how the past threatens momentarily to disappear from the
> present, which itself seems to be disappearing into the
> future.[20]

This expresses well the dizzy vortex created by the cumulative
movements of modernism, a sense of a dizzy pace which dissolved all
that lay behind, in which nothing existed; no history, no continuity,
no identity. The great black and white images of Kinetic art, where
all discrete parts flow into an endless motion *now*, symbolized,
perhaps most effectively, this giddy state of consciousness, of
perpetual revolution with no reference backwards, no cultural allu-
sion, no hint of memory or of any historical past. How appropriate a
symbol of late modernism the kinetic image is creating an effect of
endless movement based on the scientific principle of optics!

Each period, it would seem, invents its own conception of historic time and literalizes it, comes to read it in the succession of actual
events, comes to experience it as an inexorable narrative dictating the
forms of cultural life. Thus the Renaissance, envisaging itself as the
rebirth of the ancient world, created the fiction of the 'Middle Ages',
the Enlightenment, considering itself the most illuminated period that
had ever existed, came to reinvent those 'Middle Ages' as 'the Dark
Ages'. Modernism, likewise, as we have seen, has carried its own
phantasy of time, its own story, in which the past is constantly and
qualitatively superceded by the present moment. *Now*, according to
this version of time, is always better than *then*. The ethical and
aesthetic consequence of this conception have been, as we have slowly
begun to realize, quite disastrous.

Ortega y Gasset, in the essay to which I have already referred,
unwittingly gave expression to this modernist conception of time
when he wrote:

> In art, as in morals, what ought to be done does not depend
> on our personal judgement; we have to accept the imperative
> imposed by the time.[21]

In true modernist fashion Ortega continued:

> Obedience to the order of the day is the most hopeful choice

open to the individual. Even so he may achieve nothing; but he is more likely to fail if he insists on composing another Wagnerian opera, another naturalistic novel. . . . In art, repetition is nothing.[22]

In this configuration of assertions, we discern the heart of modernist understanding. Fundamentally, it confers to what is conceived as inevitable historic progress the right to determine aesthetic practice and value. Such a view is seriously flawed for it assumes that history has a hidden teleology, that this teleology can be discerned and that it must determine aesthetic and ethical values. In each case we can turn on the interlocked assumptions and ask how history could possibly have such a teleological meaning and, how, even if such an unwarranted assumption was held, one could be sure that one has grasped its meaning (and not some other meaning) and, finally, even if one granted the position, how it could possibly dictate aesthetic and ethical criteria. One could, for example, paint convincingly *against* history and ethically act against it — as innumerable Jews must have felt they were doing in the 1930s against Hitler's version of historic destiny. In brief, history does not aesthetically justify art; one could be 'of one's period' and produce artistic monstrosities, as, indeed, has been the case, with many great exceptions, during the last thirty years. Modernism was thus guilty of transferring the most dubious historic categories across to realms where they did not belong. Its essential fallacy lay in a constant and insidious extrapolation of categories. *The modernness of art does not make it either aesthetically good or ethically valuable.* The value of art lies elsewhere; in its aesthetic power, in its vitality, in its relationship to the alert senses and the open imagination, deep in its own field of execution and reference. To say that something is contemporary is to tell us nothing of its qualitative value.

Yet such a simple fallacy had, like most fallacies, many destructive consequences. It led inevitably to the cult of constant change. In 1966 Morse Peckham wrote in *Man's Rage for Chaos* that:

The conviction is almost universal that those who stick to obsolete beliefs and who refuse to change will go to the wall . . . that we must adapt or die.[23]

So the cult of the new, in its second phase, led to movement after movement, fashion after fashion after fashion. In the 1960s the practice of drawing from life, the practice of using paints and canvasses, the practice, even, of any kind of practice (for 'instant art' denied the need for any application) all but died. The cult of the contemporary made anything and everything possible.[24]

The consequences of extreme modernism become transparently clear in, for example, the following commentary by the art critic David Sylvester on the paintings of David Bomberg:

> Stylistically, Bomberg's later work was *backward looking*, added little or nothing to the language of art that had not been there 50 years before. If it is, as I believe, the finest English painting of its time, only its intrinsic qualities make it so: *in terms of the history of art it's a footnote.*[25]

Note how the intrinsic painterly qualities are made superficial and the historical qualities made all important. The history of art, according to this spurious and deadly logic, is what art must serve by constantly and quantitatively adding to its technical repertoire. The imagined march of history is what matters here; the specific art-work becomes secondary to that progression. Thus a work of art, however it may appeal to our aesthetic and imaginative capacities, deserves to be merely a footnote if it fails to match the historical moment. Here, I hope, the central confusion of categories — the *imposition of the imagined historical on the actual aesthetic realm* — is unmistakably clear and its implications disturbingly visible. It is a good example of how art can disappear into the historic category and re-emerge merely as a footnote to an imagined social evolution.

Modernism, in brief, is guilty of what Karl Popper named 'historicism'.[26] It sees itself as the inevitable outcome of the historic moment, the visible meaning of the assumed invisible imperative of history. Thus art has come to be seen and understood through an alien and, no doubt, false category. It is more than likely when people now wander around modern galleries that they do not actually *see* the paintings but merely *conceive* them as 'contemporary art', as 'modern paintings', as 'the latest developments' in 'the history of art'. So people came to understand art without responding to it! After all, the historic category does not require aesthetic gratification of any kind. It demands merely abstract and intellectual recognition: *These works are contemporary* . . .

Thus modernism engendered the tyranny of modishness (now! now! now!) and a deep exile from inherited culture. Yet, on reflection, how can what is contemporary define the quality of art? And how can great works of art, of any time, of any period, ever be outmoded? We need a better sense of art, a better sense of culture, and, perhaps, a more modest sense of history. Bristling with the weapons of ultimate

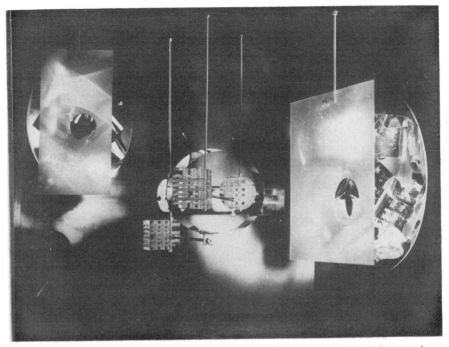

Plate 6 NICOLAS SCHOFFER *Microtime. Part of late modernism came under the influence of science and technology. In this way it uncritically served the needs of the prevailing zeitgeist.*

extinction, how can we regard ourselves at the forefront of social evolution? Perhaps it would be wiser and more fitting for artists to envisage themselves as standing at the rearguard of their civilization, reclaiming lost or neglected continuities, drawing fresh connections with our many living pasts, and re-establishing the deep aesthetic field.

Many fallacies followed upon the historicist fallacy. I would like here to briefly enumerate three that have had profoundly negative consequences on our understanding of art and of the arts in education.

The first can be called *scientism*. As the modernist movement developed, denying and destroying its own past traditions, it came more and more prone, particularly in the visual arts, to adopt the language and assumptions of science and technology. After all, these intellectual disciplines seemed to be the true pace-setters, determining, through another kind of relentless innovation, the forms of life to come. In technology one could certainly talk, without ambiguity, of historical development and a kind of progress. Here the latest could claim, with some justification, to be, in fact, the best. Having denounced its past as obsolescent, many of the arts began to assimilate the language and the understanding of the theoretical and practical sciences. Here lay a further alienation from the primary aesthetic experience. During the 1960s and 1970s some of the visual arts longed to join forces with the dominant force of their culture. This, too, must have seemed to many artists to be no more than a matter of historic necessity, of obeying the imperative of the prevailing *zeitgeist.*

Many of the manifestos of the 1960s testify to the slip into the scientific and technological paradigm. Thus Frank Popper, declared with zest; 'Art will become an industrial product ... art will become pure research like science.' While the French artist Vasarely (see plate 00) claimed: 'From now on only teams, groups or whole disciplines can create: cooperation between scientists, engineers, technicians, architects and plasticians will be the *sine qua non* of the work of art.' In 1967 in his Preface to an Exhibition of Objective Art, Otto Hahn wrote:

> No more brushes, no more painting, no more eye, no more hand, no more play of materials, no more feeling, no more personality.[27]

Instead we have *objects*; Hahn's exhibition of objective art displayed a pair of ironing boards, a gun mounted on tyres, a wardrobe, a raincoat stuck fast to a piece of formica and other such artificial pieces. What we find here is, I believe, a total confusion about the nature of art and the nature of human nature. *Art has never been primarily concerned with the literal documentation of facts* — its first and distinguishing task has always been to give visual form to sensuous and imaginative impressions and feelings — to *perceptual experience.* It is symptomatic that in many art colleges and in many school art courses the work of the art-maker is labelled as 'a mode of enquiry', a form of 'visual research', 'an assembling of data', a method of 'problem-solving'. The language derives not from true art discourse, not from aesthetics, but from the illicit application of the methods and working assumptions of science and technology. The current practice of calling a work of art 'a statement', often 'a relevant statement', derives from the same confusion. For art is not propositional by nature, but, as Suzanne Langer has said, *presentational.*[28] It asserts nothing as unequivocal as a statement and, *as art*, can be neither proved nor disproved, for it does not operate in the realm of the sentential.

But scientism has not been the only negative and distorting force in the practice of the visual arts. There has also been a related movement towards *a blank literalism.* Defending Robert Morris' *Slab* in the

Plate 7 ANDY WARHOL COCA COLA, 1962. Under the rubric of pop art the objects of mass culture were simply reproduced and often endlessly repeated through photographic techniques.

Tate Gallery, Michael Compton in his introduction to the Arts Council brochure *Art as Thought Process* wrote:

> At a certain level of consideration there is absolutely no ambiguity about such a sculpture as SLAB by Robert Morris. No matter how you look at it, it remains clear that it is just what was intended and at first glance just what you see.[29]

A slab is a slab is a slab. Here lies the idea for another movement in art: SLABISM. But, of course, it is not necessary to invent. It already exists under the name of pop art. As we know, under this fashion the objects of mass culture were simply reproduced and often endlessly repeated through photographic technique as in Andy Warhol's *Marilyn Munro* and *Coca Cola* (see plate 7). One major tendency in late modernism has been to shift the contents of Woolworths or MacDonalds into the Guggenheim or the Tate, certainly wholesale into the annual exhibition of the Hayward Gallery. In this 'tradition' the object of the art-maker was to reproduce the mass-produced and insert it in a high-class institution. Without a real tradition, without prolonged apprenticeship, without the loving continuation and

Plate 8 Roy Lichenstein O.K. Hot shot, *1963. The rapidity with which Lichenstein's 'blow-ups' came out of advertising and returned to it was amazing.*

extension of traditional practices, such a dependence on the immediate environment for symbolic material was, no doubt, inevitable. Besides weren't all these bottles and plastic plates and polythene bags and polystyrene strips of the moment, the *right now* of our historic lives? Then, surely, artists had to use them or be merely displaced by them? For obvious reasons, artists preferred the first choice to the second; but, in the outcome, the second choice was only a more subtle version of the first.

The 'inspiration' of pop art was not exploratory or recreative. It was static and reproductive. The implication was 'These things are real for contemporary society, therefore they should be the real objects in art.' Invariably under such a rubric, art became a blind extension of pop culture. It celebrated the same values: instant success, momentary fun, endless chop and change, brashness, casualness of style. Art became more ephemera and mere ephemera; an ephemera which was grotesquely fossilized when it was purchased and hung up in museums and art galleries. The rapidity with which

Lichenstein's 'blow-ups' came out of advertising and returned safely to it was amazing (see plate 8). Here *was* immediate relevance, an instant historic connection, a stunning contemporaneity: *GOT CHA! WHAM! WOW! BANG!* Modernism, shunned and maligned in its early years, had under the influence of pop art, become suddenly modish. But the mass-produced imagery of the consumer society has little endurable resonance and no artistic integrity and its blank reproduction by art-makers can only lead to the condition of anaesthesia. Such a facile dependence on the images of mass culture, once again, further impoverished art-making. In pop art, blankness merely reproduced itself becoming, at best, social commentary of the most obvious kind and leading to a further loss of deep aesthetic response. Such a mechanical dependence on the counterfeit symbols of mass-culture only served to dramatize the state of aesthetic loss, of sensuous and imaginative and spiritual exile. The literal reproduction of things entails the imprisonment of the mind in those things and when those things are spurious then the mind is corrupted in the very process of faithfully reproducing them.

Pop art, it was argued, is a social protest. And in this argument we perceive the third fallacy of late modernism, a fallacy closely related to the historicist fallacy outlined earlier. This fallacy concerns the overt and continuous politicization of the arts. If art is secondary and history primary, then art is most effectively judged through the historical and ideological dimension. This has happened on such a scale in our own time that we hardly notice it. In his contribution to this volume Rob Watson shows how the obsession with ideology has severely distorted awareness of film. In the study of literature at university the dominant practice is to decode 'a text' in order to delineate its ideological content and then, in political and social terms, to cast judgment. As we have seen, Terry Eagleton would have all literature measured against his own notion of 'real history', thus erecting a category of socio-political relevance as the final arbiter in literary judgment. John Berger, in a similar manner brings overt political categories to bear directly on works of art.

> John Berger used to say that in front of pictures he always asked the question 'How do these works help men and women to know, and to claim, their social rights'.[30]

How, one wonders, does he respond to Chagall's *Lovers in Lilac* to Gwen John's sensitive cat paintings, to Henry Moore's archetypal *King and Queen* (see plate 9) or to Constable's lyrical water colours of moving clouds? What relevance do they all have to the political

Plate 9 HENRY MOORE King and Queen, 1952–53. It is difficult to see how such powerful mythic icons can relate to John Berger's desire for men and women's social rights. Perhaps they serve another function.

struggle? And why, more fundamentally, *should* they possess such political relevance? For art has its own deep transformative powers, its own interior meanings, its own aesthetic challenges and demands.

The elevation of the historical category must lead not only to a misconception of the purposes of art, it must lead also to the triumph of an ideological criticism which seeks to discursively relate the secondary manifestation of art to what is conceived as its primary historical meaning (known only by the critic). Out of the cult of the historical emerges the omniscient critic whose unique function is to elaborate on what the art is *about*, relate it to its historic moment and provide its ideological interpretation. Thus, the intellectual eminence now given to the high priests and secular theologians of 'texts' and 'art objects'. The elevation of criticism brings about a further distancing from the aesthetic realm, for the question becomes not one of

Plate 10   CECIL COLLINS The Sleeping Fool, *1943. Under the fashions of late modernism certain painters, working the imaginal and aesthetic field, have been badly neglected.*

prolonged *aesthetic* engagement but one of *conceptual* meaning and the task not one of creation or performance or appreciation, but one of ideological placement or, more frequently, displacement. Feminism *as a method of literary and artistic criticism* is, of course, the most recent of these movements away from primary aesthetic engagement and encounter. It basically *uses* art to get to ideological perception and commitment. What tends to be lost in such an approach is any dynamic engagement with the medium and form of the artistic work. Invariably, the metaphor is literalized, the complexity simplified, the art negated.

Underlying all these tendencies one senses the underlying fallacy of historicism. For it is a belief in the historic now which accounts for the shift into the scientific and technological, which explains the attraction of literally reproducing the dominant commercial world around us and which underlies the increasing and mediating power of ideological criticism.

It is time now to consider the different but related movement of Progressivism.

Plate 11   *Rousseau composing* Emile *in the countryside.*

Rousseau's Emile and the Progressive Movement in Education

Like modernism the concept progressive bears within itself an overt orientation towards time, conceived as linear and developmental. The *Oxford English Dictionary* offers the formulations: 'marked by continuous improvement', 'continuous and successive advance' and 'straight forward or onward'. The word derives from the Latin PRO GRADI meaning *to step forwards*. The present and future tense are thus strong but the past tense is absent. Today the word 'progressive' has little precise meaning; it has become, significantly, an emotive word which can easily subdue any critical reflection. For who could be against an attitude which was 'progressive'? Who would wish, in opposition, to be considered 'regressive', or worse, 'reactionary' and 'backward-looking'? The Conservative party claims: 'we are the genuine progressive party'. Thus as Raymond Williams proposes in his *Keywords*:

> It is certainly significant that nearly all political tendencies now wish to be described as *progressive*, but ... it is more frequently now a persuasive than a descriptive word.[31]

Yet the fact that the word *is* 'persuasive' across all political parties tells us that we have touched upon an informing category of our own civilization. There are cultures which talk about 'walking backwards' into time. Our civilization, till recently, could only understand stepping forwards, striding forwards, from the now into the future, unhampered by the past. Progress.

It is, surely, no accident that the word 'modernist' and the word 'progressive' both reveal an orientation towards time which rubs out and cancels the past, which denies any kind of ancestor worship. Thus in the progressive movement in education we will find that what is valued unconditionally is self-expression and individual growth, while inherited culture and a personal sense of cultural solidarity, *of belonging to an historical past which gives depth and meaning to the present*, is actively undermined. As with modernism 'now' is elevated above and radically disconnected from 'then' and the value of skill, of tradition, of the whole invisible aesthetic field, severely occluded. In euphoric style, Dr. Montessori who, along with Froebel, was perhaps the most influential of all the child-centred educationists, wrote in 1914:

> Science evidently has not finished its progress. On the contrary, it has scarcely taken the first step in advance, for it has hitherto stopped at the welfare of the body. It must continue, however, to advance.... On the same positive lines science will proceed to direct those latent creative forces which lie hidden in the marvellous embryo of man's spirit.[32]

And, again, in similar vein:

> My method is scientific, both in its substance and in its aim. It makes for the attainment of a more advanced stage of progress.[33]

It is not difficult to detect in these sentiments the same transference of scientific categories across to human existence as well as the same kind of historicism — the sense of inevitable growth, of the inherent 'laws' of historical 'advance' which are, therefore, to determine all future forms of activity — which has so perverted the modernist arts movement. It is chillingly ironic that less than a life-time later, the image of science working on 'the marvellous embryo' has become a common image of dread and deep foreboding. 'Science evidently has not finished its progress' . . . but now in such a sentence 'progress' carries a negative charge of irony, anxiety, and disorientation. Our feelings about time future are no longer those of Montessori.

It is a liberating truth that such iconoclastic and biblioclastic movements as modernism in the arts and progressivism in education come to form traditions; are doomed, as it were, to create conventions and methods, however depleted. Their feet, too, become marked and sticky with the clay of historic time. For the progressive movement is a tradition as old as the enlightenment. It runs back in time to Rousseau who published his philosophical romance on child-centred education in 1762. In *Emile*, that charter of the child emancipated from historic time and the cultural continuum, Rousseau, with lyrical power, advocated the methods of learning through discovery, of allowing self-regulation (a term that AS Neill in our own century, was to make central to his educational work) and of relating learning to the progressive stages of child-development (anticipating here all the major tenets of Piaget). In his curious and higly influential masterpiece Rousseau claimed of his ideal pupil: 'Nature should be his only teacher and things his only models' and 'present interest the only motive power'.

To secure a true education for his fictional Emile Rousseau has to sever him from his own civilization and from all historic culture. All inherited culture is seen as imprisoning, as imposing what Blake was later to call 'mind-forged manacles'. Against 'the man of culture' Rousseau was to place 'the natural man' who lived in the present tense and only for himself:

> Our wisdom is slavish prejudice, our customs consist in control, constraint, compulsion. Civilized man is born and dies a slave. The infant is bound up in swaddling clothes, the corpse is nailed down in the coffin. All his life long man is imprisoned by his institutions . . .[34]

> The natural man lives for himself: he is the unit, the whole dependent only on himself and his like. The citizen is but the numerator of a fraction, whose value depends on its deno-

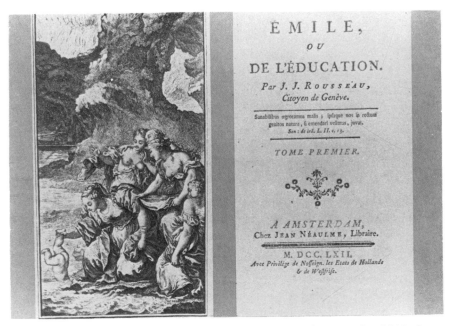

Plate 12 Frontispiece to a 1793 edition of Emile: *the woman immerses the child in the waters of nature.*

minator; his value depends upon the whole, that is, on the community.[35]

Thus, we observe in the founding father of the progressive movement the following juxtapositions; nature against culture, spontaneity against civilization, the individual against the community. The purpose of education was thus located in the progressive unfolding of the individual outside of history, outside of culture, outside of any actual community. *Rousseau's education is an education without ancestry or ancestors.* An impossible aim, of course, for the individual can only ever be born into some portion of history, into an actual culture and into the tangible solidarity of living relationships. Thus it is, and not otherwise. The fate of Emile is to be immersed in the culture provided by his tutor — the culture of endless discovery — and to be dependent on that single pedagogic relationship for emotional sustenance. It is truly strange that Rousseau did not even see that removing Emile from the community and from all intimate family relationships was perverse. So strong is his vision of the self-regulated child that he perceives nothing problematic in the annihilation of inherited forms and connections. Progressivism came to be an educational philosophy based on a fundamental discontinuity, on an ahistorical sense of human time. Like modernism it wanted to achieve an immediate 'now' uncomplicated by any past events, free from the obligations posed by any cultural past. Thus Emile, in a sense, is a child of modernism, 150 years before it became an event; a fictional figure presaging the future; the disinherited self-regulating individual, living for himself, beyond all received cultures, with no debts to the past, with no past to have debts to.

It is also highly pertinent to note that Emile is not given an aesthetic so much as a pragmatic education. Of the visual arts Rousseau writes:

> All children in the course of their endless imitations try to draw: and I would have Emile cultivate this art; not so much for the art's sake as to give him exactness of eye and flexibility of hand.[36]

The arts, as we would say, to serve 'life-skills'. 'I would rather have him a shoemaker than a poet', writes Rousseau, 'I would rather he paved streets than painted flowers on china'. The same applies to imaginative literature. Here Rousseau is particularly, and tellingly, severe. Rousseau writes 'Reading is the greatest plague of childhood' and 'the chief cause of unhappiness'. Imagination merely distorts the pragmatic reality of nature to which, to be happy and whole, each individual must adapt. For a long time only one book is allowed to Emile; it, says Rousseau, constitutes his entire library and facilitates their pedagogic work on the natural sciences. The literary work will serve project-work and thus be made doubly useful! Thus Rousseau, like many English teachers today, avoids past work and selects a contemporary documentary novel which has 'relevance' and is about 'the real world' and uses it to get to further empirical knowledge. Knowing exactly what a revolution in learning he is advocating, Rousseau writes in rhetorical style:

> What is this marvellous book? Is it Aristotle? or Pliny? or Buffon? Oh no, it is Robinson Crusoe.[36]

The rejection of the humanist and classical heritage, in favour of the present and the scientific is here both highly self-conscious and deeply defiant.

In defending his single 'relevant text' Rousseau enumerates the criteria informing his choice:

> Robinson Crusoe alone on his island, without the help of his fellows and the tools of the various arts, yet managing to pro-

cure food and safety, and even a measure of well-being: here is something of interest for every age, capable of being made attractive to children in a thousand ways ...

I want his head to be turned by it, and to have him busy himself unceasingly with his castle, his goats and his plantations. I want him to learn, not from books but from experience, all the things he would need to know in such a situation.[37]

As one reads on and considers Rousseau's desire for the child to imagine himself 'clothed in skins, with a large hat, a large sabre and all the grotesque equipment of his character, even to the umbrella he will not need' one is forcibly, if momentarily, reminded of many a modern drama lesson where children without reference to a past are invited to learn through a discovery process something of immediate relevance or, as Rousseau puts it, real utility: a 'simulation' experience to aid survival. Such continuities between Rousseau's pedagogy and some current practice in the teaching of the arts, without a doubt, exist.

One can see why Rousseau chose *Robinson Crusoe* as his set text, although his reading of it differs markedly from that of the author. Here is a narrative of a man, shipwrecked and isolated from all others, having to build up a world cut off from his historic civilization. It is a perfect analogue for the condition of Emile. The island is a visible image of time without history, of the possibilities of pure experience without reference to a prior culture, of nature without artifice; a paradise without libraries, without galleries, without concert halls, without theatres, without a recorded past. The subsequent progressive movement was, in many ways, to collectivise this phantasy. In the twentieth century the most radical experiment in English education was to turn Robinson Crusoe's isolated paradise into a school called Summerhill.

The progressive movement has its origins not in Rousseau's actual teaching (which was said to be irredeemably bad) but in his remarkable work *Emile*. In Pestalozzi, in Herbart, in Froebel, in Montessori, in AS Neill, one can find the direct shaping influence of his formulations. Again and again, the emphasis is on 'indirect learning', allowing 'spontaneous inner formation', allowing 'no obstacle between the child and his experience,' of letting the child follow 'its own laws of growth'. In the progressive tradition the characteristic tendency is to place the teacher in the background and the child in the foreground. Montessori wrote:

> The children must develop themselves by their own experience ... you will know that the teacher in our method is more of an observer than a teacher, therefore this is what the teacher must know, how to observe.[38]

The teacher, in other words, not as a custodian of culture but as psychological spectator, as observer of a natural process which only requires insulation from outside cultural influence. Montessori's words could have been written by Rousseau; they were, as we know, certainly deeply influenced by him.

According to the Plowden Report of 1967, a Report which was not at all unsympathetic to the child-centred movement, the progressive movement reached its height between 1920 and 1930, at roughly the same time as the flowering of Modernism and Psychoanalysis. *The Plowden Report* comments:

> This was a period when a great many descriptive books, of considerable practical help to teachers, were being written about both infant and junior schools, backed by H.M. Inspectors and local inspectors, began to work on lines similar to those already common in infant schools. For a brief time 'activity' and child-centred education became dangerously fashionable and misunderstandings on the part of the camp followers endangered the progress made by the pioneers.[39]

We know that in America in April 1912 *The Montessori Method* sold out of the first edition of 5000 copies in four days! In a time before the publisher's 'hype' that is a quite extraordinary figure. Between the two World Wars progressive education came into its own. The ideas of Rousseau had found a favourable cultural climate; they seeded, took root and spread widely. It is to this period that we must now turn.

The Flowering of the Progressive Movement

At the beginning of the twentieth century, at the same time as the modernist movement began in the arts, the progressive conceptions first formulated by Rousseau reached critical mass and effected a revolution whose good and necessary effects, particularly in our nursery and primary schools, still form a vital part of our educational inheritance. Against the uniform methods of a prescriptive rote-learning emerged a freer and more sympathetic practice; the child was no longer seen as a mere recipient of acquired knowledge but as an active agent, a participator in the act of understanding. The accent fell on freedom rather than constraint; on activity rather than passivity; on expression rather than regurgitation. At the centre of learning, it was claimed, was not the curriculum, not the teacher, not the culture, but the actual subject, the child. Hence the progressive's concept of education was rightly called 'child-centred'. The direct action in learning belonged to the child, while the indirect action belonged to the teacher, who became, under the power of these now common-place notions, a facilitator using what was generally described as a 'negative' or 'indirect' methodology. The essence of good teaching lay in subtle indirection, in the sensitive indirect promoting of what was seen as the child's natural biological tendency towards growth and fulfilment.

As early as 1912 in his *Playbooks* Caldwell Cook claimed that his teaching methods at the Perse School in Cambridge were based on the following interrelated principles:

  (i) Proficiency and learning come not from reading and listening, but from action, doing and from experience.
 (ii) Good work is more often the result of spontaneous effort and free interest than of compulsion and forced application.
(iii) The actual means of study in youth is play.

Experience. Spontaneity. Play. Here were three key words in the progressive's vocabulary; they were all to merge into the concept of 'self-expression' which was to remain, particularly in discussion of the arts in education, such a powerful yet deeply problematic notion. In our analysis we will have reason to return both to 'self-expression' (which was to cause so much misunderstanding in aesthetic education) and to Caldwell Cook (who, in many important respects, transcended the progressive tradition to which he yet so obviously belonged). In his actual teaching at the Perse School in Cambridge, Caldwell Cook drew with intuitive inspiration upon all the diverse elements that belong to the aesthetic field. He was both a remarkable innovator and a remarkable traditionalist. Of his methods he asserted: 'The only originality claimed is a fresh realization of the oldest truths.' He was able in his teaching to make the literary and dramatic heritage live in his pupils' imagination through the techniques of progressive education, the methods of Rousseau, Pestalozzi and Montessori. He was able to bring the child and the culture into dynamic relationship thus creating that creative transpersonal space in which the aesthetic act flourishes. But in this rare achievement he was not representative of the progressive movement. He used their techniques to ensure quite other meanings. Between, let us say, AS Neill in Summerhill (at Leyston) and Caldwell Cook in the Perse School (at Cambridge) there is an unpassable rift.

A year before the *Playbooks*, Edmund Holmes, another influential figure in the early educational debate, had claimed in *What Is and What Might Be* that 'for a third of a century, from 1862 to 1895, self-expression on the part of the child may be said to have been formally prohibited'. The allegation was, doubtless, true; now there was to be, for a number of decades, in the best educational practice a dramatic reversal. 'Self-expression' was to be formally promulgated as the essential key to education and to the teaching of the arts. In fact, Rousseau's vision of the child was to possess with an all but numinous intensity the imagination of thousands of teachers; or if not Rousseau's vision, then that of Wordsworth or Blake. Exhibitions of child-art, organized by Cizek, and later by Marion Richardson and Herbert Read, were to travel, with enormous success, across Europe and America. Books with such titles as *The Child Vision, Child Drama, Children as Artists, Art and the Child, The Play Way, Play in Childhood, A Child's Path to Freedom, The Education of the Poetic Spirit* (opening significantly with a long quotation from Wordsworth's *Prelude*) came in a steady flow from the educational presses and all explicitly proclaim the focus of concern. The interest in play — and play as a method of imaginative learning — was, of course, extended and greatly deepened by contact with the writings of Freud, Jung, and Susan Isaacs and later by the writings of Winnicot, Klein and other members of the Post-Freudian English school of psychoanalysis. Margaret Lowenfeld in an influential book *Play in Childhood* wrote:

> It (play) makes the bridge between the child's consciousness and his emotional experience, and so fulfils the role that conversation, introspection, philosophy, and religion fill for the adult.
>
> It represents to the child the externalised expression of his emotional life, and therefore in this aspect serves for the child the function taken by art in adult life.[40]

With such comprehensive claims for the play of the infant, it is not surprising that play often came to be viewed as the paradigm for all modes of learning, for all educational practice, and particularly the practice of the arts.

As far as the arts were concerned, the progressives certainly had a more positive conception of their place in education than their founding father, Rousseau. It was also common for them to consider all the arts together; Caldwell Cook in his *Play Way* delineates class-room work which while centred on English literature includes, both radically and generously, drama, dance and music. Marjorie Hourde's seminal work *The Education of the Poetic Spirit* was concerned equally with drama and literature and, more deeply, with the common symbolic process which informs all aesthetic activity. Herbert Read, likewise, envisaged the arts as one symbolic community and saw his central task as the articulation of a coherent aesthetic philosophy. He wrote:

> The theory to be put forward embraces all modes of self-expression, literary and poetic (verbal) no less than musical or aural and forms an integral approach to reality which should be called aesthetic education. The education of those senses upon which consciousness and ultimately the intelligence and judgement of the human being are based.[41]

Through the progressives' influence on the curriculum: in our state schools children composed poetry, made their own drama, began to dance, created forms expressive of their own lives and sensibilities. The intention of all this aesthetic work was not to create the specialist, but to create the sensitive human-being; it was, as the title of Herbert Read's most influential book makes clear, an education *through* art; indeed the aesthetic mode was seen by many as the key to the whole curriculum.

Without doubt the progressive 'revolution' was a remarkable achievement. It exerted an influence on our ways of thinking about children and learning so deep that many conceptions we have absorbed from its arguments strike us now as mere common sense, a matter of ordinary understanding, a matter of ethical decency. Of course, its revolution was partial and fragmentary. Other prescriptive practices, developed by the Victorians, continued and probably had greater sway, at least, in numerical terms. But now like modernism, the progressive movement seems to be largely exhausted. Like modernism it also cast a dark shadow, worked with assumptions which now seem deeply fallacious, carried its demise within its own partial premises. It is to these failings that I now want to briefly turn, particularly in their relationship to the teaching of the arts.

The Fallacies of Progressivism

In *Emile* Rousseau had written:

> Childhood has ways of seeing, thinking and feeling peculiar to itself: nothing can be more foolish than to seek to substitute our ways for theirs.[42]

During the romantic period the child's way of seeing became linked for the first time in Western civilization to a kind of sublime visionary perception. William Blake, for example, had declared that 'the vast majority of children were on the side of imagination and spiritual sensation'. The child became the symbol-carrier of wholeness and unity. Perhaps, possessing so little of history, the child invited the symbolic projection of those who were trying, like Rousseau, to shed the burdens of civilization. Whatever the reasons — and they were plural and complex — the child became not merely a child but *an angelic image of ahistorical existence* — and this image worked powerfully on the imagination of most of the progressives.

In *Education Through Art* Herbert Read referred to 'the innocent eye' of the child:

> But when we cognize a quality in a child's drawing which we describe as 'naive', we are indicating a certain 'vision' of things which is peculiar to children, and perhaps to certain rare adults who retain the child-like faculty. I have described it elsewhere as 'the innocent eye' ...[43]

While in *The Redemption of the Robot* he claimed:

> The most simple, direct and elementary affirmation of life, of the vital principle in our being, requires that we should make the effort to restore the Age of Innocence — or, if we must express the same ideal in a different phraseology, re-establish the human organism's primary unity of motivation and behaviour.[44]

The two languages are not, of course, identical. The psychological language masks rather than delineates the personal dynamic beneath, namely the nostalgia for an imagined state of innocence symbolized by the figure of the *puer aeternus* or the *puella aeterna*. But the problem lies, of course, in the very nature of the projection and the function it served.

Throughout the literature of the progressive movement one detects an idealized and somewhat euphoric image of the child; a child which nobody really wants to grow up because what it is imagined to possess is valued more highly than anything which might follow and be put in its place. Against the children of paradise, history seems a slow and tedious thing and the hard-won products of culture essentially futile achievements.

Kenneth Clarke, who was an urbane advocate of Marion Richardson's imaginative methods for developing impressionist-style paintings in the classroom (described more fully in Robin Morris' contribution to this volume) yet noted:

> We may even feel the symptoms of a reaction, an impatience with felicities of line and colour achieved at little cost. *Is art, then purely an instinctive acitvity? Is all the science of representation accumulated during the last five hundred years a waste of time? Are these years a waste of time? Is there really no point in growing up?*[45] (My emphasis)

Is there any point (to adapt Rousseau's image and to ignore the novel) in Robinson Crusoe, happily adapted to his island, returning to the cultural mainland?

The poetic image of the child is not the actual child, of course, and it quickly leads to sentimentality, to emotional indulgence, to an ahistorical psychology. Here, for example, is Dr. Montessori dedicating her own teacher's handbook to Helen Keller:

> Helen, clasp to your heart these little children, since they, above all others, will understand you.... They alone, then can fully understand the drama of the mysterious knowledge your soul has known. When, in darkness and in silence, their spirit left free to expand, their intellectual energy redoubled, they become able to read and write without having learnt, almost as if it were by intuition, they, only they, can understand in part the ecstasy which God granted you on the luminous path of learning.[46]

'*Able to read and write without having learnt*'. In such pious encomiums children become pseudo-mystics possessing all that adults are deemed to have lost. A child-centred education, on such terms, must remain perpetually child-centred for children in their mere primary existence are seen as superior to us all, and as teachers to us all.

It was, though, given the premises of Rousseau, Froebel and Montessori, all but inevitable that progressive education came to be more about the singular self-regulating self than about the self-in-the-world and the self-in-a-cultural-continuum; that it came to be more preoccupied with inner 'adjustment' than with any kind of symbolic mediation and mastery. Sixty per cent of parents sending their children to Dartington Hall claimed that they did so because they wanted their child to be 'happily adjusted';[47] in the case of Summerhill that figure would probably have risen to nearly 100 per cent. Neill was not concerned with any kind of cultural excellence. His commitment was to child-happiness. The overwhelming concern for psychological adjustment meant that the arts were invariably conceived as therapeutic activities, again rather like play. The word 'self-expression', first coined as late as 1892, came thus, more and more, to falsely characterize the quintessential purpose of the aesthetic curriculum. Yet art is embodied *symbolic*-expression and demands knowledge and skill, a formal context and a continuous culture and while having certain structural similarities with play has a variety of other functions that childhood play does not possess. Above all, art belongs to a cultural continuum and a public world; it simultaneously includes and transcends the creative play of the growing child. As all the essays in this symposium demonstrate, the misconception about art as 'self-expression' was to badly distort the development of all the arts in the primary and secondary curriculum, particularly, as Anna Haynes and Christopher Havell show, the arts of dance and drama.

The accent on self-expression left the mastery of technique unaccented, even mute. For the progressives if a work was in some way expressive of self then, by definition, it became laudatory, whatever the artistic merit. But, in all the arts, what is made is called *a work* (an *opus*) because it has required from the artist not only self-expression but also self-discipline and self-constraint in the prolonged engagement with the medium through which the art finally emerges, complete and *other*. The *expression* lies, ultimately, not in the self but in the intrinsic form of the art-work. Many children in 'free' art lessons may have expressed *themselves* only too well but produced, for want of technique and initiation into the symbolic medium, artistic non-entities. Good art is made out of a complex engagement, a reciprocal play between self and technique, between impulse and medium, between feeling and tradition. In the long term, the limited and limiting notion of self-expression could only lead to impoverished practice, the endless reproduction of the same minimal gestures, formulae, notations, brush-strokes, possibly *original* but not for that reason necessarily of any *artistic* worth.

In the same way as the progressive teachers tended not to develop the actual techniques of art, so they also tended to neglect the various traditions of art-making. A desire for immediate spontaneity of expression ousted stylistic constraints — and, hence, the formal possibilities — of inherited culture. In the 1960s many English teachers (myself included) genuinely thought in the name of 'relevance' and 'process' that one could discard the great literary inheritance of, say, Homer, Sophocles, Shakespeare, Wordsworth and Donne. What we valued was sincerity. What we largely overlooked was the need for a bed of culture in which feelings need to be rooted, to be given both *depth* and *connection*. In 'stimulating' feelings without sufficient reference to technique and traditional achievements, we tended to cheapen and exhaust the psyches of our pupils. In the wake of the second phase of modernism, we too said, as it were, *Now! Right now!* But because of our exclusive interest in the present tense, in the 'now' unrelated to a 'then', many of us felt unable to develop whatever we had released in experience. With some classes 'creative writing' deteriorated into a ritual of writing a series of short emotive lines each with an explanation mark. Stimulus — response; with little mediating tradition and few formal conventions. Professor Bantock's criticism of this kind of work in the English classroom is pertinent to our own critique and not, I think, in retrospect, unjust:

> One of the difficulties, however, has been the naive notion also encouraged by romantic progressivism, that 'creativity' was largely endogenous, a capacity with which a child was born and which needed only opportunity and encouragement rather than something on which to bite, whether technical or experiential. This, also, has tended to stultify progressive efforts to incorporate aesthetic elements into the curriculum — the consequent outpourings have been more remarkable for their becoming manifest than for their quality.[48]

While creativity may well, in fact, be endogeneous it yet needs a bed of culture to flower, the richer that bed, generally, the better the flowering. Hence the defense of tradition in this symposium.

Finally, there was an even deeper problem which it is not possible to develop here. It concerns the very meaning of art. To describe the nature of art the progressives tended to employ the language of *affectivity*, as if art was a matter of expression only, of emotion, of feeling, of subjective impulse, as if, that is to say, it was not also an intellectual and cognitive matter. As I have tried to show elsewhere[49] in reacting against the dominant rationalism of our civilization the progressives merely endorsed its cardinal fallacy: the fallacy that there is a definitive split between reason and feeling, between knowledge and expression, between science and art. The progressivist and the positivist views are two sides of the same equation; they emerge out of the same conceptual matrix, one tacitly agreeing to work on one side, the other on the other side. Yet our experience of art, both of making and receiving it, supports a different conception. Through art we *know* the nature of our experience. Art holds up in presentational symbols the conceptions of feeling, the conceptions of actual and possible worlds. Through art we recognize, *re-cognize*, the permanent elements of our human experience. Art, like science, though in a different field, is a mode of comprehension, a mode of knowing, a mode of intellection.

It is this epistemological conception of art which has finally ousted the progressive's viewpoint. In the influential Gulbenkian Report *The Arts in Schools* (1982) the second heading of the first chapter is entitled 'the different forms of human rationality'. The Report envisages art as the *transpersonal representation of meaning through expressive symbolism*. Thus the old dichotomy between science as objective and art as subjective is transcended and a much more comprehensive understanding of knowledge boldly inaugurated. We need a philosophy of art and a practice of art which comprehends aesthetic experience as cognitive in its own right, as intellectually exploratory of life in its own symbolic medium.

Locating an Alternative Conception of Art and Education

In modernism and educational progressivism we have encountered two major related failings. Firstly, there was the failure to recognize the essential autonomy of the aesthetic realm; secondly, there was the failure to recognize the essential place of historic tradition in the making of art, the need, that is to say, for a repertoire of inherited skills, exemplars, high works of achievement all needed to nourish and root the individual and social imagination. In the first case, modernism was guilty of transposing aesthetic terms into historic and ideological terms and thus, in effect, erasing them; while the progressive movement conceived aesthetic experience largely in psychological and hedonistic terms. For them the arts were more a matter of 'adjustment' and 'happiness' than a distinctive kind of symbolic experience. In the second case, concerning the denial of tradition, I have tried to demonstrate that modernism was guilty of a reductive historicism while the progressivists were deluded by a kind of naturalism that attempted to avoid confronting the obvious truth that we are born into communal relationship and, potentially, into an ever richer cultural continuum. The progressives were nostalgic for an imagined innocence beyond culture, which they proceeded, quite unconsciously to project onto the child. The result was an educational practice which tended to view the cultural achievements of the past not as a means to liberation and renewal but as oppressive obstacles, cataracts, as it were, threatening otherwise innocent eyes. My argument has been that these two 'traditions', intertwining in diverse ways throughout the course of our century, have led finally to a deep philosophical and pedagogic confusion.

In that contentious essay to which we have already referred *The Dehumanization of Art* Ortega y Gasset asked of the then emerging Modernism the following questions:

> Should that enthusiasm for pure art be but a mask which conceals surfeit with art and hatred of it? ... Is it conceivable that modern Western man bears a rankling grudge against his own historical essence? Does he feel something akin to the *odium professionis* of medieval monks — that aversion after long years of monastic disciplines against the very rules that had shaped their life?[50]

Hatred for pure art; a grudge against inherited culture: these penetrating judgments couched in the opening years of modernism are close to our own obituary written at the end of its life. Rather like Freud, but in radically altered circumstances, our task in this symposium is, once again, to release the repressed, to lift the taboo on the imaginative power of the inherited past, to expose the liberating energies of artistic conventions, the Hebraic and Hellenic narratives, and, indeed, the stories of all past cultures, particularly those of myth and cosmology; reclaiming them, that is, for present use in the continuous aesthetic field of art-making. In this task the teacher becomes not neutral facilitator on the edge of child-learning but the active custodian of culture, the agent who draws together, for further creative achievement, the creative achievements of all past culture. Teachers become co-artists working with their pupils for symbolic connection and cultural renewal.

It is this conception of an aesthetic field that I want finally to bring against the widespread anaesthesia of our 'modern' and 'progressive' thought. It is not, needless to say, a *new* conception. Interestingly, it can be found in some of the best modernist art-makers and some of the most distinguished progressive teachers. Paradoxically 'making it new' for Ezra Pound meant making it more and more ancient: for his masterpiece, *Hugh Selwyn Mauberley*, (like so many early modernist works), is steeped in the classical culture of the past — just as later his *Cantos* were to be steeped in the arts and philosophy

of many traditional cultures, particularly Chinese. Whatever iconoclasm existed in the early works of literary modernism, it merely
served to reactivate and reconstitute the whole symbolic field of
literature. And in such practice we can observe a vital principle at
work which actually negates or radically alters the demand for endless
innovation we described earlier.

It was TS Eliot, another highly traditional modernist, who gave
the notion of cultural continuum a memorable formulation in his
essay *Tradition and the Individual Talent*. Eliot, in that early essay,
defined a notion of *a dynamic tradition within which all artistic expression
has inevitably to work*. He wrote:

> Yet if the only form of tradition, of handing down, consisted
> in following the ways of the immediate generation before us
> in a blind or timid adherence to its successes, 'tradition' should
> positively be discouraged. We have seen many such simple
> currents soon lost in the sand; and novelty is better than
> repetition. Tradition is a matter of much wider significance. It
> cannot be inherited, and if you want it you must obtain it by
> great labour. It involves, in the first place, the historical sense,
> which we may call nearly indispensable to anyone who would
> continue to be a poet beyond his twenty-fifth year; and the
> historical sense involves a perception, not only of the pastness
> of the past, but of its presence; the historical sense compels a
> man to write not merely with his own generation in his
> bones, but a feeling that the whole of the literature of Europe
> from Homer and within it the whole of the literature of his
> own country has a simultaneous existence and composes a
> simultaneous order. This historical sense, which is a sense of
> the timeless as well as of the temporal and of the timeless and
> of the temporal together, is what makes a writer traditional.
> And it is at the same time what makes a writer most acutely
> conscious of his place in time, of his own contemporaneity.[51]

Eliot's insight unifies, as it were, both modernist and traditionalist positions by placing them in a larger, more comprehensive,
cultural field. Needless to say, such a recognition of Eliot's conception
of the dynamism of tradition does not commit us to his political or
religious views. If a few of the literary modernists were acutely aware
of the need for a living past — and thus important exceptions to the
argument developed earlier — so, also were a few of the progressive
teachers who actively developed a pedagogy placing their pupils, with
due sensitivity, at the centre of the aesthetic field. Two teachers stand

Plate 13 TS ELIOT as teacher transcribing the diagrammatic models of action of The Cocktail Party. *Eliot delineates in his work a dynamic concept of tradition essential in the aesthetic field.*

out; Marjorie Hourd whose practice was recorded in her own classic *Education of the Poetic Spirti* (1949) and Caldwell Cook whose approach was outlined in *The Play Way* (1914). Here there is only space to refer to the latter.

Caldwell Cook begins, he informs us, with the progressive's dictum 'Start with experience!' He writes:

'Let's have a go!' is the right spirit in which to undertake any enterprise of play. It is far more healthy for the beginner that he learn his earlier adjustments of balance empirically at the

> risk of (and better still at the cost of) a few real sprawls upon the hard ice, than that he sit secure and idle, and admire the evolutions of his skilled instructor.[52]

This, of course, is pure Rousseau! The empirical and psychological language is precisely the language through which Emile's ideal education is described. And as in Rousseau's utopia, so in Cook's actual classroom, the skilled instructor is put initially in the background, a potential menace to authentic learning. But then Caldwell Cook continues:

> After a series of preliminary exercises, a few free kicks, a few nasty sprawls, the pupil returns to his master — ready now for the instruction to begin.[53]

The return to the master as potential instructor is not found in Rousseau but for Cook it corrects the freedom and restores the centrality of the teacher. What does the teacher do? According to Cook the teacher's task is to imaginatively place the pupil in the very best of the received culture:

> When an important play is afoot, the experiment of evolving your plot is so difficult and attended with so much risk of disaster that it is wiser to follow the example of Chaucer, Spenser, Shakespeare, Milton, and all our other great poets, and found your story upon the firm rock of some traditional tale.[54]

But the tradition is not there as a series of inert texts, for Cook then urges that his pupils *play* with the received material, create and recreate within it and through it:

> Having borrowed their story, take what you have need of, and set aside the rest. You may add, divide and multiply. But you must start by borrowing. The creative skill of the speakers and their choice in text are the test of their Promethean virtue.[55]

Having liberated the imagination to work on the great narratives, having encouraged, also, free group discussions on the work 'in process', the teacher then steps into the heart of the classroom action and gives what Cook calls the 'Master's Lesson' on related conventions or background material relating to 'the history and literature of the period'. Finally, the creative work, after further 'fashioning and

Plate 14 CALDWELL COOK *teaching English in a progressive manner around 1916. His methods show a fine balance between form and informality, between self and culture, between tradition and innovation.*

shaping' is performed to an audience 'with all due ceremony' with music and dance.

Caldwell Cook himself listed the following eleven stages in this essentially literary mode of 'playmaking':

   (i)   Reading and telling of the story.
  (ii)   Informal discussion.
 (iii)   Sub-committee stage.
 (iv)   Preparation of rough notes.
  (v)   Acting in the rough.
 (vi)   Master's lessons.

(vii)   Discussion of special points.
(viii) Careful fashioning, shaping and writing.
 (ix)   Careful acting, as in rehearsal.
  (x)   Final revision of text of speeches.
 (xi)   Performance with all due ceremony.[56]

What we see in action here is neither obviously progressive nor in any way simply traditional, but a model which envisages the teaching of art as complex aesthetic practice; as dynamic and dialectical; as constantly moving from the teacher to the pupil, from the pupil back to the teacher; and constantly moving, also, from the cultural heritage to the expressive act of the pupil and from the expressive act of the pupil back to the heritage. Thus we see a subtle, continuous reciprocal movement between complementary poles guided by the teacher, now through direct intervention, now through indirect sensitive observation. The teaching method allows for the various diverse and demanding phases of the creative act and culminates in performance, a performance which connects with the arts of music and dance. Here, I suggest, is an early and brilliant example of a teacher working (often intuitively) the whole aesthetic field and providing his pupils with an aesthetic education worthy of the name.

Thus within modernism (taking one of TS Eliot's notions) and progressivism (taking the practice of Caldwell Cook) we can begin to identify a creative answer to the many aesthetic and educational problems they spawned.

Defining the Aesthetic Field

What then do we mean by aesthetic field? And how can such a notion provide a conceptual matrix for the organization of the arts in the curriculum?

The word 'aesthetic' has never been a particularly easy one in our language. Coleridge, who was largely responsible for bringing the word into English under the influence of Kant, wrote in 1821: 'I wish I could find a more familiar word than aesthetic for works of taste and criticism'. And as late as 1842 the status of the word remained uncertain for in his *Encyclopaedia of Architecture* Gwilt had called the word 'a silly pedantic term' and 'one of the useless additions to nomenclature in the arts'. Yet the word instead of folding up and instantly dying, was to become shortly after Gwilt's peremptory dismissal the acclaimed word of a controversial artistic movement.

The aesthetes were to congregate together holding to Walter Pater's conception of 'love of art for art's sake' as it was eloquently propounded in the last chapter of *The Renaissance*. Aestheticism, for them, meant a refined hedonistic grasping of beautiful experience and of beautiful objects. Yet the word was to survive its temporary annexation and again broaden out to mean a specific mode of responding, making, and knowing which was both autonomous and autotelic. In this broad sense, broadened beyond, but including the category of beauty, it retained its essentially Kantian sense of sensuous perception. Thus in the Gulbenkian Report, *The Arts in Schools*, it is stated quite unapologetically that:

> one of those distinct categories of understanding and achieve-
> ment — the aesthetic and creative — is exemplified by the
> arts: music, drama, literature, poetry, dance, sculpture and the
> graphic arts.[57]

Aesthetic refers here to a distinct category of understanding. Throughout the symposium this is our concept of the word as well.

Aesthetic denotes a mode of sensuous knowing essential for the life and development of consciousness; aesthetic response is inevitably, through its sensory and physical operations, cognitive in nature. Through aesthetic activity we half-apprehend and half-create a world of understanding, of heightened perception, of heightened meaning. Art, we might say, exists for the meaning's sake but that meaning cannot be grasped outside of the form in which it finds expression. Thus we want to say that the aesthetic mode is one distinctive mode for the creation of meaning, of significance, of truth. We have moved a considerable distance from the progressives' talk of 'self-expression' and ' emotional release', a long way, also, from talk of 'art for the sake of art' and the cultivation of 'the exquisite' or, even, 'the sublime and beautiful'. Our symposium is, in part, an attempt to reclaim and reanimate the word aesthetic and to put it to new purposes in our educational practice.

But what characterizes the aesthetic mode? How does it work in practice? What are its distincitve features? The etymology of the word gives a vital clue. Aesthetic derives from the Greek word *aisthetika* meaning *things perceptible through the senses*, with the verb stem *aisthe* meaning: *to feel, to apprehend through the senses*. Here in this small cluster of words: perception, sensing, apprehending, feeling, we begin to discern the nature of the aesthetic mode. We can see how the various meanings that the word has been given in our culture cohere: from 'good taste' (the first use of the word) to 'the a priori principles of sensuous knowledge' (Kant's understanding) to the appreciation of the Beautiful and Sublime (the general Romantic conception). The unity of these diverse meanings lies in the essential perceptual nature of the activity.

It is important that *the sensing* is observed here. In its root meaning the word *taste* includes the meaning: to feel, to handle and *to touch*. While the word 'touch' itself refers both to sensing an object or texture (through touching) and to being emotionally moved ('it was a touching moment'). The word 'feel' can, likewise, denote an affective disposition or the act of touching an object. By a similar inner logic the Latin word for feeling (tactare) has given the English language both the notion of tact (having feeling for other people's feelings) and of tactile (where sensory touch is indicated). According to the *Oxford English Dictionary* the word anaesthesia, first used in 1721, decades before 'aesthetic' came into the language, denotes 'loss of feeling or sensation: insensibility'. The aesthetic, then, must be concerned with all that works through and on feeling, sensation and sensibility ... *Touch, taste, feel, tact:* these are the words, suggesting in their uses the intimate relationship between sensation and feeling, which best bring out the nature of the aesthetic mode. However high art may aspire it is yet always rooted in bodily response and primitive engagement. Of the characteristics of the poet, Coleridge wrote:

> ... a great Poet must be implicité if not explicité, a profound Metaphysician. He may not have it in logical coherence, in his Brain & Tongue; but he must have it by *Tact/* for all sounds & forms of human nature he must have the *ear* of a wild Arab listening in the silent Desart, *the eye* of a North American Indian tracing the footsteps of an Enemy upon the Leaves that strew the Forest —; the *Touch* of a Blind Man feeling the face of a darling Child'[58]

Clearly, this is an aesthetic notion of poetry and, by analogy, of all art which does not lead to aestheticism but, as Edwin Webb also insists in his essay on English, to *cognition and understanding*. Coleridge elsewhere refers to a thinking that takes place when 'a succession of perceptions' is 'accompanied by a sense of *nisus* and purpose'. Thus, inherent in the perception is the whole complex intentionality of the person — feeling, willing, remembering, judging, thinking. It is all but never simply a matter of sensation, for sensation is only the manifest and mediating shaft of the whole mentality, the whole person. Robert Frost describing somewhere the genesis of art-work offers a simple description of the process: 'A poem begins as a lump in the throat, a homesickness, a lovesickness. It finds the thought and the thought finds the words.' Through sensation into meaning, into understanding, into, literally *meta*-physics. As we have implied in our defence of tradition and culture, Robert Frost's account is far too simple a concept of art-making; however, what we are keen to establish here is, firstly, the nature of the perceptual mode through which we create and engage with art and, secondly, to show that the perceptual mode is inherently cognitive in its action. All aesthetic activity as it is developed through the manifold forms of the arts is simultaneously perceptive, affective and cognitive; it can offer an education, therefore, of the highest order not through the analytical intellect but through the engaged sensibility.

What then of aesthetic *field*? I have taken the word 'field' from Quantum Mechanics to act not as a precise analogue — the arts have no need of any analogue outside of their own activity — but merely as a suggestive metaphor. I want to suggest that art should not refer to a series of discrete artefacts or what some critics call 'art objects' but to a highly complex web of energy linking the artist to the audience, and both artist and audience to all inherited culture as now an active, now a latent shaping force. Ideally, art requires for its understanding, a dynamic language of participles and verbs, not of inert nouns referring to discrete objects. Just as in the study of sub-atomic particles so in the field of art our terms should be those of motion, of interaction, of transformation. Just as the nature of matter cannot be separated from its activity, so the art-work should not be conceptually separated from the complex field in which it operates. Just as in quantum physics the field gives birth to a variety of forms, which it sustains, then takes back, then recreates, so the aesthetic field may throw up endless combinations which are, in turn, dissolved and recast again, culture after culture, work after work, symbol after symbol; the 'simultaneous order'.

Field, then, in our context, implies an intricate web of energy where the parts are seen in relationship, in a state of reciprocal flow between tradition and innovation, between form and impulse, between the society and the individual, between the four phases of *making, presenting, responding* and *evaluating* which mark the four essential elements of the aesthetic field. The concept of an aesthetic field in which all art moves and has its being can be diagramatically portrayed as follows:

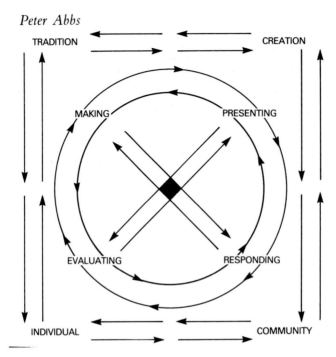

Figure 1 Diagrammatic Representation of the Aesthetic Field

The arts teacher can break into the aesthetic field at any point and be led by an invisible pattern of relationships into the whole circuit — for the parts are not self-contained but gain their meaning through connection with all the other parts. All points, therefore, can be starting-points *and there can be no one way of sequencing the teaching of the arts.* What is important for the teacher is to discern *the whole complex interaction of the field and to use that knowledge in the organizing and planning of work.*

For our own purposes we will break into the aesthetic field at the point of making (M) move to presenting (P) continue by considering responding (R) and close with evaluating (E). What matters, though, is not the establishment of one of the parts but the vivid realization of the whole field. As we shall see in Part II of this book, we are often still very far from achieving this in the teaching of the arts, and in some arts, as with film, the aesthetic field hardly exists at all.

Making

Igor Stravinsky describing his own method of composition wrote:

> All creation presupposes as its origin a sort of appetite that is brought on by a foretaste of knowledge.[59]

That seems an eloquent definition of the origins of art-making: *appetite moved by the foretaste of knowledge*. The appetite — the impulse to expression — animates the specific medium of the art-maker, (in the case of Stravinsky the 'twelve sounds in each octave and all possible rhythmic varieties') and in the encounter between appetite and medium the art-work begins to take shape. Soon after naming 'appetite' Stravinsky goes on to stress the importance of technique in the process of making:

> This foretaste of the creative act accompanies the intuitive grasp of an unknown entity already possessed but not yet intelligible, an entity that will not take definite shape except by the action of a constantly vigilant technique.

Appetite-knowledge: creative art-technique. Here are the essential reciprocal forces at work in the process of composing the art-work.

The medium, it is worth observing, is not a neutral space through which the creative act passes; it is rather the tangible material which makes the act possible and, as tangible material, it has its own character, inviting certain movements of the art-maker, resisting or confounding others. The material also carries with it a history, a repertoire of previous uses, of working conventions, of established connections and meanings, both covert and hidden. In engaging with the material the art-maker thus engages both consciously and unconsciously with tradition, with the forms already used and the modes and the techniques those forms have employed and passed on. Indeed, sometimes, the art-maker in the process of composition will actively study other artists' work. And so, art does not come solely out of appetite but also out of other art. Each work of art in its making manifests the whole field.

In his account Stravinsky compares the activity of the composer to that of an animal grubbing about, using his senses and his body to instinctively locate what he needs. This is an evocative image for *the perceptual mode*. And, again, Stravinsky is emphatic about the impor-tance of *working*, the absolute value of the exploratory and cumulative action, the meandering through progressive revision to embodied vision:

> The idea of work to be done is for me so closely bound up with the idea of the arranging of material and of the pleasure that the actual doing of the work affords us that, should the impossible happen and my work suddenly be given to me in a

perfectly completed form, I should be embarrassed and non-plussed by it, as by hoax.[61]

In the movement from expressive impulse to engagement with the medium to the realization of symbolic form one notices also a movement in the art-maker from a passionate identification with the material — being, as it were, lost in it — to a more distant stance as the work takes form and the art-maker senses that he has, perhaps found himself or, at least, his *conception of feeling* within it. Towards the end of the process, the art-maker thus feels ready to release the art into the world, to let it have its own independent existence. Indeed, a sense of an audience has been, invariably, a shaping influence, at least in the latter stages of the art-making process. The completion of the art is deceptive, then, for its apparent completion merely sets into motion further aesthetic actions, another set of related interactions and developments still in the perceptual mode.

Presenting

John Dewey observed that the completed artefact is not *in itself* an aesthetic object but an object that invites aesthetic response from others:

> The product of art is not the work of art. The work takes place when a human being cooperates with the product so that the outcome is an experience that is enjoyed because of its liberating and orderly properties.[62]

If there was no-one to view a Cezanne the painting would be devoid of aesthetic meaning for aesthetic meaning can only reside in the dynamic interaction between the work and the person looking. Here again, we locate a field concept of aesthetic activity. *The work exists in its action on the senses and imagination of the audience.* No audience — no aesthetic. Merely as 'an art object', to be classified by historians or sociologists or archaeologists, the work exists on the other side of the aesthetic field, devoid of its artistic life. In practical terms, this means that the work needs to be shown to a reponsive audience. It requires presentation in a specific context which draws out its essential aesthetic import, its liberating and ordered properties. To use Caldwell Cook's formulation it needs 'performance with all due ceremony'. Thus our account turns away from static 'art objects' to further aesthetic interaction.

In the various arts presentation takes various forms. In drama, dance, mime and music — often known as 'the performing arts' — the recreation of the dance, score, play or the narrative demands fresh and exacting acts of creative indwelling and expressive projection which closely parallel the making process already outlined. In some cases, as in jazz, and certain forms of drama, dance and mime, the performing act is itself the primary act of creation with no fixed form prior to its expression. In such cases the art-making and the art-performing exist simultaneously in the achieved moments of continuous improvisation. In the other arts presentation may be overtly less dramatic but, nevertheless, it remains essential — a key element in the aesthetic field. The finished paintings and sculpture are *exhibited* and *displayed*; the novels, stories, poems are *published* or *broadcast*; the films are *shown*. The actual size of the audience may not matter. A small responsive group can form a better audience than an anonymous crowd. What really matters is the drawing of the work into the community, into the imagination and sensibility of human experience. The audience needs the art-maker as much as the art-maker needs the audience — though in aesthetic education the students move constantly from one position to the other, now making, now responding, now performing, now evaluating.

Under the virtual tyranny of the discursive and ideological mode, the performing element in the teaching of literature has been neglected, particularly so with poetry. It has been argued by certain poets[63] that the poem exists aesthetically only at two moments: the moment of its *composition* and the moment of its *performance*. In this view, if the poem is conceived as a kind of potential sound-event which rather like scripted drama or the musical score needs for its full aesthetic realization to be rendered to an audience. Each poem has its own voice or, like *The Waste Land*, a polyphony of voices — and the poem lives in the auditory imagination only when the voice or voices are spoken out, given dramatic utterance. From this perspective — a perspective which accords well with the aesthetic field model — our present teaching of poetry (the '*looking at* meaning' approach) works at a considerable remove from its aesethetic nature. Once again, the discursive method of teaching bypasses and negates the presentational.

Responding

Aesthetic presentation invites aesthetic response. Such response is initially pre-conceptual — when it is impulsively formulated it is often expressed in such phrases as 'Great!', 'Terrific!', 'I want to hear it again!', 'I like it!', 'I want to touch it!', 'Deeply moving!' or, when the response is negative: 'Dreadful!', 'A right mess!', 'Simply awful!'. Sometimes, the immediate response is to the whole work and represents a kind of intuitive assent (or dissent); at other times it is more a response to a part, some compelling fragment, which we attend to and which like Ariadne's thread takes us down into the labyrinthine complexity of the actual work; or we may be drawn to the work but yet somehow confounded by it and wish to submit ourselves to it further so that it may slowly release the power it appears to have and yet, on first response, witholds. All these responses — and many more of their kind — are not logical but *intuitive apprehensions working through our senses and our feelings*, through our sensibility.

Responses to art, *as art*, are sensuous, physical, dramatic, bodily, pre-verbal. For this reason the often heard casual remark: 'Well, what's it *do* for you?' is aesthetically much sounder than the intellectual question 'What is it *saying*?' or 'What did the artist *intend*?' Premature answers to these latter questions take us quickly out of the aesthetic realm into the documentary or discursive. Too much theory, too much knowledge, in isolation from aesthetic experience, can block and impede the immediate bodily response, the imaginative indwelling of mind in the pattern of sensation.

The point and purpose of the art lies in the field of its action. Often in educational contexts the desire to explicate needs to be explicitly suppressed. What needs to be nurtured is trust in the authority of the aesthetic form: trust in the power of the story, the narrative, the non-discursive symbol; trust in the organs of imagination and sensibility through which they posses their power of meaning. We need, in brief, to cultivate the aesthetic response before works of art; not the political or historical or conceptual.

Yet is is neither possible nor desirable to leave the aesthetic field with these three elements. For we *do* wish to judge aesthetic work and we *do* wish to understand the media it so magically transforms into living symbols, and, at many crucial moments in responding to art, we *do* require information (historical, technical, cultural) to make sense of what we see. To respond fully to many Renaissance paintings, for example, one needs to know the Bible narrative, Greek myths as well as certain emblematic codes. It is this need for understanding and for evaluation which brings us to the last element of the aesthetic field.

Evaluating

'Well, what did you make of it?' is a natural response after any performance or presentation. In the evaluation of art we struggle conceptually to *draw out the value* it has for us.

Evaluating is, then, in large part, an attempt to organize the complex elements of our aesthetic response — to state intellectually our relationship to the work of art, to formulate the aesthetic response (as near as we can get to it) conceptually. In part, this is the attempt both to organize and analyze — which will lead us to a consideration of the *form* of the piece itself, and to that matrix of associations and traditions in which it operates. Discriminating, for example, how the associative network of images in a poem combine to produce their effect, heightens and, in some way, justifies the value of the work's effect upon us. This can come close to an intellectual pleasure in itself — the pleasure we derive from seeing how something works, how it has been made. The symmetries, the flow of movement in the lines of a visual presentation, the modified nuance of a theme repeated in music, the pace and placing of cuts in film, the organization of space in theatre production — these, and many other characteristics of art-products may be identifiable elements of the total.

To some extent such judging of the work tests out our knowing of the work in the immediacy of our responding to it — for such evaluation is essentially reflective. It is post-event. We put some sort of psychic distance between the event of the art and our formulation of judgment. It is a critical act, but one which — in extreme practices — can become wholly detached, pure cerebration, an intellectualization alone. The fact of established critical vocabulary can here actually promote this disengagement. In the best evaluation, however, there is actually a further engagement: the intellectual and the aesthetic combine *to make sense* of the sensuous. Evaluation makes *intelligible* (and communicable) the aesthetic response.

Here, at its most productive, our knowledge of traditions, our awareness of history and culture, our understanding of the craft, will develop and deepen our aesthetic judgments. the essential elements of reference may be schematically indicated as follows:

(i) An awareness of conventions and of techniques.
(ii) An awareness of the historic development of the art tradition including an understanding of historic background.
(iii) An awareness of some of the best critical and interpretive literature.

In some arts these three areas are well developed — while in others, dance and drama for example, they hardly exist. Yet a discursive understanding of these elements makes discourse possible, gives the means of clarifying and defending aesthetic judgments. Of themselves, of course, they do not constitute aesthetic response, and, therefore, they can very easily miss the point. Thus we can know that Mozart is considered a musical genius, but if we do not *hear* it in the auditory imagination the proposition is void of aesthetic meaning.

What is important, then, is that the intellectual knowledge is turned back into the aesthetic field and continuously linked to the primary elements of making, presenting and responding. It is merely a part of a greater whole and its meaning derives not from itself alone but from its intrinsic relationship to that totality. On our own cyclical journey through the field, the evaluative habit dissolves and constitutes itself once more as the art-making process; a process enriched by the stages it has travelled through. As in any field of energy there is no final stopping place, so criticism and discourse move on and art, as that awesome activity of creating, begins again.[64]

Conclusion

Into this dynamic aesthetic field we would wish to place all the expressive arts in the curriculum. The implications are as complex and momentous as they are urgent and necessary. The arts have come into the curriculum at different points of time, for different reasons and under different philosophies. All of them have been affected by both modernism and progressivism. What is called for, then, is the historic reconstruction of each discipline in the light of a common aesthetic. In the six chapters which now follow we will find ourselves encountering in the teaching of the arts, not only many examples of good aesthetic practice, but also many examples of distortion, of confusion, and of isolation. Thus, for example, we will find that dance entering the curriculum as physical education found it extremely difficult to locate its aesthetic nature or to make formal, or even informal, connections with the other arts. We will see how English began as a critical discipline, developed into an aesthetic one and has tended, during the last twenty years, to become more a general discursive and linguistic discipline. We will observe how film has always been badly neglected in the curriculum but how it is now making its advances not as an aesthetic activity but as an ideological one within media studies. In complete contrast, we will read how drama under the influence of progressive child-centred philosophy came to be, perhaps, over-preoccupied with process and neglected 'performance' and 'evaluation', neglected theatre and the need for critical discourse. We will see, also, how music had yet another pattern of development — begining richly and yet often, in practise, becoming little more than a curious mixture of extra-curricular virtuousi playing and class singing; while the visual arts tended to work with most elements of the aesthetic field but, under the distorting influence of modernism and progressivism, gave too little attention to tradition and often dispensed with the need for critical discourse.

We can bring the aesthetic field to each arts discipline and ask crucial and wholly practical questions: *How much making? How much presenting? How much responding? How much evaluating?* It gives us a coherent way of looking, it provides the conceptual elements of a unified aesthetic. Yet the arts in our schools are so divided and fragmented. If we are to bring the six great members of the aesthetic family together — art, drama, dance, music, film, literature — we must first listen, with care, to their histories. Only then can we move forwards together into the new ground of a unified aesthetic education. We now turn to the historic and aesthetic reconstruction of each arts discipline.

Notes

1 This current understanding, at a popular level, is well exemplified by the GULBENKIAN REPORT (1982) *The Arts in Schools*, Calouste Gulbenkian Foundation. At a higher critical level it can be seen informing such infuential and diverse critics as Peter Fuller, Roger Scruton, David Best and David Aspin (see bibliographies).

2 FRANK KERMODE in BERGONZI, B (Ed) (1986) *Innovations*, Macmillan, pp 83–4.

3 ORTEGA Y GASSET (1968) in *The Dehumanization of Art*, Princeton University Press, pp 12–13.

4 Consider, for example, MARGARET DRABBLE'S remarks in *The Oxford Companion to English Literature*: 'Modernist literature is a literature of discontinuity both historically, being based upon a sharp rejection of the procedures and values of the immediate past, to which it adopts an adversary stance; and aesthetically'.

5 ROY STRONG (1980) in *The Listener*, 20 November.

6 I have documented part of this movement more fully in 'Art and the loss of art in an age of spilt science' in *Continuity and Deception*, Welsh Arts Council, 1979. The most eloquent voice against the excesses of visual modernism has been that of Peter Fuller. See, for example, *Aethetics after Modernism*, (1982) Writers and Readers; see also bibliographies.

7 KERMODE, F (1968) *op cit*, p 80.
8 HERBERT READ's paper 'The limits of permissiveness' sounding a note of alarm about modernism by its arch exponent is reproduced in ABBS, P (Ed) (1975) *The Black Rainbow: Essays on the Breakdown of Contemporary Culture*, Heinemann Educational Books.
9 Josef Herman in an open letter to *Tract* printed in *Tract 28, Crisis in the Visual Arts*, Gryphon Press.
10 HERMAN BAHR (1920) in *Expressionism*, translated by RT Gribble, London, p 35. First published as *Expressionism*, Munich, 1916.
11 NICOLAS TARABUKIN 'From the easel to the machine' quoted in FRASCINA, F and HARRISON, C (Eds) (1982) Modern Art and Modernism, Harper and Row.
12 See, for example, the conclusion to EAGLETON, T (1983) *Literary Theory*, Basil Blackwell, where history is at once reified and turned into self-justifying category in a typical Marxist manner.
13 In her definition of modernism in *The Oxford Companion to English Literature* Margaret Drabble refers to *Art Now* and quotes its demand for 'an abrupt break with all tradition'.
14 HERBERT READ, quoted by MARGARET DRABBLE in *The Oxford Companion to English Literature*.
15 HERBERT READ (1935) in *Five on Revolutionary Art*, Artists International Association, p 21.
16 *Ibid*.
17 From the Brazilian Manifesto for *Concrete Poetry*, Noigandres, No 4, Sao Paulo, 1958.
18 ROBBE-GRILLET quoted in *A Dictionary of Literary Terms* under the entrance 'noveau roman'.
19 GEORGE MATHIEU (1960) in *From the Abstract to the Possible*, Paris, p 9.
20 LESLIE FIEDLER (1968) in *The New Mutants*, reproduced in BERGONZI, B (Ed) *op cit*, p 25.
21 ORTEGA Y GASSET (1968) *op cit*, p 13.
22 *Ibid*.
23 MORSE PECKHAM (1966) in *Man's Rage for Order*, New York. For a brilliant critical evaluation of this book see GOMBRICH, EH (1968)' Art at the end of its tether' in BERGONZI, B (Ed) *op cit*.
24 See, for example, MICHAEL DALEY's account in *Tract 28, Crisis in the Visual Arts*, Gryphon Press.
25 Quoted by PETER FULLER (1980 in *Beyong the Art Crisis*, Writers and Readers, p 147.
26 For a full study of this fallacy see POPPER, K (1957) *The Poverty of Historicism*, Routledge and Kegan Paul.
27 OTTO HAHN quoted in PARMELIN, H (1977) *Art-Anti Art*, Marion Boyers.
28 For SUZANNE LANGER's philosophy of art see her classic study (1953) *Feeling and Form*, Routledge and Kegan Paul.
29 COMPTON, M (1974) *Art as Thought Press*, Arts Council.
30 FULLER, P (1986) *Marches Past*, Chatto and Windus, p 31.
31 WILLIAMS, R (1976) *Keywords*, Fontana/Croom Helm, p 207.
32 MONTESSORI (1972) in *Dr Montessori's Own Handbook* first published in 1914, Schocken books, p 32.

33 *Ibid*, p 36.
34 ROUSSEAU (1950) in *Emile*, Everyman's Library, p 10.
35 *Ibid*, p 7.
36 *Ibid*, book III.
37 *Ibid*.
38 MONTESSORI (1972) *op cit*, p 14.
39 DEPARTMENT of EDUCATION and SCIENCE (1967) *Children and Their Primary Schools* (The Plowden Report), Volume 1, HMSO, p 190.
40 MARGARET LOWENFELD quoted in HODGSON, J (Ed) (1972) *The Uses of Drama*, Methuen, p 53.
41 READ, H (1958) *Education Through Art,* Faber & Faber, p 7.
42 ROUSSEAU (1950) *op cit*.
43 READ, H (1958) *op cit*.
44 HERBERT READ quoted in WOODCOCK, G (1972) *Herbert Read: The Stream and the Source*, Faber and Faber, p 274.
45 CLARKE, K 'Introduction' in RICHARDSON, M *Art and the Child,* University of London Press, p 8.
46 MONTESSORI (1972) *op cit*, p 26.
47 For research findings and further analysis see PUNCH, M (1977) *Progressive Retreat a Sociological Study of Dartington Hall*, Cambridge University Press.
48 See BANTOCK, GH (1981) *The Parochialism of the Present*, Routledge and Kegan Paul.
49 See particularly (1985) 'Art as a way of knowing' in *Aspects of Education*, 34, University of Hull.
50 ORTEGA Y GASSET (1968) *op cit*, p 45.
51 In KERMODE, F (1975) *Selected Prose of TS Eliot*, Faber and Faber, p 38.
52 CALDWELL COOK quoted in *The Uses of Drama*.
53 *Ibid*, p 147.
54 *Ibid*.
55 *Ibid*.
56 *Ibid*.
57 GULBENKIAN REPORT (1982) *The Arts in Schools*, Calouste Gulbenkian Foundation, p 20.
58 COLERIDGE quoted in WHALLEY, G (1953) *Poetic Process*, Greenwood Press.
59 STRAVINSKY, I (1973) 'Artistic invention' in LIPMAN, M (Ed) *Contemporary Aesthetics,* Allyn and Bacon, pp 373–9.
60 *Ibid*.
61 *Ibid*.
62 JOHN DEWEY (1934) in *Art as Experience*, Minton Balch and Company.
63 See, for example, VALERY, P (1964) *Aesthetics*, Volume 13 of the Collected Works of Paul Valery, Bollingen Foundation.
64 I am indebted to Edwin Webb for part of the formulation of the above account of the evaluating element in the aesthetic field.

Part II
The Arts in Education:
Their Collective History and
their Future Development

2 *English as Aesthetic Initiative*

Edwin Webb

Introduction

The case of English, its content and philosophy, suggests something like a running battle. The history of its teaching may be characterized as a clash between 'content' and 'process', between 'subject-centred' and 'child-centred' approaches, and between a 'literary' conception of English and that of a 'language' concern. The terms of reference for the debate change in time and emphasis — but they are still there, explicitly and implicitly.

In the first section of this chapter I shall review the history of English teaching, identifying some of its principal features at each stage throughout this century to the present time. In the nature of the undertaking this will be a pen-sketch, one which requires shadings, detailing and amplification — but one which, by drawing upon telling influences, will trace a retrospective outline of events. The purpose here is two-fold: (i) to supply a context for present thinking; (ii) to supply significant points of departure for further development.

In the second part of this chapter I shall go on to draw the sight-lines within which I take a personal view of the critical contribution English teaching has to offer to an aesthetic education. This I see as a major commitment of the English programme, within a conception of English which is arts-based. It is one founded on aesthetic engagement and activity through which both individual and shared experience may be realized and shaped. It too is a pen-sketch; of prominent considerations which shape the perspective.

Edwin Webb

The Teaching of English: 1900 to the Present Time

In the opening decades of this century, English in state schools was virtually synonymous with grammar: the naming of parts of speech, the parsing and analysis of (selected or specially-prepared) sentences. Such instruction was justified on the grounds that it trained the mind, developing disciplines of analytical and logical thinking; and that such knowledge 'about' language was essential if the pupil was to read and write correctly.

To these ends literature too had its contributions to make. Passages of prose and verse could offer useful models for imitation — sometimes simply by being copied out by the pupil, or by supplying a linguistic style to be mimed. Literature also supplied ready-made passages for training and testing the pupils' ability to read out loud. Passages of verse were especially useful as material to be learned by heart and recited; again, as a means of training the mind, as well as testing speech production.

Formally instituted as a compulsory subject of study for state schools by Board of Education Regulations (1904), the teaching of English language and literature had low status and limited objectives. First, it was seen by many as a poor substitute for the study of Classics. Second, it was seen as an instrumental means of combating illiteracy. Third, the dominant philosophy of the time conceived of education for 'the masses' as having rigidly restricted aims: to educate up to, but not beyond, a proper social place within the economic empire of production. Hence English was an instrument of social conditioning and a discipline of narrow intentions.

Derived from Latin, the grammars (for there were many of them) of English were constructed as a kind of Linnaean taxonomy, minutely detailed and complex. In the attempt to devize his own fully comprehensive system, Linnaeus went mad. And there can be little doubt that learning some of the more fully-blown of these grammars would have been positively harmful to mental health.

The faith in prescriptive grammar teaching dies hard. Parsing was still regularly taught to the late 'fifties at least. And there are many adults who still believe that there are certain things you are to never split, and other things you must never start or end a sentence with. There are, too, a few teachers of English who still believe that 'spelling, punctuation and grammar' are the key-notes to literacy, just as there are parents and employers who hold to the same creed.

Prescriptive grammar teaching may be countered on a number of fronts. Knowledge *of* grammar does not guarantee an increased quality of language-production. However 'common-sense' it might appear that doing language exercises *must* increase language performance, there is no evidence to support such a view. There is the fact, in the words of the 1927 *Handbook of Suggestions for Teachers*, that 'grammar was made for language, not language for grammar'. The study of grammar makes, at best, grammarians. Clearly, you do not need to know your auxiliary from your modal in order either to say or write, 'Thou shalt not kill' or 'I should not have done it, your Honour'. Indeed, there seems to be a point where drilling in the formalities of grammar is actually counter-productive; is, in fact, an inhibition to the production of language.[1] The Bullock Report (1975) *A Language for Life* reviewed and passed judgement on the matter of prescriptive grammar teaching (paras. 11.15 to 11.25 especially), concluding:

> What we are suggesting, then, is that children should learn about language by experiencing it and experimenting with its use. (11.25)

At the same time as grammar teaching had its most forceful advocates there were voices raised not only against its usefulness but also the whole form and purpose of education which it symbolised. Such objections were accompanied by, and were in some senses a product of, a reaction against the view of children as raw material to be moulded to some ulterior, adult motive.

Among those voices was Edmond Holmes who, in *What Is and What Might Be* (1911), presented forcefully the case for education as a liberation, as a freeing of the essential spirit of the pupil towards the aim of 'self-realization'. Such a philosophy recalls the earlier moral stance of Matthew Arnold and his sustained attack — both in official reports and other writings — upon the deadening effects of the Revised Code (1862). Where the dominant model of state education sought to educate children up to, and not beyond, their proper social place, Arnold saw that such provision (both of content and means) would be socially-divisive. He looked to education, in the broadest terms, to civilize and to humanize. The agent of this change was to be 'culture' — by which he had in mind literature specifically as the chronicle of that heritage:

> The poor require culture as much as the rich; and at present their education, even when they get education, gives them hardly any of it.   (*Literature and Dogma*, 1873)

[Culture] seeks to do away with classes; to make the best that

> has been thought and known in the world current everywhere;
> to make all men live in an atmosphere of sweetness and light,
> where they may use ideas, as it uses them itself, freely, —
> nourished and not bound by them. (*Culture and Anarchy*, 1869)

The teaching of English Arnold saw unequivocally as 'the greatest power available in education'[2] — an argument which would reappear subsequently in the work and influence of FR Leavis.

In the first decades of the twentieth century there were other voices too arguing for radical changes in the conception of education. The influence of Maria Montessori, and her insistence that the creative enterprise, through 'activity methods', be put at the centre of education, spread beyond the primary school level. What she counselled, the child's 'need for self-expression', could be seen to have application at other levels.

Notable among those practitioners and writers of the time who also founded their educational beliefs upon 'self-expression' and 'creativity' were Greening Lambourn and Caldwell Cook. Both sought to encourage the innate imagination of the child, and to foster creative writing as a means of realizing that potential. Certainly they, as others at the time and subsequently, shared the same fundamental predispositions: that education should be child-centred, and that the first requirement of education was to provide opportunities and encouragement for the child both to express, and in expressing discover, a sense of self. There are here, at times, tones of a Romantic picture of the child — even of a Rousseau-like version of 'the noble savage', or the Wordsworthian infant 'trailing clouds of glory'. Such a faith in the untutored, natural gifts of the child — whose genius required merely opportunity for its realization — can be seen as a critical weakness in the scheme of belief held by the progressive movement in several of its versions and explored more fully by Peter Abbs in this book.

Nonetheless, it is clear that the shift towards a curriculum which put the child at the centre of operations began here; and that seventy years of educational provision since then have been much concerned with the task of working out in practice the implications of this reversal of philosophy.

Caldwell Cook[3], for example, whose exemplary practice was described in the first chapter, asserted that *activity*, the actual doing of things, was the key to learning — not the passive reception of information. Further, that through the writing of stories, poems, plays, descriptive accounts, and so on, pupils would necessarily engage with matters of spelling, punctuation and grammar as a means of achieving important modes of expression, and not as a detached learning 'about' language. On these matters he was both scathing and farsighted. The mechanics of language, he proclaimed, were best acquired through acts of producing and shaping language, as they are needed, *in order to express meaning.* Cook's insistence upon 'play', as he termed it, as the natural focus of a child's interest, of course opened his philosophy to attack; for 'play' can be seen as purposeless, a free exercise of time demanding no discipline. If seen, however, as that process by which a child experiments among alternatives, directed to specific outcomes — in the course of which 'discoveries' are made — then Cook's outline is perfectly consonant with an accumulation of findings from child psychology. For what Cook had identified was a programme of work based on the needs and interests of his pupils, and achieved through the processes of talking, reading, and writing. By these means of engagement with their experience, the pupils were the more ready to enter the created worlds of established writers in imaginative interplay.

The year 1921 has a unique significance in the history of English teaching. In that year were published the Newbolt Report, *The Teaching of English in England*, and George Sampson's *English for the English*. The significance of these publications together identified the central importance of English within the curriculum. On the place of English, the Committee's Report affirmed:

> ...we state what appears to us to be an incontrovertible fact, that for English children no form of knowledge can take precedence of a knowledge of English, no form of literature can take precedence of English literature: and that the two are so inextricably connected as to form the only basis possible for a national education. (para. 9)

The Committee of Inquiry, under the Chairmanship of Sir Henry Newbolt, included distinguished scholars, critics, and educationalists, such as Professor CH Firth, Sir Arthur Quiller-Couch, Caroline Spurgeon, George Sampson and John Dover Wilson. Their names gave immense weight to the Report's reflections. Today, however, in the altered circumstances of society and of the practice of education, the exclusive identification of literature with English literature would need to be challenged. There are literatures written in English shaped by other cultures, as there are literatures in translation, and valid claims to be made for their introduction into the classroom. Literature can be more broadly conceived than the English which the

Committee of Inquiry asserted to be 'the essential basis of a liberal education for all English people' (para. 13). And at the practical level of implementation it is quite clear that the members of the Committee were not able to free themselves of some of the dominant attitudes which had determined, and continued thereafter to influence, much of the teaching of English. The Report, for example, still held to the notion of 'correct' English in its standard form — 'to secure clearness and correctness both in oral expression and in writing' (para. 13), as it was concerned also 'to secure correct pronunciation and clear articulation' (para. 13), behind which evidently resided the notion of received pronunciation in speech.

A consequence of these assertions was in fact to give further impetus to the reinstatement of grammar teaching and language exercises, including précis and comprehension.

Nonetheless, it is important to acknowledge the fact that the Report enhanced greatly the status of English and of teachers of English; and that literature had distinctive and intrinsic contributions to make to the concept of a liberal education. For literature afforded unique opportunities for personal experience, a greater understanding of self and others, and was in itself 'a source of delight'.

George Sampson, in his personal testament to the place and value of English, in some ways went further than the Report. He echoes repeatedly the ethics of Matthew Arnold: like Arnold he saw English as a potentially humanizing influence. He too saw the possibilities of a common culture overriding class differences. He too saw English as a liberation of the essential spirit, and literature as a counter to the dulling consequences of industrialization with its tedious, mechanical drudgery. In the light of contemporary 'innovations' being brought into the State secondary curriculum to 'prepare' pupils for the world of work, Sampson's comments should give an arresting pause for thought:

> I am prepared to maintain, and indeed, do maintain, without any reservations or perhapses, that it is the purpose of education, not to prepare children *for* their occupations, but to prepare children *against* their occupations.[4]

On the question of grammar, Sampson would reduce drastically the extent of its direct teaching — whilst retaining modified versions of the learning as a means to clear expression. Parts of speech should receive some attention as they 'come up for notice', and dealt with 'shortly and practically ... in relation to the art of writing' (p. 97).

Much of what Sampson records offers an illumination to critical thinking about the nature and purpose of education — and a reflection on English teaching which pre-dates a great deal of later development. It was Sampson, for instance, who identified positively the need to distinguish between English as a 'content' and as a medium of instruction. The former 'is not really a subject at all'. It is more important than that:

> It is a condition of existence rather than a subject of instruction. It is an inescapable circumstance of life, and concerns every English-speaking person from the cradle to the grave. The lesson in English is not merely one occasion for the inculcation of knowledge; it is part of the child's initiation into the life of man. (p. 44)

In the decades following Newbolt and Sampson, the battle between the 'traditionalists' and the 'progressives' continued to be fought out. Crudely summarized, the conflict was between those who asserted the need for *training* students in the 'correct' forms of language, written and spoken, and those who put first the need to see the teaching of English as a creative discovery and definition of the pupil's sense of self. One saw language development as directed towards an *a priori* model; one saw it as a realization prompted through the needs of articulation itself.

A further powerful drive towards a cultural function for English teaching was given by the work and influence (and the influence of those he influenced) of FR Leavis. The English tripos at Cambridge finally became independent of the modern languages board in 1926, and English literature as a discipline in its own right was there established. Trenchant and uncompromising, Leavis's stance borrowed from the tradition of Arnold the sense of literature as being the lodestone of culture — its principal documentation and most assured messenger. The pursuit of literature, as with Arnold, had for Leavis a dominantly moral purpose: a 'delight in itself' it undoubtedly was, but its final worth was in the values it proposed, and the reflections it would induce. Not all literary products lent themselves to such high ideals, of course — hence the need to define the tradition. Not all students were capable of responding to the challenge literature posed. So to his detractors Leavis has always been open to the charge of being the priest of a high, minority culture:

> In any period it is upon a very small minority that the discerning appreciation of art and literature depends: it is (apart from cases of the simple and familiar) only a few who are capable of

unprompted, first-hand judgment. They are still a small minority, though a larger one, who are capable of endorsing such first-hand judgment by genuine personal response ... Upon this minority depends our power of profiting by the finest human experience of the past; they keep alive the subtlest and most perishable parts of tradition. Upon them depend the implicit standards that order the finer living of the age.[5]

As to the substance of what Leavis had to say in the first part of that passage, there could be adduced the evidence of IA Richards' *Practical Criticism* (1930), a work of new criticism which directly set out to test powers of literary discrimination. The second part of the passage shows the divergence between Arnold's hopes for universal improvement through access to fine literature, and Leavis's own belief that guardianship of the heritage would in fact depend upon the few.

The undoubted advantage for literary study issuing from the work of Leavis, and of new criticism generally, should not, however, be undervalued. For knowledge 'about' a text, the history surrounding it and biographical facts of the author (which had constituted a good deal of literature teaching til then), was substituted a fundamentally reconstrued approach. Above all, there was the literary work itself; to be analyzed through close reading, its levels of meaning to be identified by an understanding of the textual network of image, metaphor, and matters of tone, style, and structural organization. For it was upon these significant features of the work that genuine, first-hand appreciation depended.

By his example Leavis exercised an important disciplining of attitudes to the teaching of literature — one which was more fully developed in terms of classroom teaching by others such as Denys Thompson, Frank Whitehead, William Walsh, Gavin Bantock, Fred Inglis and David Holbrook.

While the traditionalists were still pressing the case for English as a constitution of mechanics and rules, and the Cambridge School was advocating literary-critical analysis, a resurgence of interest in the child-centred, 'expressive' approach to English teaching was also gathering. The impetus emerged from two particular sources. One was Herbert Read's *Education Through Art* (1943): a work which stressed children's own art-making as a principal means by which they project experience, and thus come to apprehend it. The second was Marjorie Hourd's *The Education of the Poetic Spirit* (1949), a work specifically concerned with the teaching of English and Drama.

Hourd's work looked back to Susan Isaacs[6], and that pioneering attempt to see education as a continuous process of realization from fantasy and play, through imaginative constructions of reality, to the development of intellect. Hourd looked back, too, to the romantics — to Coleridge especially on the imagination, and to a view of the child which saw it as fully-possessed of an image-making faculty. What the child required was *opportunity* to express these images so that they might represent the nature of experience and feeling. Hourd herself employs the word 'vision' to point to that perception or realization which inheres in the products made by the child. By being allowed to be 'free' the child will organize experience through the shaping or synthesizing of these possessions of experience.

Hourd's propositions remind us of things it is often easy to overlook: that children *do* have their own inner life — and that it requires, first, an act of faith on the part of the teacher to generate opportunities for those resources to be tapped. But for their realization to take place the argument, as Hourd makes clear, must be taken further. For example, children may not already *be* in possession of those very images which would enable syntheses of experience to take place. Their own private, or esoteric, vocabulary of materials might require supplementing from that vaster, richer source of image and symbol which is culture. Induction into, or discovery of, these resources actually confers *a greater freedom of choice* in that selection which will then 'express' self — the public resource thus becoming a personal possession. And another vital amendment is this: the origin of the word 'poem' in the Greek *poiema* reminds us that poetry is also 'a making', something crafted. The expression, or expulsion, of images alone does not constitute a poem — it might possibly make something closer to 'automatic writing'. Expression and understanding must go together: only when the products of the imagination cohere, has anything coherent been articulated. To these ends the existing forms and structures of artistic-poetic productions have themselves an enormous potential contribution to offer for the suggestions they contain as to the 'how' of making, of shaping experience.

The distinctive contribution of David Holbrook[7] to the field of English teaching has been the attempt to apply the principles of Leavis — and work out in practice the implications of these for the subject. Like Leavis, Holbrook is wholly committed to the position of literature as the most powerful instrument of culture; and to its educative power to develop 'right feeling', to humanize and to civilize. But, unlike Leavis, there is a strong democratic urge to go beyond the mere acceptance that there will be few capable of gaining access to the benefits literature can confer. Holbrook addressed himself to this concern in a number of ways. To engage with a work of literature was to engage, above all else, with the nature of the experience contained in the work. Where pupils could not do this directly, it was the task of the teacher to devise some means of mediation, *via* which the pupil could gain access. Similarly, just as there were activities which enabled the pupil to connect *to* the work, there were activities leading out *from* the text. Both of these would enable and encourage the pupil to realize personal connections *with* the experience contained in the work. In this way feeling and personal biography could be identified and explored in a suggestive context. The major means of seeking these connections would be that of creative writing — writing which expressed, imaginatively, the pupils' sense of involvement with self and text: an 'essay' in an old sense, but not its form. And as means towards these realizations, Holbrook proposed the use of stimulus and reflective materials, including music and song, as well as the literary.

It is true that Holbrook's position has been greatly influenced by psychoanalytic theory — and that there is a tendency at times to equate pupils' imaginative writing with psycho-therapeutic purposes. Some of Holbrook's critics would see this as a deficit in his scheme of things. Others might say: but there *is*, in a good deal of creative, literary writing (mature as well as novice) an impulse to come to terms with inner disturbance and emotional conflict. That is one especial advantage of the literary mode, and of encouraging such an undertaking. And where else in the school curriculum, if not in English and the arts, will occasion be provided for pupils to give shape to such experience so that they might recognize it?

Such is the 'maturity' which Holbrook sought to develop — an imaginative enlightenment and a closer knowledge of personal identity, together with an enlargement of sensibility within a culture.[8]

Holbrook's conception of 'maturity', whilst sharing some important sympathies, is not the same as that of 'personal growth' outlined by John Dixon. Dixon's report[9] on the Anglo-American Conference of some fifty British and American teachers and academics (held at Dartmouth College, New Hampshire in 1966) has been greatly influential in opening up a much wider focus as to what constitutes the business of English teaching. His account proceeds from an 'observation of language in operation from day to day' (p. 4), built on the premise that 'the most fundamental aim of language is to promote social interaction between people' (p. 6). Identity develops in relation to others — out of which interaction the individual constructs a unique reality. Such observations lead to an 'operational' view of English teaching; because language 'belongs to the public world' then English is to be defined 'by process, a description of the activities we engage in through language' (p. 7). The following summary predicates the working principles:

> ... language is learnt in operation not by dummy runs. In English, pupils meet to share their encounters with life, and to do this effectively they move freely between dialogue and monologue — between talk, drama and writing; and literature, by bringing new voices into the classroom, adds to the store of shared experience. Each pupil takes from the store what he can and what he needs. In so doing he learns to use language to build his own representational world and works to make this fit reality as he experiences it. (p. 13)

Dixon's account, in the unambiguous stress upon social context, sets out much of the theoretical framework within which English teaching over the last twenty years has come to be conceived and debated.

Many of these outcomes may be identified as consequences of a 'sociolinguistic' approach to English — one which, on most occasions, references literature, but whose basic attitude regards all language as a social phenomenon, and all its products as linguistic 'specimens'. And all of these specimens, in the detached view of a neutral observer, are equally deserving of attention. And that view itself raises further questions; for example, the question as to whether literature has a place by virtue of the fact that it undoubtedly *is* a linguistic product, or whether there is not something 'special' about it — not just a new voice, but a unique way of speaking. For literature, arguably, provides *significant* voices; *mature* voices which articulate experience in an *achieved form*; and which are grounded in that accumulation of *collective experience* which we call *culture*. Is literature to be provided because it offers opportunities for the study of 'language-situations'? or does some other purpose inform its use? Does literature have 'values' not necessarily shared by other language-productions? or should one not make value-judgments in any case?[10]

James Britton, for example, has offered a perspective of literature which likens it to a written form of 'gossip'. Presented as a paper at the Dartmouth Conference, he had already offered an illustrative working of the idea in 1962, in a lecture given at London University[11]. In broader terms, too, his thinking has been decidedly influential; most markedly as the model-maker of those language categories he labelled expressive, transactional and poetic[12]. 'We classify at our peril', he once wrote, yet these notional assignments of written language have become embedded as more or less incontrovertible descriptions — wholly taken up in the Bullock Report, for instance. Britton was a member of that Committee of Inquiry, and his presence there certainly provided a most influential, theoretical contribution to its formulations.

A Language for Life itself displays a progression of the sociolinguistic way of thinking. The insistence upon talk as the prime means by which the pupil moves towards a construction of reality is there endorsed. Such an insistence continues the line of development begun by Andrew Wilkinson's concept of 'oracy'[13] — an invaluable reminder of the potential liberation of ideas, thoughts, and feelings, which interactive discussion can, and does, precipitate. The Report asserted:

> We welcome the growth in interest in oral language in recent
> years, for we cannot emphasise too strongly our conviction of
> its importance in the education of the child. (para 10.30)

The Report was approving also of the direction of English teaching developed by the Schools Council Programme in Linguistics and English Teaching — and the practical suggestions for implementation devised by the team[14]. As a handbook of suggestions for lesson content and methods it generates a wide range of possibilities for examining language in many contexts; and in such a way as can equally well be incorporated into 'general studies', 'liberal studies' and 'communications' courses.

The major benefits deriving from sociolinguistic activity have been two-fold. First, it has freed English of the notion of 'correctness' in expression. It has done this by studying the ways in which language is actually used, for stated or taken-for-granted purposes, in relation to supposed or actual audiences, as a means of making meaning. What such an approach discovers is that language as used among and between persons is far more extensive, complex, and even unpredictable, than formal prescriptions would either acknowledge or permit. Thus the language used on each occasion is appropriate and effective rather than 'correct'. The second benefit, directly accruing from the concepts involved in language registers, has been to give closer attention to language across the curriculum, and the specific demands posed by each subject of study. Here the work of Douglas Barnes[15] has been directly influential, and has been endorsed by the Bullock Committee of Inquiry in its insistence that effective language policies need to be devised and implemented. The consequence of such a policy would be to impose upon the teacher of each and every subject a responsibility for the language of that subject. If the teacher of a given subject insists, say, on a use of language which is both impersonal and passive, then it is the responsibility of that teacher not merely to insist upon its adoption, but more importantly to develop and *justify* that usage. More than fifty years after George Sampson quite clearly enunciated the proposition that 'every teacher is a teacher of English', the Bullock Committee of Inquiry formally endorsed the view — and called for direct action.

So in these and other ways the sociolinguistic approach to English has certainly produced an altered way of looking at language as a social phenomenon. It has also contributed its own vocabulary to the exercise of analysis and appraisal.

A sociolinguistic model for English would argue for the need to experience as wide a range as possible of linguistic variety. Competence then, so it is proposed in the words of the Bullock Report:

> ... grows incrementally, through an interaction of writing,
> talk, reading, and experience, and the best teaching influences
> the nature and quality of this growth. (Conclusion 1.3)

Since *A Language for Life* English has progressed further, or become more diffused, in a number of directions. English has disappeared altogether in some contexts, or is retained as an 'English-for-special-purposes' (writing memos, letters, making telephone calls ...). A proliferation of 'communications' courses has emerged, various of these having become formally accepted by some examination Boards. In this setting English (written and spoken) becomes one of many other communicative forms for study and practice — including graphic and other visual representations of information, as well as the statistical and quantitative ('numeracy'). English has been replaced by 'language skills' or embraced by 'social and life skills', 'core skills', 'coping skills' — and even 'media studies'. The trend is most firmly established in further education, but the advance into the secondary sector seems assured.

Some of these applications it has to be said are built on a very suspect, at times intellectually shoddy, rationale. The 'skills model' of language, for example, seems to have acquired respectability, despite its lack of either linguistic or cognitive evidences. Its argument goes thus: the reason why pupils and students do badly in tests of language is that they do not have the necessary 'skills' which will enable them to do what is asked of them. Therefore, in order to make language work, they must first be given those language 'skills' which will enable them to use the language. The notion that one first learns a skill, then by practising it, learns how to use it is, at best, a product of tautological thinking.[16] At worst, it is of a piece with the urge (accelerated by economic recession) to find fast, instrumental answers — means-ends solutions, and mechanistic schemes of work.

In the confusion of courses which are concerned with language, in the fact that all courses *should* be concerned with language for learning, English has lost its identity. English has become synonymous with language. It is time for English to reassert its essential vitality, its concerns, its aims. And these are to do with the promotion of self-realization within the literary culture, to do with the making sense of experience through and with imaginative forms and structures. Imagination in the sense Coleridge identified it — the synthesizing power by which the mind assembles its possessions. Here is located the art of English within the aesthetic field: a making and remaking of meaning in a personal mode, and language as the agent of discovery.

Language as the Agent of Discovery

Late in life, reviewing the career of his own sensibility, Charles Darwin wrote:

> My mind seems to have become a kind of machine for grinding general laws out of large collections of facts, but why this should have caused the atrophy of that part of my brain alone, on which the higher tastes depend, I cannot conceive ... If I had to live my life again, I would have made a rule to read some poetry and listen to some music at least once every week ... The loss of these tastes is a loss of happiness, and may possibly be injurious to the intellect, and more probably to the moral character, by enfeebling the emotional part of our nature.[17]

The testament of Darwin reminds us that the full development of the individual can be blunted, where one feature of personality is excessively elaborated at the expense of those other experiences which contribute to well-being. It is a common finding of psychology, of those involved professionally in counselling and therapy. It is a self-discovery noted also by John Stuart Mill. His education, as is well known, was exclusively intellectual. In maturity, however, he was able to perceive for himself the need of a fuller integration of personality. Of his finding of the poems of Wordsworth, he wrote that:

... they expressed, not mere outward beauty, but states of feeling and of thought coloured by feeling, under the excitement of beauty. They seemed to be the very culture of the feelings, which I was in quest of.[18]

What these reflections of Darwin and of Mill show us is something absolutely vital to the conception of art itself, and hence to the need for the experience of art (including the literary) in education. For engagement with art provides the opportunity not simply to acquire cultural knowledge, knowledge about art; the crucial opportunity it generates is for self-possession — for an awareness and understanding, through the art, of one's personal world. And through engagement with a literary work is induced sympathetic understandings of the world of experience in ways which exceed the merely egocentric, by its revelation of the states of feeling and behaviour of others, their motivations, their hopes and fears, *their* engagement with the confusions and the messy business of living; the pain and the momentary joy alike. For in the impulse to create literature we find also the need to make sense of experience.

The consolation which art then affords us is the knowledge brought forth in the train of these realizations: that such a world is also to some extent shared. Art-products enter the public world of events (each one *is* an event). However self-referential in its initial impulse, each work of art which is 'achieved' is also a communication — and hence a potential communion with others.

The artistic, and the literary with which I shall be expressly concerned, have these advantages over other forms of knowledge: (i) that their construction is free to range over, and incorporate, *all* elements of human experience; and (ii) that such experience can accommodate the 'subjective' as well as the 'objective'.

In many forms of education, knowledge is proposed as a compendium of information quite detached from the learner. Such subjects presume an independence of things existing in their own right irrespective of the individual. One consequence of this form of learning is that the learner can become alienated from that which is known. Just such a process was identified by William Golding:

I was educated to be a scientist, until the prospect got too much for me and I turned to other things. The truth is that my teachers thought I should never make a scientist, not because I thought science was dull, but because I felt it was comic. Dullness they could accept, but frivolity was unforgivable.[19]

The work of Michael Polanyi of course throws in doubt the question as to whether, and certainly to what extent, science, for example, can be viewed as an 'objective' undertaking. The speculations of Coleridge remind us that the terms 'objective' and 'subjective' are in any case doubtful divisions — what is known is a product of the knower, an activity of consciousness.[20]

In literature the artist seeks to enter regions of experience in their wholeness — whether these be the histories of personal experience, or those projections of event, circumstance and personality we call 'fictions'. (For these too are manifests of the writer's whole psyché). What takes place is an encounter between the individual and her or his world of experience. The literary form which issues is a product of the complex of that interaction in which significant experience is symbolized or embodied.

To construe experience is to put a construction upon it. In part this is the pattern-making of art: the shaping of those materials of experience, the exploration of their connections and contiguities, the experimentation which produces alternatives, and the demand to make choices which these propose. Thus experience connects with further resonant experience — so that the final product can rarely be predicted from the start of the activity of the encounter. The pathways through experience are various, diverse, and sometimes perverse. Such authentic encounters will therefore contain their own surprises, or discoveries, in that improvisation which we call the composition of literature. The description of the poetic process offered by the Australian poet AD Hope represents just such an involvement. He wrote:

> As for the poet, he has to learn to be conscious of the effect as a whole but he is rarely aware of the details of his 'score'. He works by habit and trial and error, until he recognizes the effect he is searching for ... There are no rules for it and no prescriptions; because one has to be able to recognise the 'rightness' of something not existing before the moment of its emergence, and often in a context not yet clear to the composer. The composition of a poem is a series of epiphanies.[21]

Hope's words remind us of the bifocal nature of this creative encounter. It is, first, an encounter with one's personal world. But it is also an encounter, in the literary, which takes place through the medium of language: a symbolization which is at once individual and yet a social possession, an accumulation of history, and a vital carrier of that inheritance we know as culture. So that in the exploration of experience, with and through language, so is language itself explored, improvized, rehearsed, extended and selected. Here is a powerful, dual argument for insisting that our pupils are encouraged and enabled to engage creatively both with personal experience and with their experience of literature.

The nature of this engagement, the endeavour to make a projection of experience so that it is realizable (and therefore available for reflection and scrutiny), is in important respects like the act of speech itself. The Danish philologist Otto Jesperson noted this remark of a young girl in a contemporary novel of the time:

> I talk so as to find out what I think. Don't you? Some things one can't judge of til one hears them spoken.[22]

The remark is almost identical with one ascribed to EM Forster: 'How can I know what I think till I see what I write?' For speech is utterance: utterance is an 'outering' — that is, a making manifest of what is tacit, unformulated. We are subliminally, or pre-consciously, aware of much more than we actually *know*, in the sense of being able positively to identify, to specify, to explicate. The making of personal literature, and the reformulation of literature in our own terms, are both potent means of coming into awareness, of the movement by which we come to know.

One distinct advantage of the imaginative engagement with literature, both in its making and our creative responses, is precisely this: that some sort of integration of personality, however provisional, may be achieved. What is produced is neither exclusively 'objective' nor 'subjective' — though there will be, to varying degrees, evidences of both. Object and subject are brought into imaginative relationship — objective embodiments which have subjective credibility, and a subjective extension of oneself into the objective world. It is in this very interrelatedness we should seek to justify the aesthetic experience of literature, of prime making and of the making of expressive response.

Where this integration is denied, as the testimonies of Darwin and Mill remind us, the personal world of one's habitation becomes partial and unsatisfying. Outside of the arts and literature, everywhere else in the curriculum we are devoted to the development of rational, 'objective' thinking and the processing of experience, the collection of data and their deductive analyses. These, too, are important means of making meaning and developing understanding — but they are processes which essentially are brought to bear upon pre-existing content, our formal representations of things and the orthodoxies of formal knowledge. But rational analysis and logical deduction do not *generate* the prime materials themselves — those images of the senses, our metaphors and symbols by which psychic possessions and perceptions are first bodied forth. Logic, reason, explication, analysis and exegesis may well operate upon these products of the psyche — once they are known. But first they must be constituted in some way, projected *via* some means, even when rational thinking operates upon them virtually simultaneously with the activity of their generation. For creative engagement is not an unthinking activity; but it is one which does not function by reason alone. Rollo May, from the perspective of a psychotherapist, expressed it this way. Referring to 'the intensity of consciousness that occurs in the creative act', he wrote:

> ... it involves the total person, with the sub-conscious and unconscious acting in unity with the conscious. It is not, thus, *irrational*; it is, rather, supra-rational. It brings intellectual, volitional, and emotional functions into play all together.[23]

The aesthetic discipline of literature — its making, remaking and possessing through art-speech — must be founded exactly here: in that integration through which it proceeds from the unknown to the known, an imaginative movement by which experience may be composited. The labour of the poet, in the words of Archibald McLeish (in *Poetry and Experience*) is one which 'undertakes to "know" the world not by exegesis or demonstration or proofs, but directly, as a man knows apple in the mouth'.

The literary experience, the aesthetic activity, attends to knowing in its own distinctive ways.

Most significantly, it attends to those processes of being which we name 'feeling'. As Peter Abbs makes clear in the introductory section to this book, the aesthetic mode itself operates directly through the senses — an immediate apprehension. And feeling, it seems to me, is the most signal artificer of those senses which will both shape personal response and generate the impulse to create. Yet feeling, as a concept, is notoriously elusive when we try to trap it in definition. In part the difficulty resides in the fact of (English) language itself; as Gilbert Ryle pointed out, such a term is

> ... not a case of something being too delicate to be caught by our gross linguistic tools, but of its being too amorphous to be caught by our over-delicate linguistic tools.[24]

Because literature is such a crucial carrier of feeling, some of the implications of the term must nonetheless be considered here. For

these are central to the argument for conceiving English as an essentially aesthetic discipline.

The knowledge which we create through the aesthetic experience
is one which is tacit and personal, to begin with — though capable of
being shared with and mediated by others. As a clinical psychologist,
Miller Mair has pointed to these contexts of feeling in the following
way:

> Knowing personally is intimately involved with feeling. Feel-
> ing is a fundamental means of knowing in the realm of the
> personal ... In coming to know ourselves or others person-
> ally we will need to find ways to realize the invisible, to enter
> private worlds and get close enough to touch what hitherto
> we have refused to feel.[25]

Feeling is related to mood, the total organic state of the organism
at any time. It is psycho-physical: it includes both bodily mechanisms
(creating sensation), and mental states which include perceptions and
cognitions. Such feeling is unlike emotion in that it has a single re-
ferent: emotion is outgoing, is directed to persons or things other
than the individual (one is angry *about* something, or directs anger *towards* somebody). The distinctive mark of feeling is that it relates back
to the individual who is feeling: it is an amalgam of the individual's
mental and physical energies at that time. That amalgam may be
global — a mood: it may be a composite of some of these energies —
what one is (predominantly) feeling at the time.

Feeling (a noun-substitute for 'what one is feeling') is in this
sense pre-verbal — it is as yet experience which is unformulated.[26] It
resides as a potential perception. To be realized, feeling must be projected *via* some means which will *embody* (though not necessarily explicate) its nature. All art-forms offer their own possibilities for such
shaping — visual, plastic, kinetic, verbal. Once embodied in devices
of images, symbol, rhythm, contiguities and relationships, the product of feeling, as I've argued, is then made available to rational, intellectual, appraisal and discrimination.

In the case of literary forms, this mode of 'thinking' induced by
feeling and the processes of language itself are contemporaneous in
the act of composition. DH Lawrence pointed to the interaction of
thought and language — and to the later reflections brought to their
issues — in the following way:

> The novels and poems come quite unwatched out of one's
> pen. And then the absolute need one has for some sort of

satisfactory attitude towards oneself and things in general makes one try to abstract some definite conclusions from one's experience as a writer and a man.[27]

These 'inferences made afterwards from the experience' are the 'polly-analytics' to which Lawrence refers.[28] And there is a further dimension which applies both to the creating and re-creating of literary texts — known in their shorthand as writing and reading. It is this. By their very constitution in language literary forms tend to 'tap' areas of experience to which they connect in suggestive ways. Language seizes upon the opportunity of the moment, the total state of the individual at that time. For words are not merely nominative — they are active constructions which then construe versions of the reality being composed. Coleridge precisely noted the point:

> Be it observed, however, that I include in the meaning of a word not only its correspondent object alone, but likewise all the associations which it recalls. For language is framed to convey not the object alone, but likewise the character, mood and intentions of the person who is representing it.[29]

The mind, through language, brings things into relationship with each other — which brings all those things into relationship with the mind. The poem, for example, upon completion may not be a direct analogue of that experience which initiated its composition. Such 'ideal creations' as Coleridge termed these poems 'discover', as it were, intrinsic conjunctions with other areas of experience (including experience of language itself):

> ... where the ideas are vivid and there exists an endless power of combining and modifying them, the feelings and affections blend more easily and intimately with these ideal creations than with the objects of the senses ...[30]

What Coleridge asserts seems to me to have vital pertinence to the argument that in English teaching pupils must have opportunity to produce their own creative writings. For these are opportunities to connect not simply with objects and things and thoughts, but with their selves. And because language can connect intimately with the whole of experience, language is also explored when experience searches it out, tests, qualifies, amends, and actively sets out to fashion its likeness. Here also is an 'operation' of language — an intimate understanding of what language can do, a potent means of researching its resources.

Implications for the Practice of English Teaching

It is considerations such as these, I believe, which justify the concern of English in the classroom with 'aesthetic education': of art-making and art-mediation. There are obvious affinities with Michael Polanyi's concept of 'tacit knowledge', those matters we are aware of (and may even act upon) but do not *know* in the ordinary sense by which we hold a fact or items of information. In this respect English has a dual focus of operation.

One, to which some attention has been given, is the development of the pupil's own creative work — to which other activities will contribute and to which they will lead. Talk, the talking *through* of experience will be vital; talk as exploratory and talk as Lawrence's 'art-speech' by which one moves between art and individual experience. Various forms of writing — poetic, narrative, dramatic, journal accounts — will be available. The heritage of culture here provides not models to be imitated, but forms within whose organizing principles areas of individual experience may be most fittingly accommodated. Such forms themselves direct attention to function; *how* elements of experience may be embodied. Form itself proposes selections, organizations, arrangements.

The second focus directs attention as to how to make literary texts a personal possession — one which locates, refines, extends individual experience. Whatever the methods adopted (rôle-play, recasting, translating from one form to another, using visual realisations ... and so on) they share in the same fundamental endeavour. They are expressive as well as analytic. They are active workings out of relevance. In finding a personal expression of the work, the terms of reference for subsequent analysis are subsumed, proposed in the fresh individual making. Subsequently, if not at the time, these projections posit both recognitions *of* the text, and connections with one's own inner life.

In presenting a poem, for example, the challenge is to find a means by which the articulation of the text can be transformed into personal utterance. In brief,[31] such a response begins in finding a way to *say*, with one's own voice, the words of the poem. The words of a poem — there are some exceptions which are intended for the visual effects of graphics — are 'organized speech'. Experimenting and improvizing with different ways of saying those words forges important realisations of the language. Take the opening of John Clare's 'I am':

I am, yet what I am none knows nor cares ...

At one level, the level of 'paraphraseable meaning' the words are obvious. But when the poem is audited, rather than scanned as print symbol, the implicatory system of meaning begins to reveal itself also. How, for example, are the first two words to be said? and thus heard? Is *this* 'I am' the intonationally flat statement of fact ('I am an engineer, a teacher, a writer...')? is it the self-assured announcement (cf. Betjeman's 'I am a young executive')? is it the petulant foot-stamping of a small child ('I am, I am, I am.!')? is it a shout, a scream even, defiantly hurled against the odds? and so on, through many other variants. And each version is a potential of those two opening words — and each version supplies its own cargo of suggestive meaning. As *this* utterance is further contextualized, some of the range of possible auditory realizations will be discarded, others will be suggested. Worked at in such a fashion, pupils will learn to *hear* what they might *overlook* because meanings are being actively rehearsed. Pupils' intuitive understandings of the ways in which speech carries meaning and implications *via* tone, pitch, pace, pause and intonation are here being employed. This understanding (or 'tacit knowledge') is considerable — they themselves make meaning in such ways every time they say anything at all. So, in the context of Clare's poem the second 'I am' will be significantly different in character. Experimenting with the poem along these lines compels attention to the feelings which inhere in the poem — not as literal statement, but as an embodiment of the psychic *condition* which impelled the fabrication of the poem. The private impulse which generated the public articulation has become, again, a personal possession — but mediated in the social domain because pupils and teachers have worked together on their recreations of meaning.

As with poetry, so may literature generally connect with the pupils' own self-development. This, of course, is not literature made into ideology, an illustration of social or political themes; these may accrue, an organic networking of personal response with wider contexts which, too, locate a sense of self implicated therein. This is literature which invites, first, an imaginative engagement through which the responses made are also to some extent realizations of individual personality. To respond to literary forms in this way is to enter into literary criticism *expressively*: it is to offer re-statement *in one's own terms*. And in producing their own writings and talk in response, pupils have a means of access to their own thinking and feeling — by developing a language which will enable them to come into that possession.

For literature, to generalize to the theme which founds such an aesthetic of English, is not concerned with spondée-spotting or tropé-hunting. Nor is it, in the first instance, a body of information to be learned, or a compilation of cultural facts. It does not so much contain knowledge *per se*, as it contains a powerful means of 'coming to know'.

English as an Aesthetic Activity

In offering these reflections, neither a programme nor a method, I have attempted to put those considerations, as I see them, which inform the view of English as an aesthetic activity. It is a view which sees the making of meaning (in acts of creating and recreating) as central to that educational process which is concerned with developing the individual's fuller sense of self and others. It regards literature, the pupils' own and that of others', as the prime motivator — for the modes of awareness which its constructions both realise and promote.

This aesthetic of the English discipline is not concerned with abstract and abstruse *contemplation* of the literary. It is, however, one very much concerned with developing 'art-speech' — not, in the first place, as a set of vocabulary items and concepts as they figure in the language of literary criticism. But art-speech as the individual's articulation of response to a literary work as well as a means of expressing imaginatively, and therefore developing, a sense of self and a relationship to other potential or actualised worlds. This is the language of first-hand experience, however tentative and fumbling, by which personal realities are identified. It is the language through which we clarify, refines, and *extend* experience so that we may come to know it — a representation of the impulse to confer meaning, for ourselves and others.

Here is an aesthetic which is dynamic, operating through the pupils' active engagement in the making of the representations. The terms of reference for this process are no less than the sum-total of each psyché, contents of being to be recognized and re-cognized *as they are discovered to be* through their exploration. Such crucial evidences of being which the artistic attends to will include the conscious and pre-conscious, thoughts, volition, sensation, feeling and emotion. Image, metaphor, symbol, and rhythm will be the coordinates for these projections of experience – not preformulations of knowledge to be learned. Those intellectual schema by which we seek to account for reality are in any case partial — coded extrapolations within defined limits: rules, prescriptions, analyses, formulae, theories and received knowledge. These too serve their purposes, and generate their own significant intellectual advance in our comprehension of things. The aesthetics of the literary (and the artistic generally) confront the 'Idol of Objectivity', to borrow a phrase from Susanne Langer. Our concerns for living and being do not resolve themselves, are frequently not even *known*, through detached, evaluative observation. They are, rather, identified and come to terms with by engagement, by the encounter which actively and imaginatively enters the world of experience.

In an age of quantification, of procedural methods and operationalism, in a current educational ethos which seeks mechanistic solutions, to reassert these fundaments of being and becoming is of necessity to stand opposed. The aesthetic discipline of English is questing, provisional, tentative: there are no rules by which to raid the inarticulate or to force the unknown to reveal its identity. Learning the rules of 'spelling, punctuation and grammar' will not help either. Then there is no evidence that teaching these rules will increase the pupils' ability to *make meaning* with language, in any case. First one must *possess* the language. Tacit understanding of how language works by experimenting with what language can *do*, will more certainly release the pupil into her or his own use of language. And it is· this tacit understanding which we seek to foster through the aesthetic experience. The rule for riding a bicycle, as Michael Polanyi pointed out[32], will not help you at all to ride a bicycle.

The aesthetic of English must not be thought of, however, as an exclusively esoteric engagement. The extension of one's personal world is both social and cultural. There is the fact of one's sharing of experience with others, and the entry into their worlds. There are the cultural forms of literature to enter — and their relationships with self and others to be explored and accommodated.

This extension of self through the response to literary texts is vital. It develops the range of one's cognizance, just as the first-hand making of literature also promotes recognitions beyond the strictly autobiographical. In this context we might recall the remark of TS Eliot on John Donne — that he was 'expert beyond experience'. Through the introduction of, and induction into, mature literatures we also guard against the fallacy that such creating is equivalent merely to 'self-expression'. Peter Abbs has previously explored this notion. I should like to add that there is no especial merit in expressing oneself freely — heaving a brick through a window might achieve that expression. But in the artistic *activity* of composing a poem, a picture, a concerto (as opposed to the *act* of brick-throwing) the impulse itself and the state of being of which the act is somehow expressive, are also examined, related, come to terms with. Self-expression can be gratuitous; detached from history, including personal history, which is memory. Such acts are autistic. Each act might 'expel' disturbance of one sort or another. But it does not articulate.

Genuine artistic activity, however, can never detach itself wholly from that history, which is culture, in which it shares. 'Every picture owes more to other pictures than it does to nature', remarked Ernst Gombrich. The proposition is a useful reminder, too, of the medium within which the literary operates — and of its potential relation with other artistic modes. For all of these offer themselves to aesthetic experience, and all parts of that experience may offer themselves as the occasion calls them forth for distillation in the literary. Language may interact with all the expressive modes of art: through 'art-speech' we may embody something of the experience of music, drama, dance, film, the visual arts. We *place* them within our sensibility, in speech and writing which can inter-penetrate their especial sense-modes and activities. We do not *replace* them with talk — that is 'cocktail-party art' which substitutes the aesthetic experience for the social gaming of conversation. We use language in relation to the other arts (where almost certainly we shall be compelled into metaphor) in order to explore their relationship to self — their effects, movements, images, as they connect with and suggest significant experience. We *transpose* experience across the arts in order to try to find another and different angle of approach. In that process we shall discover what *does* make each picture different from every other picture. Its difference is precisely what it does owe to nature, to the nature of the individual artist, and to the constitution of experience of those who participate in the art by their responses. Here alone is scope for inter-action among and between the arts, including the literary. For in the end I take it that the business of literature is the pre-occupation of all the arts: namely, to come to terms with experience and try to develop a sense of meaning.

These then are the sight-lines within which, I believe, we form the view of English as an aesthetic enterprise. English teachers will be called upon, undoubtedly, to service other requirements, other applications of language. But without regard to the literary-creative experience, then the English programme will be impoverished, and a potent power of being denied our pupils.

Our medium is the exploring word. We should recall that Helen Keller's discovery of 'water' (the word to construe sense-impressions) changed her world. It also changed utterly the means by which she would continue to experience the world. The aesthetic discipline of English insists that denied the imaginative encounter with their world and that of others, our pupils will be dispossessed both of a vital experience, and of a significant potential *for* experience.

Acknowledgements

In the account given of English teaching in the first part of this chapter, I have drawn upon the detailed documentation of DAVID SHAYER's (1972) *The Teaching of English in Schools 1900–1970*, Routledge and Kegan Paul. I should also like to record my thanks to Lesley Pearson for making available to me her unpublished study 'A History of English Teaching 1880–1980'.

Notes

1 See WILKINSON, A (1971) *The Foundations of Language*, Oxford University Press, pp 32–5 for a summary of findings as they pertain to the general issue. For the results of a particular enquiry see HARRIS RJ (1963) 'An experimental enquiry into the functions and value of formal grammar in the teaching of English', reported in BRADDOCK, LLOYD JONES and SCHOER, *Research in Written Composition*, NCTE. Of this research the Bullock Report concludes: 'In the writing test the "non-grammar" classes gained significantly higher scores than the "grammar" classes, and overall there was no effective correspondence between high scores in the grammar test and improvement in writing' (*A Language for Life*, 1975, p 171).
2 General Report for the Year 1871, in *Reports on Elementary Schools 1852–1882,* p 142.
3 In the *Perse Playbooks 1912–17*, and in *The Play Way* (1917).
4 *English for the English*, edited by FRANK WHITEHEAD (1970) Cambridge University Press, p 27. All subsequent references are to this edition.
5 From the essay (1930) 'Mass Civilization and minority culture', reprinted as appendix III of *Education and the University*, 1943, London.
6 *Intellectual Growth in Young Children*, 1930.
7 First in *English for Maturity*, 1961, and in *English for the Rejected*, 1963.
8 HOLBROOK everywhere stresses imagination as the vital faculty: for

example, 'Even to write a recipe for making tea clearly requires all the powers of a man's sensibility' (*English for Maturity*, p 23).

9 *Growth Through English*, first published 1967. Page references are to the second edition, 1969. A third edition with revised introduction was published in 1975.

10 Many features of this debate, in which Frank Whitehead features prominently, may be traced in ALLEN, D *English Teaching Since 1965* (1980) London.

11 'Literature', reprinted in BRITTON, J (Ed) (1963) *The Arts in Education*, London.

12 'What's the Use?', in WILKINSON, AM (Ed) (1971) *The Context of Language*, University of Birmingham School of Education. See also the riposte of FRANK WHITEHEAD, 'What's the Use, Indeed?', *The Use of English*, 29 February, 1978.

13 *Spoken English*, University of Birmingham, 1965.

14 DOUGHTY, P PEARCE, J and THORNTON, G (1971) *Language in Use* Arnold.

15 First in *Language, the Learner and the School*, Penguin, 1969; then in *From Communication to Curriculum*, Penguin, 1976.

16 John Holt expresses the falseness of thinking in this way: 'As Whitehead said years ago, we cannot separate an act from the skills involved in the act. The baby does not learn to speak by learning the skills of speech and then using them to speak with, or to walk by learning the skills of walking and then using them to walk with. He learns to speak by speaking, to walk by walking ... We cannot separate skills and acts, and we make a disastrous error when we try. Talking is not a skill, or a collection of skills, but an act, a doing. Behind the act there is a purpose ... we talk because we have something we want to say, and someone we want to say it to, and because we think or hope our words will make a difference' (*Instead of Education*, Penguin edn, 1977, p 18).

17 Quoted by HOGGART, R (1970) 'Literature and society', *Speaking to Each Other*, II, p 27.

18 *Autobiography*, Columbia University Press, 1924, p 104.

19 Introduction to school education of *The Brass Butterfly*, Faber, 1958.

20 I have attempted a fuller exposition of Coleridge's thinking in '*Reality's Dark Dream*: Coleridge's language of consciousness', *Critical Quarterly*, 25, 1.

21 *The New Cratylus*, Oxford University Press, 1979, p 64.

22 *Language: Its Nature, Development and Origin*, Allen and Unwin, 1922, p 253.

23 *The Courage to Create*, Collins, 1976, pp 48–9.

24 'Feelings' in *Collected Papers, 1929–1968*, vol. II, Hutchinson 1971, p 284.

25 'Coming to know' in SALMON, P (Ed) (1980) Routledge and Kegan Paul, p 113.

26 A proposition which I have explored in greater detail in 'Literature and the education of feeling', parts One and Two, *Liberal Education*, 24 and 25, winter 1972/73 and spring 1973; and in 'Poetry and the culture of feeling', *New Universities Quarterly*, 32,4, autumn 1978.

27 Foreword to *Fantasia of the Unconscious*, Heinemann, 1961, p 9.

28 *Ibid.*

29 *Biographia Literaria,* edited by GEORGE WATSON, corrected edn., London, 1965 XXII.
30 *Ibid,* II.
31 An approach more fully argued in my article 'The sounds of poetry' *The Use of English*, 37,1, autumn 1985; and, with Edward Lee, produced as classroom materials (audiocassette and teacher's handbook) in *The Sounds of Poetry*, Sussex Publications Ltd., 1985.
32 '... for a given angle of imbalance the curvature of each winding is inversely proportional to the square of the speed at which the cyclist is progressing' *Personal Knowledge*, 1958, p 50.

3   *Towards the Condition of Music:*
The Emergent Aesthetic of Music Education

Marian Metcalfe

Introduction

Although music has been included in educational courses from the
earliest times it has suffered more than any of the other arts disciplines
in Britain (with the possible exception of film) from lack of a clear
exposition of its place in both education and community. Even today
there still exists some distrust of its abstract and ephemeral nature,
its bonds with religion, pageantry, culture and ritual, a certain unease
at its properties of enhancing emotional states and particularly at
its pervasive influence on the young. For many parents, pupils,
employers, administrators, and even some teachers themselves, still
remain largely unconvinced of the value of music in the general
education of the unmotivated or disaffected teenager who is not
aiming to be André Previn or Toyah Wilcox.

Why should this be so? Why, when music is so clearly a major
part of all our lives, listened to by most of the population for some
portion of each day, with radio stations devoted entirely to its dissemination and multi-million pound industries to its production and
distribution, with more and more young people making their own
music, going to live performances, buying instruments, recording
and reproduction equipment, assiduously practising and attending
rehearsals, why, with this massive affirmation of the importance of
music to the human condition, is it so little understood, so widely
undervalued and so generally under-resourced in our schools, colleges
and universities today?

The answers to these questions must surely lie in the nature of
our society itself and therefore outside the terms of this chapter.[1] But
by outlining developments in Britain over the last 100 years or so
some measure of understanding of the present position may be gained

and a way forward illuminated. This chapter therefore falls naturally into two sections. The first makes a brief historical survey of the thinking behind music education in British secondary schools[2] in order to provide both a background to and a context for the present situation; the second looks at those current trends most likely to generate good practice in the teaching of music in schools and to identify areas and possible points of departure for strengthening the future development of music education as aesthetic experience operating within the aesthetic field. For it may be that after a century of passionate but often inadequate debate, we have now reached the point in music education where a comprehensive philosophy and practice, *a practical aesthetic of classroom music*, has finally emerged but into economic conditions that are inimical to its growth. To understand this properly, however, we must trace the development of music in the curriculum from the beginning of the century.

Section I

1900–1960

From the inception of the secondary schools in 1902 music was never classed as a valuable or high-status subject and indeed the first set of *Regulations for Secondary Schools*[3] made no mention of it at all. Largely as a result of the founding influence of religious and charitable bodies, class singing was virtually compulsory in the elementary schools. Here it was regarded as an important moralizing force, as a way of diffusing passionate emotions and redirecting them towards habits of industry, thrift, contentment, sobriety and patriotism. This legacy was to a certain extent inherited by the new secondary schools, where classes were often combined for massed singing — generally for administrative reasons rather than musical ones!

There were, however, three main reasons for the general disregard of music in the secondary schools. The first was that they were nearly always modelled on the already established public and grammar schools where music, when it existed at all, was almost entirely extra-curricular. Significantly, much of the tuition was provided by visiting teachers which only served to confirm its peripheral nature. Secondly, in the school certificate syllabus[4] music was made a 'group IV' subject in which a pass did not count towards the award of the certificate. This further reinforced its position as non-academic and, therefore, of low status. And thirdly, the existence

of a large army of private music teachers[5] meant that the consciences,
if any, of the decision-makers could be quietened by the thought that
music instruction could always be obtained privately. Progress could
be monitored externally by graded examinations[6] and therefore there
was no pressing need to provide music in schools.

By the early twenties the narrowness of the timetable was
becoming a matter of national concern and the first of the great
consultative committees chaired by Sir William Hadow[7] was set up to
reconsider the organization and suitability of the school curriculum.
The first of these Reports[8] recognized the paucity of opportunity for
development in the arts and recommended that a more prominent and
established place should be assigned to them in schools for their value
in 'stimulating the growth of the imaginative, critical, and creative
faculties'.[9] It emphasized that:

> The study of music, rightly undertaken, can be of the highest
> educational value. We are in error if we dismiss it as a recrea-
> tion, or seclude it as a remote and technical study which is out
> of relation to the rest of our intellectual life. Its range is not
> less wide than that of literature; it appeals to the same faculties
> of emotion and judgment; it is ... subject to the same general
> aesthetic principles ... All the arguments which can be used
> for the inclusion of language and literature in our ordinary
> scheme of education may be used with equal force in the case
> of music.[10]

To this end the Committee recommended that in order to strengthen the position of the arts in the curriculum, music should be
accorded parity with other subjects in the school certificate
examination. Hadow and Arthur Somervell[11] drew up the first draft
syllabus and published it as appendix IV to the Recommendations. It
contained sight-singing[12] and aural tests of the type common in many
music examinations ever since, elementary harmony and form, an
outline knowledge of musical history and the study of one or more set
works.[13]

It is ironic that this draft examination, intended to lay the foundations for a major growth in aesthetic education, succeeded in
smothering the development of music as a creative and practical
subject for the next fifty odd years. For although the music lesson had
often not been very inspiring in its staple diet of class singing, the
pupils were at least *making* and *hearing* live music. But the legitimization
of music as a 'subject', by making it examinable, served only to
deflect it from its practical and experiential direction towards paper

exercises on a theoretical body of knowledge which could be studied and examined in the same way as 'academic' subjects. And yet at the same time the fact that it was still not acceptable as a matriculation requirement by the universities continued to emphasize its low status. Music had been caught in a Catch 22 situation, a kind of destructive double-bind, neither able to develop as an intellectual study nor as an aesthetic one.

However, notwithstanding this misguided attempt to promote music, many of the early major Board of Education documents do express the feeling that music is essentially to do with 'creativity', with 'expressiveness' and with the 'non-verbal'. The documents struggle to articulate felt concepts that the arts express a symbolic dimension of life not otherwise present in the school curriculum. Following hard on the heels of the second Hadow Report[14] and very much influenced by it, the 1927 edition of the *Handbook of Suggestions*[15] contained the following remarkable passage:

> ... the real function of music begins at a point where words, intellectually apprehended, have no place. Its inherent significance is outside the range of the purely rational mind. A special exercise of the imagination is needed in order to recognize a musical idea in a particular series of sounds, or to recognize in musical ideas a disciplined expression of deep and obscure human emotions.[16]

Here we see clearly a conception of music which predates Susanne Langer's work by a number of years, which anticipates the arguments of the Gulbenkian Report: *The Arts in Schools* (1982), and which is central to our symposium.

I want to emphasize the point that the potential for making the arts, and music in particular, a vital part of the curriculum for all children has been there almost as long as the secondary school itself. A philosophical basis was provided in those early Reports on which to build strongly expressive music courses for all children throughout their education and it was continually reinforced in later ones. For instance a 1931 Report[17] contained the following famous statement: 'the curriculum is to be thought of in terms of activity and experience rather than of knowledge to be acquired and facts to be stored. Its aim should be to develop in a child *the fundamental human powers* ...'[18] (my emphasis). Another splendidly conceived piece of thinking emerged from the Spens Report[19] which, although already showing the influence of progressivism in reaffirming that 'subjects' are not 'bodies of facts to be stored' but 'modes of activity to be experienced',[20] said:

we think too much of education in terms of information and too little in terms of feeling and taste[21] ... a school ... (must) also foster the creative impulses needed not merely for new enterprises and adventures but even for the daily adaptation of routine and technique to changing situations ... the activities which are the richest in the creative element have the strongest claim for a place in the curriculum. *For these spring from the deepest needs of human nature.*[22] (my emphasis)

But the fact remained that the potential inherent in the Reports was not widely understood and seldom translated into coherent directives or practice. For by the 1944 Education Act there had been forty years of music in secondary education. And yet, despite official thinking, it was in a parlous state. Much had been accomplished and certainly the music curriculum had developed enormously from the days when it had consisted merely of singing songs, a few vocal exercises and sight-reading. Now secondary music classes included not only singing and theory of music, but musical appreciation, often by means of broadcast lessons, and perhaps recorder, pipe band, or even eurhythmics as well. In addition, extra–curricular music such as choirs, instrumental groups and music clubs offered many possibilities in some schools.

However, notwithstanding the apparent progress of music in schools, by 1944 its problems were also plainly to be seen. In *Education for Music*[23] Noel Hale posited a scheme for the total reorganization of music education. This scheme covered the supply and recruitment of teachers and the complete integration of music into a comprehensive music education for the whole population. Other contemporary publications, including the Norwood Report itself[24], also show a similar concern with the problems besetting school music.

Summarized briefly, these problems appear to fall into three main groups, which for convenience I shall refer to as 'philosophy', 'people' and 'plant'. 'Philosophy' is concerned with the justification of music in the school timetable; 'people' is to do with the personal qualities of the teachers, trainers and administrators themselves, who have often either not understood or who have had difficulty in translating a philosophy into practical curricular terms; while 'plant' concerns the actual time, accommodation, equipment and funding essential to realize the implications of teaching music as an aesthetic discipline.

In 1923 Hadow's Committee first voiced some of the 'philosophy' reasons still often heard today as justification for teaching music in schools. These 'philosophy' reasons themselves also fall into three main categories: the training of the mind, or *im*pressive reasons; the training of the emotions, or *ex*pressive reasons; and the training of behaviour, or social reasons.

The impressive category includes such justifications for music as teaching mental discipline, the widening of general knowledge, an understanding of the nature of culture and cultural difference, the transmission of the cultural heritage, and the teaching of useful vocational skills such as flexibility, adaptability, motor ability, decision-making, inventiveness and so on. The expressive justifications refer largely to the channeling of emotional or creative energy into the medium of sound for the development of aesthetic pleasure and personal growth. The social reasons, subtly expressed though they may be, include a variety of pupil-behaviour modifications such as release of emotions considered to be dangerous or subversive, learning the skills of working together towards a goal, being inculcated with a spirit of unity, patriotism, social cohesion, or whatever corporate values are considered desirable — music, one might say, conceived as a form of social engineering.

At various times during this last century different categories have dominated in the justification of music in education. Fashions exist in philosophies as in other walks of life, as we have seen in the opening chapter. Hadow's heartfelt plea for more importance to be accorded the arts in the curriculum in 1923 stresses his philosophically sound reasons for it — intrinsic aesthetic reasons — but nevertheless he still included traditional *im*pressive and social reasons. For example, he argued that a study of the fine arts could to some extent counteract the effects of unfavourable environment, or be of use in developing backward children: 'skilful musical teaching had frequently produced remarkable results in stimulating supposed "dull" girls.'[25] Incidentally such claims of stimulating intelligence are still advocated today for English choir schools and the supporters of the Hungarian system of music education. But the problem was then, as it has been ever since, that of expressing in curricular terms *a creative philosophy of music education as aesthetic education*, intrinsically valuable on its own terms and needing no other justification. Herein lies the heart of the matter; I shall return to it in section II of this chapter.

The problems mentioned in the forties by Hale and others included the three 'philosophy' reasons already noted, i.e., the lack of inherited musical tradition from the grammar and public schools, the late admission of music into full status as a school certificate subject, and the availability of private instrumental tuition. This latter led to charges of privilege and elitism when the fees charged precluded so many children from taking such opportunities. Other difficulties contributing to the failure of music to achieve full status in the curriculum included: the inadequacies of the training of music teachers; the lack of recognition of the unique qualifications of music specialists (which often led to a dissociation from other members of staff and disunity amongst themselves); the fact that music was often taught by musically unqualified teachers; the limited accommodation, funding and equipment for music in schools; the general acceptance of the extra-curricular status of much musical activity; and the concentration in schools on utilitarian subjects. 'Payment by results never really died', wrote Hale. 'It lives now in assignments to prepare for vocational examinations.'[26]

In addition Hale mentioned music's abstraction, the fact that the faculties of sight and speech are more readily trainable than that of hearing, and the limited and uninspired teaching methods of so many teachers. Others cited the stultifying effect of the examination syllabus, the crowded curriculum, the lack of easily assessable and verifiable results, the timetabling and disturbance problems music presented, and lastly, and probably most importantly, its own uncertain justification for inclusion in the curriculum together with the inadequate appreciation and presentation of its case.

But a recognition of problems does not lead automatically to their solution! *Education for Music*, written with such hopes during the war years, offered a comprehensive scheme and nineteen provisional recommendations for music education in the coming reorganization.[27] It is unlikely that we would agree now with every point Hale made, for in some ways his view of the value of the arts in education was rather limited. However, his clear exposition of the problems and suggestions for overcoming them serve as a useful check-list even today. Unfortunately his recommendations were not taken up in any way, either by the LEAs to whom it was largely addressed, or by the music teachers themselves.

Perhaps it was a bad time. Britain had much to occupy her in the immediate post-war years other than concern with music in schools. The humanitarian ideals of the twenties and thirties were replaced by more immediately practical matters, for the educational documents of the late forties and fifties were mainly concerned with the reconstruction of the system, the growing concern with technological education, the wastage of the early school leaver, and the relationship and relevance of education to the increasingly industrial needs of the country for more directly vocationally skilled manpower. And yet there was phenomenal growth in some areas of school music during

this period and provision for it grew rapidly to match. The upsurge
of interest in orchestral music during the war as a result of the activities of the Council for the Encouragement of Music and the Arts[28]
led to a much greater conviction of its importance in schools. Peripatetic teachers were appointed in many LEAs to teach orchestral instruments, orchestras were established in schools and the National
Youth Orchestra founded in 1947. New music advisers and inspectors
were appointed; many schools developed fine choirs and gave performances of full-scale choral works, operas and musicals. Broadcast
school music programmes proliferated and, with the advent of long-
playing records in 1949 and the 45' single and the transistor radio a
few years later, music became much more accessible to all.

But most of this growth in schools was in the field of extra-
curricular music. Inside the classroom lessons seemed to be largely
unchanged from the pre-war years. The accent was still on singing,
musical appreciation, history of music and 'paper exercises' in
theory. Argument and confusion on the place and value of music in
the curriculum continued even in the Ministry of Education itself.[29] In
1963 the Newsom Report[30] launched a scathing attack on music in
schools, pointing out the vast differences between enthusiasm for it
out of school and boredom within. It reiterated the same old problems: an unduly narrow conception of the subject, its low status, the
shortage of suitably qualified teachers, and the fact that 'music is
frequently the worst equipped and accommodated subject in the curriculum'.[31] And in 1968 the Schools Council Report *Young School
Leavers*[32] showed that music was voted top of the list as the most bor-
ing and useless subject by 15-year-old school leavers.

Following, as it did, shortly after the Newsom Report, this 1968
research created an enormous furore. The Ministry of Education
Pamphlet *Music in Schools*[33] was revised drastically by the DES and
reissued in response to the growing insistence that something should
be done. The purpose of music in schools was now: 'to give the ordinary pupil opportunities to make music up to the limit of his
capabilities both creatively and recreatively, to extend his general
musical knowledge and to accustom him to the use of musical
notation, at least for reference'.[34] But the reasons for including music
at all were still muddled and incoherent, reflecting obvious diver-
gences of opinion:

> Music enables pupils of all ages and abilities to join together in
> a corporate effort. It fits many occasions from the daily Act of
> Worship to the camp fire. It straddles the 'two cultures', de-

manding great precision yet touching the human spirit. It is both a valuable educational medium and an absorbing hobby. It can illuminate and stimulate effort in other subjects, as it often does in cathedral choir schools. It provides realistic opportunities for work with adults on a footing of equality.[35]

Not the most lucid philosophy upon which to build an aesthetic education! And one which certainly stemmed from a general confusion on the true purpose and value of music in education. Each of the great Reports had confidently articulated sound justifications for music in the curriculum, *and yet there had still emerged no coherent philosophy and practice of music education throughout the whole history of the maintained secondary school.* In comparison one could cite the speed with which the government of the day moved to implement radically changed maths and science curricula in schools following the success of the first Russian space project in 1959.

The time was long overdue for revolution!

1960–1980

The revolution began, largely under the belated influence of the progressive movement, during the sixties. It manifested itself in a number of ways. Firstly, it appeared in the growing criticism of the lack of firm philosophical foundation for music education and inadequate attention to the formulation of realistic objectives.[36] The debate was conducted along the child-centred lines that Marion Richardson, Herbert Read, Peter Slade, Sybil Marshall, David Holbrook and others had already laid down for the visual arts and crafts, drama and written language. Thus it tended to place self-expression at the centre of music. Secondly, it revealed itself in the number of teachers who, unhappy with traditional methods and curricula, were finally experimenting with entirely new approaches in the classrooms. Some of these approaches were based upon the work of Zoltan Kodaly and Carl Orff. In developing comprehensive and systematic schemes of music education, Kodaly had been concerned to develop aural imagination through the use of the voice, while Orff had created a series of pitched percussion instruments which were instantly playable by any child. Other music teachers began working with different subject disciplines in integrated projects.[37] Thirdly, the movement gained impetus in two publications: Self's *New Sounds in Class* (1967) and Dennis's *Experimental Music in Schools* (1970). These two books introduced composition in the classroom through contemporary approaches to the manipulation of sounds and simple electronic techniques. Finally, the Certificate of Secondary Education (introduced in 1965) offered new types of teacher-created validation based directly on pupil experience which could cater for teachers and pupils working in new ways. Thus the seeds of the revolution were planted.

In 1970 a seminal book appeared. This was *Sound and Silence* by Paynter and Aston; it included a remarkable manifesto in the opening chapter:

> It is as a creative art that music is beginning to play an increasingly important role in education. Like all the arts, music springs from a profound response to life itself ... The artist does more than make a record: he projects feelings into his materials ... until the materials become like the reality of his imagination. Through his work we feel what he feels, we see with his eyes and hear with his ears ... Artists of all kinds function as visionaries and commentators: their job is not simply to entertain us. We rely on them to help us come to terms with life and its problems ... When, in school, we involve children in the creative use of language or the materials of visual art, we are encouraging them to think like poets and artists ... In this context the arts in education take on a new importance. They are accepted as ways of saying what we feel.[38]

Not since the early Hadow Reports had music teachers had such a profound and powerful statement of faith in the role of the arts to underpin a philosophy of teaching. In insisting that the raw material of music is sound, and that music consists in the organization and manipulation of sound into coherence, Paynter and Aston provided a focus for a new imaginative classroom approach in a series of projects offering suggestions for experimental and creative music-making.

Brocklehurst too, in *Response to Music* (1971),[39] insisted on the crucial necessity of formulating aims to inform and direct music teachers, and called for more research to be made into the nature and development of the affective response to music: 'it is essential that more attention be given to studying the nature of aesthetic perception in music and its development in schools'.[40] This call was in some measure answered by Robert Witkin's *The Intelligence of Feeling* (1974) and Malcolm Ross's *Arts and the Adolescent* (1975).[41]

These two publications emphasized the view that the creative arts offer a unique opportunity for children to come to know themselves and their world through developing their inner life of feeling in the making of expressive art-objects. Ross maintained that 'the arts have an increasingly important social role ... as an essential element of lifelong education',[42] and both he and Witkin argued powerfully for their hypothesis that 'the arts offer us — not so much as product but as process — a vital instrument in the education of feelings'[43] and that not to take account of human emotion in this way would be educating for sterility. Witkin's book had a marked impact on music teachers for his scathing attack on the content and methodology of their lessons caused many of them to feel very threatened and defensive, and this was not helped by Ross's accusations of 'narrowness of outlook and a deeply rooted inertia'.[44] After all, the teachers retorted, the process may very well be what is important, but in music it is the product which is so blatantly assessed!

Other institutions were also concerned about the obvious discrepancy between what was taught in schools and the musical needs of children. The University of York set up a project directed by John Paynter and financed by the Schools Council to research into the relationships both between music and the school curriculum and between music and the other arts, as linked activities, within the curriculum. This project, which ran from 1973–78, was finally published in 1982 as *Music in the Secondary School Curriculum*.[45]

The project adopted as its framework the so far almost unrecognized notion that music was *a majority participatory subject*, and that its objective was *'musical understanding' through development of the individual imagination and sensitivity in decision-taking musical activities*. Its central concern was to see music as expressive experience that was essential for all children both as individuals and as members of a pluralistic society. Rather like Herbert Read's *Education through Art*[46] it regarded professional-type training as inappropriate in school and saw music as an expressive medium necessary to the vitality of human existence. The emphasis was on process not product, on the child not the tradition, on freedom and decision, not on constraint or teacher-controlled exercises.

Much of the work on the project filtered into the schools before the publication of the final report and was taken up with enthusiasm in some cases. Its case was reinforced in 1980 by representatives of Understanding British Industry[47] who expressed delight in the exploratory, creative, decision-making aspect of the work which, they said, were just those skills industry needed. However, this type of justification, while lauded by Hargreaves in his drive to inspire arts teachers to 'sell' the importance of their subjects to all concerned,[48] was seen as dangerous by Malcolm Ross who said firmly that such an instrumental approach to the teaching of the arts was counter-productive to its case and was to be resisted at all costs.[49]

Progressivism, with its emphasis on self-expression, spontaneity and process, came late to music education compared with the other arts;[50] even so, what came to be called 'creative music' was not welcomed or even accepted as a valid means of music education by many teachers. Arnold Bentley, whose tests of musical ability were widely used by schools to select children for instrumental tuition, argued strongly for balance in music education.[51] He advocated a traditional approach including formal tuition in staff notation, and argued passionately that a disservice is done to pupils if it is neglected. He represented the views of many teachers when he rejected pro-gressive methods, and produced a study of German orchestras as proof that those who play the classical repertoire have fewer psy-chological problems than contemporary music performers. He also repudiated the idea of integrating the arts in a combined approach: music, he said, 'exists in its own right as a separate human experi-ence, and the skills involved in listening and more overt participation are to some extent unique. Integrate it with other learning situations and those musical skills tend to suffer.'[52] Changing the traditional content of the music lesson, Bentley warned, would create a danger of neglecting fundamentals and excellence, and he questioned the last-ing value of what he saw as throwing out the baby with the bath water.

Many teachers supported him, not from suspicion of the new or anxieties of inadequacy but from strong conviction that he was right, not only in that the traditional method taught children to read music, but that it transmitted the cultural heritage. 'Creative music', they argued, led nowhere and, what was worse, the pupils themselves did not see it as *music* in the way that perhaps they saw creative dance as *dance* and modern art as *art*, because what they understood as music at this particular stage in their development was based on the tonal harmony and traditional instruments they heard around them in their daily lives. So the 'creative music' lesson was seen by pupils as even more irrelevant than the traditional one it was intended to revolu-tionize. There were also concomitant problems of lack of facilities to be overcome and, more problematic, teaching creative music to groups of thirty children at a time.

Other approaches to the problem of curricular irrelevance were explored by those who began by believing the teenage culture first

noted in the Newsom Report to be an important expressive phenomenon, and looked for credibility in the classroom through the use
of pop music. This set up yet more controversy, not only between the
traditional and radical schools of thought who argued about debase-
ment of the inherited high culture and bourgeois-dominated value
systems, but also between those who, already converted to the education of imagination and feeling, thought that the use of pop as a
medium of expression would stifle creativity by promoting mass-
media dominated stereotypes. However, over the ten years since the
first appearance of *Pop Music in School*[53] pop has been accepted into the
curriculum in some measure as another valid means of musical expression.

The late flowering of progressivism in music education has meant
that there have been proportionately more theories for revolutionizing
its principles and practice launched during the late sixties to early
eighties than at any other time in the history of its development. Indeed they have jostled behind one another so closely that in many
cases teachers have not had time to examine and assess them all, and
have simply given up the attempt and 'switched off'. At the risk of
appearing simplistic it seems fair to say that there is still a sharp divide
in the profession between the 'trads', perhaps best epitomized by
Arnold Bentley and the skills-oriented approach of the traditional examination systems, and the 'rads' symbolized by a somewhat misunderstood John Paynter. However it is also fair to say that where
they conflict most strongly it appears obvious that neither side has
fully examined or comprehended the case of the other, nor even
noticed the fact that in some fundamental areas there is more agreement than disagreement. For the transmission of the cultural heritage
so important to the 'trad', and the moment of the making and the
emphasis on the individual so vital to the 'rad' can be united and
incorporated in a common aesthetic as we shall see in section II.

But there is one further point I should like to make before pro-
ceeding to an examination of what I believe should be the future
direction of music education, and that is the distortion of classroom
music by the parallel existence of a system of instrumental tuition
reinforced by the graded examinations of the conservatoires. Do not
mistake my comments for criticism of their work. It is not part of my
thesis to remark upon or judge their product in any way, and in fact I
must laud the Colleges of Music for producing some of the finest
musicians of this century. But the fact that alongside what children
learn in school, and in most cases without reference to it, there exists
an independent system of instrumental tuition assessed by formal

graded examinations, has produced a distortion in the minds of many of what music education in the classroom should be doing. Of the other arts only dance has had to suffer the same type of distortion from the similar existence of the graded exams of RAD.[54] There is no doubt that the integration of children who are already highly skilled performers with those who are comparatively musically unskilled and illiterate has created enormous problems for many teachers, and raised the questions of efficacy and value that Paynter's work was designed to answer. But at the present time of writing it appears that the division between the school and the conservatoire will remain, for neither side seems much interested in working any closer together. And with the demise of the GCE and the loss of the option which allowed a pass at grade V to replace one of the papers of the examination, it is likely that classroom and conservatoire will draw further apart. Only the future will show the effects of this division.

Section II

Music in the Aesthetic Field

The perceptive reader will have noticed the omission of two publications of major significance for music education both of which appeared in the seventies. I have left a discussion of these until now because I believe that together with other related material they constitute the most significant landmarks in the current direction of music education.

In asserting that music education must be aesthetic education Bennett Reimer's *A Philosophy of Music Education*[55] was based on the fundamental premise that the nature and value of music education are determined by the nature and value of the art of music itself. This book, which was to have a profound influence on the thinking of the seventies and eighties, was written from Reimer's concern at the desperate lack of a fundamental philosophical understanding by music educators of what they were really about. A basis for music education, he said, would begin by affirming the nature of music as music while recognizing the relation of music to life. It would confirm that the experience of music is related to the experience of life at the deepest levels of life's significance, and manifest the major function of music, as of ail art, as making 'objective, and therefore conceivable, the subjective realm of human responsiveness'.[56] For education consists largely in the development of people's power to share meanings about man and his world, and the arts are the means by which humans can explore and understand subjective reality through the presentation of a sense of feeling in the creation and experiencing of an art-work. Therefore music education is the education of human feeling through the development of responsiveness to the aesthetic qualities of sound. 'The deepest value of music education is the same as the deepest value of all aesthetic education: the enrichment of the quality of people's lives through enriching their insights into the nature of human feeling.'[57]

Reimer introduced the ordinary music teacher hitherto unused to reflecting on deeper issues to the thinking of aestheticians such as Dewey, Leonard Meyer and Susanne Langer and to the notion of the symbolic nature of music. He also made the point that they should concentrate on teaching what is teachable — *aesthetic perception* — in contexts which encourage creative reactions to that which is being perceived, a point which Swanwick was to elaborate nine years later. Reimer suggested that listening was the essential mode of musical experiencing supported by the concomitant activities of composition and performance. Also indispensable were the conceptual tools — the skills, techniques and a language in which to communicate — but these were secondary to the main thrust and purpose of an aesthetic education through the active experience of music.

An even more significant publication for music in the school curriculum appeared in 1979. This was *A Basis for Music Education* by Keith Swanwick of the University of London Institute of Education.[58] Appointed to the first chair of music education in Britain, Professor Swanwick brought to this book the distillation of years of work and experience in the field. He not only grounded his work firmly in that of Langer, Koestler, LA Reid, Reimer and others, but having established a theory of music he confidently articulated a rationale for music education. He based this upon direct musical involvement in the three activities posited by Reimer of composition, performance and listening, which he retermed 'audition', and defined as listening with intention.

Swanwick specified two levels of meaning in music: 'meaning to', characterized by recognition — understanding 'what is being said', and 'meaning for', characterized by relationship — being moved by that understanding.'Meaning for' may be understood as *value*. Only on the first level of meaning, that of understanding, said Swanwick, are teachers able to work, for values can probably be 'caught' but not taught. In a later book[59] he stated that we are always looking for signs that pupils are coming to value music but we obviously cannot predict how and when this might happen[60] and 'our influence on this second level is bound to be minimal. So much depends on the individual and his state of feelings at the time'[61]. Leading the horse to the water is the teacher's task; forcing it to drink is impossible. However on the first level of understanding much can be done, and Swanwick defined clear objectives for bringing it about through the three activities of composing, performing and audition which, he stressed, must be pursued in such a way that they assume aesthetic significance.

Here at last was the curriculum model that music educators had lacked for so long containing both a clearly stated philosophical base and defined curriculum objectives. It was welcomed by many of the music education profession and used not only as a more coherent and cogent argument from which local education authorities, advisers and teachers could develop curriculum initiatives, but also, together with Paynter's work, as the focus for the gradually emerging General Certificate of Secondary Education examination. This was to surface in a common examination at 16+ designed to replace the GCE and the CSE by 1988.

Not since Hadow and Somervell put forward the first draft proposal for a music syllabus for the School Certificate in 1923 has there been such a profound change in the approach to music examinations. For in requiring the new examination syllabuses to conform to national criteria,[62] and in basing these criteria on composing, performing and listening, a most significant step forward has been taken in the direction of music education as aesthetic education. The national criteria for Music are firmly rooted in the very stuff of music itself for they are based essentially on experiences of music both individually and in groups. Assessment of pupil work will be largely internal and much of it will be founded on course work thus enabling pupils to make, present, respond to and evaluate their own symbolic experience. Here there are not only exciting opportunities for teachers to develop new curricula rooted firmly in musical involvement, but also a form of safeguard against those who still cling to what will now be seen as irrelevant modes of teaching music.

Music educators have been lamenting the strait-jacket of the public examination system almost since the day it was first realized that raising the status of music by admitting it as an equal partner with other subjects in the old school certificate created more problems in classroom credibility than it solved. But there is no use in being anything other than realistic. As long as the examination system exists in our society as the accepted way of validating educational experience it cannot be ignored or sidestepped by those who wish to promote their 'subject'. The Gulbenkian Report[63] of 1982 was the most powerfully and weightily presented argument for the arts in education yet to appear in the public arena of debate, but to pupils, parents and employers argument alone is not enough; it is the magic pieces of paper labelled 'certificate' that count.

The way ahead for music as an aesthetic education is still by no means free of problems. The new syllabuses are not without imperfections, and there is certainly an enormous problem of equipping, acommodating and training to be overcome. Teaching music as a practical subject makes its provision and timetabling a matter for pressing attention, and the training of teachers with vision and sensibility a vital necessity.

With the impetus of the GCSE criteria and the unequivocal support of HMI[64] — it appears likely that in the classroom at least music will more and more rapidly become a practical subject. Well taught, the aesthetic field proposed in the opening chapter will become increasingly apparent as through composing, performing, listening and evaluating each pupil grows both as an inheritor of a tradition and an innovator creatively striving within or against that tradition. And through this understanding it is hoped that the pupil will also come to value music. As Swanwick puts it:

> Why we value music is ultimately not to do with belonging to a tradition or with self-development, as some have argued, but depends on a recognition that music is one of the great symbolic modes available to us. Initiation into this activity is what we look for ... the act of shaping music is a purposeful attempt to articulate something meaningful. It need not be complex or profound, earth-shattering or of cosmic proportions but it will be expressive and structured and just as 'objective' as the spoken or written word, an equation or a map.[65]

'Initiation into this activity' does not mean returning pupils to the meaningless activities which have characterized too much music teaching for too long. It is a reiteration of Paynter and Aston's 'encouraging them to think like poets and artists' (see note 38). Through the medium of individual and small group work children can be taught how to develop the smallest germ, the least prepossessing idea — a few notes or chords, a rhythmic pattern, an interesting sound effect — into compositions with structure and form to be performed, recorded and later evaluated by themselves, the teacher and the class in discussion or written response. It is both during the process of composing and at its evaluation that location of the pupil's work in the tradition of music takes place, as the teacher introduces listening material from the widest variety of sources across times and cultures. Thus the work in hand is linked with that of others who have tackled the same symbolic problems — varied a theme, made an incantation, expressed a mood or explored a sound.

Creation within tradition, innovation through knowledge, a true fusion of the new with the old, the now with the then. After over 100 years of conflicting ideas about the place and value of music in the curriculum the ground has finally been cleared and the way forward illuminated. But despite arguments for the centrality of the arts in the curriculum provided by, for example, the Gulbenkian Report (1982) and *Challenge for the Comprehensive School* (1982),[66] no assumptions can be made that the battle is won. The recent recession, the increased technological and vocational thrust in education coupled with the noticeable swing towards 'Victorian values' could lead, even now, to a wrong turning being taken.

Unless the new curricula being developed by teachers in response to the new examinations are firmly rooted in what is really important about music, the creating and recreating, the responsive listening and evaluating from a growing knowledge of *how music is*, it may cease to be of any importance at all in schools. For there is a grave danger that unless it is fully comprehended as an aesthetic discipline and properly taught it may be relegated to the realm of the unimportant. After all, a pupil may argue, I don't have to do music at school. I can learn the clarinet and pass my graded exams privately. With the distorted and fragmented nature of current provision for music education both in and out of school, where pupils may be taught by the classroom teacher, a specialist teacher, a peripatetic teacher, a private teacher, in a school, a private studio, a specialist music school, an LEA centre, or at junior classes administered by a conservatoire, and all this by teachers with widely differing qualifications or none, there is a very real possibility that music education may cease in schools altogether. Without a rapid and apparent return to the teaching of music as an essentially aesthetic discipline based firmly on reclamation of the historical tradition and a location of the symbolic moment within the cultural procession, so that music is seen not just as a soft option for 'thickoes' but as a vital mode of experiencing for every child, music stands in more peril than any of the other arts in school.

This makes the provision and provisioning of rich and vital curricula the most urgent task confronting music teachers. Music is an endangered subject[67] in this utilitarian age; the necessity of making music a living experience for every child must be attended to before it is too late. There is no substitute for music. Nothing else will do.

Notes

1 But for two interesting discussions of the topic see SMALL, C (1980) *Music, Society, Education,* (2nd ed) John Calder; and FLETCHER, PG (1973) 'Crystal slippers and the fading Cinderella — why the scenario has changed for good', *Education,* 141, 1 June, pp 627–8.
2 That is, in England and Wales; schools in Scotland and Northern Ireland are administered separately.
3 BOARD OF EDUCATION (1904) *Regulations for Secondary Schools,* HMSO.
4 Finally instituted in 1917.
5 Arising in response to the demand for piano and violin lessons as cheap mass-produced instruments became readily available.
6 A graded examination system was initiated in 1876 by the Trinity College of Music and followed shortly by the institution of the Associated Board of the Royal Schools of Music. Both systems were well established by the 1890s.
7 Sir William Hadow was Chairman of the Consultative Committee of the Board of Education from 1920–34. He was, among other things, both a composer in his own right and also a music historian and critic. His interest in the educational value of the arts, and of music in particular, informed and coloured the deliberations of the Committees throughout his term in office.
8 BOARD OF EDUCATION (1923) *Report of the Consultative Committee on Differentiation of the Curriculum for Boys and Girls Respectively in Secondary Schools,* (Differentiation Report), HMSO.
9 *Ibid,* p 67.
10 *Ibid,* p 68.
11 Board of Education Chief Music Inspector.
12 Sight-singing was always considered to be of great importance in the elementary schools. Three names are associated with the development of a teaching method — Sarah Glover, John Hullah and John Curwen, and the story of the gradual triumph of Curwen's tonic-solfa system over Hullah's fixed-doh method makes fascinating reading. Choral singing was considered to be an important moralizing force in the nineteenth century and singing was made compulsory in the elementary schools in 1872. Here it was enforced by a system of 'payment by results' whereby sixpence was granted for each child able to sing a prescribed number of songs, and a shilling if they could also sing at sight.
13 BOARD OF EDUCATION (1923) *op cit,* pp 159–70.
14 BOARD OF EDUCATION (1927a) *The Education of the Adolescent,* HMSO. This Report attempted to codify secondary education, introduce it for all children up to the age of 15, and effectively widen the curriculum. In it Hadow's Committee suggested that there were 'three great ends of

human life and activity' which education in a modern secondary school should promote, and specifically mentioned music and art as subjects to be included in a training 'to delight in pursuits and rejoice in accomplishments' (p xxiii).

15 BOARD OF EDUCATION (1927b) *Handbook of Suggestions for the Consideration of Teachers and others concerned in the work of Public Elementary Schools,* HMSO.

16 *Ibid*, p 240.

17 BOARD OF EDUCATION (1931), *Report of the Consultative Committee on The Primary School,* HMSO. This Report, also chaired by Hadow, later directly influenced secondary school practice.

18 *Ibid*, p 93, italics mine.

19 BOARD OF EDUCATION (1938) *Report of the Consultative Committee on Secondary Education with special reference to Grammar Schools and Technical High Schools,* (The Spens Report), HMSO.

20 *Ibid*, p 152.

21 *Ibid*, p 145.

22 *Ibid*, p 155.

23 HALE, N (1947) *Education for Music: A Skeleton Plan of Research into the Development of the Study of Music as Part of the Organized Plan of General Education,* Oxford University Press.

24 BOARD OF EDUCATION (1943) *Curriculum and Examinations in Secondary Schools: Report of the Committee of the Secondary Schools Examinations Council Appointed by the President of the Board of Education in 1941,* HMSO. The Norwood Report showed perceptible irritation with woolly thinking on justification for the inclusion of the arts in the curriculum, and impatience with those who would emphasize only their unique and specific values. It pointed out that the arts are not unique in carrying aesthetic sensibility and stated that they could only seriously base their claim for inclusion in the curriculum firstly on their likeness to other subjects in providing areas of experience before, and secondly, on their own specific values. (see pp. 123–4.)

25 BOARD OF EDUCATION (1923) *op cit*, pp 68–9.

26 HALE, N (1947) *op cit*, p 34.

27 The 1944 Education Act gave the local education authorities the duty to secure 'adequate provision of primary and secondary education'. As Organizer of Instrumental Music to the Bournemouth Education Authority, Hale had hoped to be instrumental in implementing his aims for music education. Some of his recommendations were actually incorporated in the Norwood and McNair Reports (BOARD OF EDUCATION (1944) *Teachers and Youth Leaders,* and some were made possible by the 1944 Act itself. (HMSO).

28 Renamed The Arts Council in 1946.

29 See, for example, MINISTRY OF EDUCATION (1956) *Music in Schools,* Ministry of Education Pamphlet no. 27, HMSO for an attempt to satisfy all parties. In a section on the value of music we read: '... power of music to draw together and strengthen a community through the corporate singing of fine tunes, to inspire and control rhythmical movement, to give the individual as well as the group a command of satisfying skills, and to

create its own world of disciplined imagination in which to strive after perfection brings immediate and lasting rewards' (p 21). Against that LONG, N (1959) in *Music in English Education* (Faber and Faber) was concerned with the problem of 'effectively pressing the claims of a study which has little utility for most of the pupils who follow it' for it cannot be argued instrumentally but only intrinsically through its distinctive values 'the very power of which depend upon the fact that it has no utility, that it is concerned not with the everyday world but with a world of imagination, ... it helps the individual not to study more efficiently but to experience more profoundly' (p 103).

30 MINISTRY OF EDUCATION (1963) *Half Our Future: A Report of the Central Advisory Council for Education (England)*, (The Newsom Report) HMSO
31 *Ibid*, para. 418.
32 SCHOOLS COUNCIL (1968) *Young School Leavers: Report of a Survey Among Young People, Parents and Teachers*, HMSO.
33 See note 29; 2nd edition issued in 1969.
34 *Ibid*, p 28.
35 *Ibid*.
36 See, for example, articles in *Music in Education*, Macmillan Journals Ltd, particularly those by John Paynter and Christopher Green. Green in 'Objectives in music education' 32, 334, Nov/Dec 1968 refers to current research findings and so provides a useful survey of publications.
37 See, for example, Schools Council Bulletin, autumn 1972.
38 PAYNTER, J and ASTON, P (1970) *Sound and Silence: Classroom Projects in Creative Music*, Cambridge University Press, pp 3–4.
39 BROCKLEHURST, B (1971) *Response to Music: Principles of Music Education*, Routledge and Kegan Paul.
40 *Ibid*, p 43.
41 WITKIN, RW (1974), *The Intelligence of Feeling*, Heinemann Educational Books, and Ross, M (1975) *Arts and the Adolescent*, Schools Council Working Paper 54, were both outcomes of the Schools Council's 'Arts and the Adolescent' Project of 1968–72 set up as a result of Enquiry One: *Young School Leavers* (see note 32).
42 Ross, M (1975) *op cit*, pp 61–2.
43 *Ibid*, p 68.
44 *Ibid*, pp 52–3.
45 PAYNTER, J (1982) *Music in the Secondary School Curriculum: Trends and Developments in Class Music Teaching*, Cambridge University.
46 READ, H. (1958) *Education Through Art*, Faber and Faber.
47 The Understanding British Industry Association was an educational offshoot of the CBI with regional headquarters throughout the country. In 1981 they highlighted ten points that industry needed from education, suggesting that six of them could be found in music education, see PAYNTER, J (1982) *op cit*, p 240.
48 Lecture given at the National Association for Education in the Arts Conference, November 1984.
49 *Ibid*, in reply.
50 DEPARTMENT OF EDUCATION and SCIENCE (1967) *Children and their Primary Schools* (The Plowden Report), HMSO, a Report of the Central Advisory

Council for Education (England), stresses how music as a creative subject lagged behind work in language, arts and crafts (see para. 687).

51 BENTLEY, A (1975) *Music in Education: A Point of View*, NFER Publishing Co.
52 *Ibid*, p 62.
53 VULLIAMY, G and LEE, E (Eds) (1980) *Pop Music in School*, 2nd ed, Cambridge University Press.
54 The Royal Academy of Dancing.
55 REIMER, B (1970) *A Philosophy of Music Education*, Prentice-Hall Inc.
56 *Ibid*, p 39.
57 *Ibid*.
58 It is fitting to note that Louis Arnaud Reid, that doyen of contemporary British philosophers, who sadly died while this book was in preparation, himself wrote the introduction to Professor Swanwick's book, thus setting the seal on this approach to music education as aesthetic education.
59 SWANWICK, K and TAYLOR, D (1982). *Discovering Music: Developing the Music Curriculum in Secondary Schools*, Batsford Academic and Educational.
60 *Ibid*, p. 128.
61 SWANWICK, K 1979 *op cit*, p 31.
62 DEPARTMENT OF EDUCATION AND SCIENCE (1985) *General Certificate of Secondary Education: The National Criteria: Music*, HMSO.
63 CALOUSTE GULBENKIAN FOUNDATION (1982) *The Arts in Schools: Principles, Practice and Provision*.
64 DEPARTMENT of EDUCATION AND SCIENCE (1985) *Music from 5–16*, Curriculum Matters 4, An HMI Series, HMSO.
65 SWANWICK, K and TAYLOR, D (1982) *op cit*, pp 124–5.
66 HARGREAVES, DH (1982) *The Challenge for the Comprehensive School: Culture, curriculum and community*, Routledge and Kegan Paul.
67 ASSISTANT MASTERS AND MISTRESSES ASSOCIATION (1984), *Music: An Endangered Subject?* AMMA.

4   *Film Is Dead — The Case for Resurrection*

Robert Watson

Introduction

In this chapter I want to reaffirm the importance of film as an expressive art whose place on the curriculum has never been adequately secured; I also want to make a clear distinction between film studies, as a disciplined exploration within the aesthetic field proposed with such clarity by Peter Abbs, and media studies, whose parasitical growth now threatens film studies with extinction.

The chapter is in three parts. An introductory section provides an outline history of the slow progress towards acceptance, followed by the displacement of film as art and the establishment of television as crown prince of media studies (with pop music, newspapers and magazines in close attendance). The second part retraces the main theories of film, and suggests that the earlier and sometimes more tentative theories, where they grew out of and were again tested in practice, still retain some validity and will tend to be encountered naturally by students involved in creative exercises in film-making as well as in their evaluative responses to film-watching. The third part consists of a few practical ideas for teaching the subject.

It used to be confidently asserted that film was a new art form, indeed, *the* new art form of the twentieth century, and yet, for all its fruitful flirtations with Russian formalism, German expressionism, surrealism, the anti-novel and so forth, it has remained predominantly naturalistic and conventional in its narrative forms (though they need to be understood in their own terms), and humanist in its most significant achievements. Effectively the cinema has managed to put good old wine into its new bottles, thus incidentally maintaining continuity with the traditions which other arts have sometimes disastrously cast aside. Despite its initial novelty the cinema has rarely been motivated by any compulsion to 'make it new'; nevertheless, the account of modernism and the progressive movement in education — especially in its latter stages — does concern us in this context, since the theoretical discourses which have evolved out of modernism have been applied to film in such a way that it is film, rather than the theories, that has been found wanting. An academic philistinism has been on the rampage, and anyone picking over the debris of the last twenty years or so in search of criteria to enhance the immediate experience of attending to a film will find virtually nothing comparable even to the impressionistic criticism of the early 1960s — *that*, at least, came from people who loved films, even if they had little comprehension of the creative processes involved in making them. What is needed now is something of a return to basics, and that is why the third part of this chapter is deliberately modest in its scope.

The exercises should not imply that practical work is intrinsically better than theoretical — writing a poem is not necessarily more educative, more rewarding, than reading one: that fallacy has been dealt with elsewhere in this book. What is so valuable in the model of the aesthetic field is its stress on the interpenetration of processes. It seems to me that by entering the various collaborative processes of film-making at whatever level, by responding to and evaluating those processes in the context of a concurrent study of major examples in the art, the student of film will become necessarily and rewardingly involved in the aesthetic challenges of other verbal and visual arts. It would be utopian at this time to propose film studies as a central meeting-place for integrated-arts studies. Nonetheless, even the brief suggestions which close this chapter should indicate some of the ways in which teachers of English, Drama and Art could ameliorate film without diminishing the work in their own aesthetic fields. I see little prospect of this uniquely hybrid and yet distinctive art being nourished by media studies. At the same time it seems to me that it has an invaluable contribution to make within the arts' community.

The Development of Film and Film Studies

Any early defence of the film as art had to make its way against an influential, and not unreasonable, critique of the cinema as mass entertainment. In *The Principles of Literary Criticism* (1924), for example, IA Richards drew attention to its supposed effect on audiences:

> They tend ... to develop stock attitudes and stereotyped ideas, the attitudes and ideas of producers: attitudes and ideas

which can be 'put across' *quickly* through a medium that lends itself to crude rather than to sensitive handling.[1]

Leavis and Thompson's *Culture and Environment*, nine years later, showed a similar concern with, and a determination to combat, the deleterious effects of the popular cinema on standards of taste, and as late as 1938, in *The Principles of Art*, RG Collingwood could dismiss the film's pretensions to art as if no substantial claims had yet been made for it:

> 'Why', one hears it asked, 'should not the modern popular entertainment of the cinema, like the Renaissance popular entertainment of the theatre, produce a new form of great art?' The answer is simple. In the Renaissance theatre collaboration between author and actors on the one hand, and audience on the other, was a lively reality. In the cinema it is impossible.[2]

I think it's worth adding that at this time virtually no serious study of audience response had been undertaken. The documents collected in the sociological studies of JP Mayer (*British Cinemas and their Audiences*, 1948), do not altogether support Richards' observations, suggesting, rather, a sensible resistance to stereotypes and a capacity to discriminate in many other instances. Mayer concluded that there was both 'a tendency of the film medium towards art and the increasing concern with the interpretation of collective and individual value patterns' and that there existed 'a considerable percentage' of the audience waiting and wanting to appreciate that art. However, he did not think that a deliberate policy to raise the cultural standards of films could succeed within the existing capitalist structure, and therefore, by implication, the critical stance of leading intellectuals continued to be justified, at least insofar as it related to popular film-going.[3] It would be impossible to determine the extent to which that blanket dismissal retarded the advance of serious appreciation of the film; certainly a chronological tabulation highlights the painfully slow progress towards the acceptance of positive approaches to film study on the curriculum:

1925   The Film Society was formed in London, and began making the most interesting developments in international films available, not only by preparing them for exhibition but also by encouraging discussion and translating theoretical works (though contemporary advances in the Russian cinema were not made available for the first four seasons).[4]

1932   The Report of the Commission on Educational and Cultural

Films was published as *The Film in National Life*. It summed up the situation with regard to the educational potential of film as follows:

> It was difficult to bring films into real relation with class syllabuses, and the limitations of the cinematograph within the scope of subject appropriate to an elementary school were more narrow than was at first supposed. Reviewing all circumstances, therefore, including the high cost of projectors and the limited number of films, the Committee saw no grounds for advising the Council to depart from the policy of encouraging private enterprise in out of school displays of a high quality, but would hesitate to propose any policy which might involve expenditure on equipment or attendance at displays in school time.[5]

1933   The principal recommendation of the report was implemented with the foundation of the British Film Institute, whose objects would be to encourage 'the use and development of the cinematograph as a means of entertainment and instruction' and to set up a national repository of films.[6] For the next fifteen years some of the Institute's resources were necessarily used for building up the stock of films as teaching aids, and it was in this sense that 'film in education' was generally understood, though as RS Lambert noted in 1937 there continued to be isolated examples of film-making and appreciation in schools.[7]

1943   The British Film Institute summer schools were inaugurated by Ernest Lindgren, developing out of his work at the City Literary Institute and responding to the steadily growing demand for an education in film itself.

1946   The National Committee for Visual Aids in Education was formed, with specific responsibility for developing the uses of film in education.

1948   The Radcliffe Report on the British Film Institute gave official sanction to this separation of functions. Henceforward the Institute was free to

> encourage the development of the art of the film, promote its use as a record of contemporary life and manners and foster public appreciation and study of it from these points of view.[8]

1950   The post of Film Appreciation Officer was created so that someone could implement the report's recommendations and enable film to become the subject of study in schools and colleges. A voluntary body, the Society of Film Teachers (now the Society for Education in Film and Television, or SEFT) was formed at about the same time to develop materials and courses.

1957 The BFI's Education Department was formed, its work

> based on the belief that the cinema, a great contemporary art and one of the powerful media operating in society, must find its place in the curriculum. The department thus exists primarily to service teachers and lecturers who are concerned to introduce and pursue this work. ('Service to Education', BFI)[9]

1958 The first postgraduate course in film studies was initiated at the Slade School of Fine Art.

1959 A joint working party of the BFI and the Association of Teachers in Colleges and Departments of Education (ATCDE) explored the possibilities for extending the study of film and television in teacher training.

1960 Their Report, *Film and Television in Education for Teaching*, was published, and led to the introduction of the first three-year course adopting a number of their suggestions, at Bede College. Initially an option within main English, eventually a main course in film and television was established there. In the same year the Pilkington Report on Broadcasting was published, with its useful strictures on the trivialization of content.

1963 The Newsom Report, *Half our Future*, stressed the value of media studies for the less academic children. Treating film and television together, the Report regrets that 'in the majority of schools they are used only as visual aids for the presentation of material connected with other subjects':

> Little attention is paid to the degree to which film and television enter into and influence the lives of our pupils and to these media as legitimate means for the communication of personal experience alongside literature, music and painting.
>
> The culture provided by all the mass media, but particularly by film and television, represents the most significant environmental factor that teachers have to take into account.[10]

1972 The Associated Examining Board's 'O' level film study consortium was set up.

1973 The Higher Education Grants Committee of the BFI assisted the first university lectureship, at Warwick University.

1975 The Bullock Report on English teaching, *A Language for Life*, advocated the extension of film and television study, though mainly as sources of thematic material for English work.

1976 The BFI conference at York, *Film and TV Studies in Secondary Education*, concluded that film should be studied within the larger context of media studies.

1977 *The Use of Film in Higher Education* (BFI), listed fifty-five institutions where film was being studied in some form.

1979 By this date there were four 'O' level consortia in the regions, and seven university lectureships assisted by the Institute.

1979 The BFI conference in London, *Film and Media Studies in Higher Education*, (published 1981), examined methods and course structures in the light of recent theoretical fashions. The opening paper made the following assertion:

> ... film is by any standards today, of entirely marginal intellectual interest *per se*. It cannot possibly justify itself as the basis for a substantive discipline or field of study.[11]

In the introduction to the published papers a plausible explanation for this extreme point of view is offered:

> ...if a film is to be analysed as mass culture and ideological effect, then in the seventies and eighties, television, journalism and soon video have a greater claim to centrality; if film and society or cultural analysis are the issue, then the disciplines for the study of society have equal claim with the specificity of particular media ...[12]

And towards the end of a useful paper on 'Institutions and Course Structures' the current Head of Education at the BFI sees the 'tendency to treat film as a *medium* rather than an *art*' as 'both pedagogically and politically desirable'. He quotes with approval the point that the new theoretical approaches to reading films open out

> ... the text onto or into a number of different processes. The text is no longer frozen into the timeless vacuum which it had been permitted to inhabit by virtue of its eternal value as *art*.[13]

Clearly, by the end of the 1970s, *art* had become a term of derogation for some theorists. In retrospect the implications of this are detectable even prior to the publication of the Newsom Report: if aesthetic and moral criteria disintegrate, the criterion of immediate social relevance — however narrowly defined that may be — tends to become central. Film as a *medium* has no greater intrinsic value than other media, and if other media such as pop music and magazines constitute more 'significant environmental factors' in the lives of contemporary schoolchildren, then the study of these media is bound to be more rewarding than the study of the film medium. What is at issue here is the nature and scope of education, and the function of art in education and in our lives.

The 'de-centring' of film has continued. In 1983 the DES Report, *Popular TV and Schoolchildren*, was published, to be reprinted two years later in the BFI's collection of essays on *TV and Schooling*. Increasingly, educational aims and objectives are designed to accommodate the study of ephemeral media, and although the new GCSE syllabuses in media studies and communication emphasize the value of practical creative work, the rich potential of that work for developing expressive skills is severely limited by its study context. Planning and making a promotional pop video, a simulated 'soap', an advertisement or a news or current affairs programme, to take several examples, will demand as much creative intelligence as students can offer, but that intelligence, once released, has nowhere much to go — it is confined by the very models it can understand only to emulate or be dismissive of. There exists, in short, a qualitative difference between *medium* study and *art* study; only the latter offers that enormous range of challenges to the developing consciousness which both includes and transcends its responsive capacity at the moment of study.

Accounting for his wariness of 'systematic criticism and of any form of critical terrorism' — in other words of the four disciplines which have become influential largely in the last twenty years, 'Marxist/materialist, structuralist, semiological and psychoanalytical in orientation' (he missed feminism there) — Richard Roud pointed out that

> Most critical movements in the past (in literature, music and art as well as in cinema) have arisen in an attempt to justify or defend new creative developments. But by and large, the films to which these scientific methods are applied have already been accepted, even by the impressionistic critics.[14]

'The new film critics', he added, 'are interested in criticism as an end in itself'. Lindsay Anderson has made the same point:

> Under the twin deadly influences of sociology and aesthetics, critics have tended to write more and more as though criticism were an end in itself, comprehensible only to the academically elect, expressible only in its own hieratic jargon.[15]

And Luis Bunuel:

> I ... was introduced to several professors, including a young man in a suit and tie who blushed a good deal. When I asked him what he taught, he replied, 'The Semiology of the Clonic Image'. I could have murdered him on the spot.[16]

Factors distinct from, and even ideologically opposed to those which often motivate the various forms of 'systematic criticism and ... critical terrorism', are contributing to the institutionalization of media studies. My concern here is neither to isolate these nor to criticize media studies as such but simply, by drawing attention to what is being lost, to make a case for film in education, for film as art.

Defining the Art

Fox Talbot, recording that with a magnifying glass he was able to count every one of the 200 panes of glass in his photograph of a window at Lacock Abbey in 1835, was expressing wonder at what would soon be taken for granted — a photograph's photographic accuracy. Baudelaire, in 1859, saw that very accuracy, or 'truth to nature', as a sort of disease already infecting and impoverishing the fine arts.[17] Muybridge's analytical sequence of the movement of a horse was accepted as real in 1877 because, it was assumed, the mechanically recorded image would not lie; the photograph was *proof*, even of what could not be verified by observation. By 1880 he had developed the Zoopraxiscope, which enabled the analyzed movement to be reconstituted, the single images synthesized into movement projected on to a screen.

The first public exhibitions of films by the Lumiere brothers, at the end of 1895, included a train arriving at a station, and the sense of reality was so strong that audiences panicked at the train's approach. Subsequently, when, by means of editing, an audience could see a whole person one moment apparently cut off at the waist in the next, there was initially consternation, even nausea, and some producers feared that customers would demand their money back if they were only shown parts of people.

The *artifice* of the film, then, was glimpsed in that confusion with the sense of reality it imparted, but then rapidly accommodated within narrative structures serving essentially naturalistic ends, already familiar in literary and dramatic forms of popular melodrama.

But there was also a qualitative difference between the truth to nature of a still photograph and the reality of a film. A still photograph stops something and holds it to that moment (Baudelaire tried to make a distinction between mere truth — which might be accurately recorded by purely mechanical means — and beauty and wonder: the artist could no longer be content merely to copy nature). The film has something of this quality of being a copy, and something else again: it does not stop a moment, it starts a movement, and our strongest sense of movement is visual (though we may feel the breeze or smell aromas lifted by the breeze). When we see movement on the screen we are really seeing movement, not a simulation.[18] Necessarily the images have been recorded and therefore come to us from the past, but their movement contradicts this pastness, being continually present, or continually replaced as each movement is naturally succeeded. If Baudelaire was right to see that accuracy in a copy of nature was no measure of artistic worth, then the film, achieving both photographic accuracy and the reality of movement (as well as, in due course, synchronized naturalistic sound) would seem to have even less potential as an art form than still photography.

The first films were not edited. The camera, containing about fifty feet of film, would be fixed in position, the film wound through, removed, processed and then projected, each complete film consisting of one shot lasting a little under a minute. Soon several of these films would be cemented end to end for continuous projection in programmes, and within a few years the narrative potential of this expedient was exploited, pre-eminently by Georges Méliès and Edwin S Porter. As early as 1902, in *The Life of an American Fireman*, Porter was alternating scenes occurring simultaneously in 'real' time for dramatic effect, cutting away from a woman and child trapped in a burning house to the fire alarm, then to the fire engines. Because he was building up his film with stock footage, Porter inadvertently involved several different fire services in the same rescue, accidentally demonstrating that the edited narrative film could deploy time and space in its own terms. DW Griffith made more effective uses of these and other devices, and it was Griffith whose work ahd a major influence on the Russian directors and, therefore, on the development of montage theory (initially known to the Russians as American montage, it has subsequently been thought of as Russian montage).

At its simplest, montage is the French word for editing, which already implies more than merely joining one length of film to another: it implies selection, correction and the rearrangement of the pieces to form a satisfactory whole, be it a sequence or a complete work. Elements of creative choice were always present, of course, in the positioning of the camera, the subject matter and so on, but editing gave the director far greater control over the filmed material. He assembled his film from discrete sections, imposing or creating a rhythm and a meaning not necessarily apparent in any individual shot. The Soviet experiments extended to the shot, but the shot as the servant of montage. In itself the single shot was inert. It became active in juxtaposition: A plus B generated something new, effect C.

In *Film Technique*, (1929, revised 1933), Pudovkin analyzed scenes from Griffith's films and gave detailed accounts of the montage experiments undertaken by Kuleshov and, subsequently, himself. These included the demonstration that the expression on an actor's face would be 'read' differently according to the shot which preceded it and to which it was supposed to be a reaction, that juxtaposed images could work as metaphors to suggest a state of mind, a concept like freedom, or the director's attitude to his subject, and that montage effects could be classified according to rhythm, variable speed filming, contrasting planes of composition, etc. Eisenstein saw the essence of montage, and of art, in conflict, and was critical of Kuleshov's metric editing, but many of Eisenstein's essays were unavailable until *The Film Sense* and *Film Form* were published in the 1940s, so I think it is true to say that montage theory, as it was understood in the West from the early 1930s, derived from Pudovkin's account and its application to the study of Russian films. Its ideological component — it was a dialectical process encapsulating the concept of progress — was stressed by the Russian theorists despite the apparent contradiction in their discovering the principles of montage in American cinema, and despite Eisenstein's long search for analogues and antecedents in other arts and other cultures. This insistence on montage as the essence of cinema and the aesthetic exemplar of dialectical materialism, together with its inevitable undervaluing of the shot and the consecutive sequence, made the theory appear inapplicable to subsequent developments. However, although montage theory is not comprehensive, its principles have remained fundamentally valid.

Rudolf Arnheim (1933) accepted the importance of montage,

with reservations about some of Pudovkin's claims to be able to calculate and achieve specific effects with images. It was in his detailed attention to the inherent weaknesses of the film as a vehicle for transcribing reality, however, that Arnheim formulated his aesthetic: the limitation imposed by the frame, the two-dimensional image, the distortions of perspective, the black and white tonal range, the absence of synchronized sound. Each limitation could be used creatively to make in film-time and film-space coherent works which redefined spatial and temporal relationships — simply, sequences need not unfold chronologically, time could be retarded or accelerated, events occurring simultaneously in different places could be placed in immediate proximity, details could be heightened or eliminated, lighting and composition could be used expressively to intensify an emotion or comment on an action. That is, Arnheim added to montage all the compositional and temporal qualities of the filmed shot, demonstrated that film did not in fact replicate nature but made only partial and distorted representations, and argued that these limitations were properties that could be used artistically. His attitudes to sound and colour were somewhat contradictory, but insofar as they enabled film to get nearer to the objective recording of reality he tended to see such developments as likely to reduce the artistic power of film.[19]

This work — hugely simplified in my brief account here — constitutes the first and most important phase in film aesthetics, endorsed and developed by Raymond Spottiswoode (1935) who also drew attention to the importance of economic and political factors, then arranged into what was to become a standard teaching text by Ernest Lindgren (*The Art of the Film*, 1948), popularized by the indefatigable Roger Manvell through the forties and fifties, and revised by Stephenson and Debrix, (*The Cinema as Art*, 1965).[20]

The second phase was a reaction against artifice in praise of realism, led by André Bazin. In a sense it takes the challenge back to Baudelaire, for Bazin argued that the distinctive aesthetic strength of film was to be located precisely in its capacity to record the real objectively: 'King montage' was dead, replaced by Italian neo-realism, the documentary-style narratives of ordinary lives observed in natural locations with natural sound and natural lighting where possible, without an imposed dramatic structure in terms of editing for effect, or other overt manipulations of palpable reality — a direct cinema, whose drama evolved out of the lives observed rather than the skilful use of cinematic devices. Bazin saw the deep-focus lens, which allowed for composition in depth, and the extended shot as two major developments encouraging this greater naturalism. Effectively, one ideological interpretation of a technological development was ceded to another.

There is a more prosaic determinant which does not reduce basic principles of film-making to political or ethical allegiances, and it is simply mimetic. In the first films there was no alternative to relatively brief shots, and these established an habitual way of seeing reality in film. Joining such shots extended the duration and the expressive potential of the film without challenging the timespan of each individual shot — an unavoidable characteristic became a convention, even when film magazines made much longer takes technically possible. Cutting within the shot — from medium shot to close up, for example — further reduced that timespan, while vastly increasing the expressive range. Montage theory was a response to a convention already established through usage; it failed to anticipate or adequately perceive alternative uses of film because habit obscured them, rather than because ideology proscribed them. Synchronized sound, at first only practicable with cumbersome equipment, made brief shots and fluid editing technically difficult: long, static takes were easier to record. Subsequently, although more portable equipment was developed, the longer take became part of the acceptable visual and aural habit, and could then be used dramatically where appropriate. Hitchcock subordinated montage completely in *Rope* (1948) where each shot lasted for ten minutes — a full magazine of film — and the edits were as unobtrusive as possible. The unrelenting gaze of the camera, combined with its ropelike movements, helped to create an unpleasantly claustrophobic tension connecting audience to spectacle, but because the experiment was unique and unfamiliar it drew attention to itself. Consequently *Rope* has been one of the most underrated films of the 1940s, as has *Under Capricorn* (1949) in which the ten-minute take was modified and conventional montage reintroduced.

The importance of a few directors — Griffith, Chaplin, Ford, Hitchcock, for example — was acknowledged by contemporary critics and audiences, Griffith for technical and artistic advances rather than for the melodramas they shaped, Hitchcock for light but compelling entertainment, Chaplin and Ford for serious social content as well as skilfully contrived entertainment, but generally the commercial cinema was thought to be inferior to the art cinema of Europe. A group of young French critics associated with Bazin and *Cahiers du Cinema* helped to establish a third phase by instigating a deliberate *politique des auteurs*. Until the 1950s most critical attention had been devoted to establishing aesthetic principles, a theory and grammar of the film; for the ensuing decade or so it was concentrated on director study.

Inasmuch as this policy rescued for serious consideration a number of directors previously more or less hidden within the studio system — all tarred with the same brush — it was an invigorating one which liberated criticism from prejudices about the worth of popular entertainment, but once the initial discriminations had been made — *auteurs* on one side, mere directors, or *metteurs-en-scène*, on the other — there was a curiously indiscriminate attempt to present as equally valuable every example of an *auteur's* work. Bazin soon wrote a careful corrective article — '"*Auteur*", without doubt', he concluded, 'but *of* what?' —[21] but the policy was taken over largely unchanged by the English critics associated with *Movie*, whose first excited blast appeared in June 1962.

By demonstrating persuasively that certain directors pursued the same theme or deployed the same stylistic devices in film after film, despite changes in writers, cameramen, genres and so on, the *auteurists* were manifestly celebrating the director's cinema, but simply uncovering clusters of themes with variations and then identifying them under the name of the *auteur* did little to develop those criteria with which we recognise the work of the artist as a work of art. There was a concern with meaning and value, but the value tended to be located in a meaning limited to an *a posteriori* revelation of latent ideological configurations or simplistic themes, rather than in the more complex human experience communicated through the art of the film itself. Thus 'transference of guilt' was what one found in Hitchcock, 'wilderness versus garden' in Ford, 'role reversal' in a Hawks comedy, 'professionalism' or 'the male group' in his action films.

At its most interesting — in, for example, Robin Wood's studies of Hitchcock and Hawks — detailed investigative and impressionistic criticism of the director's cinema provided an accessible and persuasive account of achievement rather than potential: film could now be regarded as a mature art form, complete with great masters and masterpieces. Taken out of its original polemical context, however, the policy of the *auteur* looked vulnerable to the persistence of the very conditions it had attempted to cut through. The study of Hollywood screen-writers revealed consistencies in individual bodies of work much as director-study had done. The study of the output of the major studios revealed consistent predilections for particular genres or styles. The study of the star system again had its own conventions and ideological framework. Indeed, the study of the classic period of

Hollywood film production became a comprehensive critique of stylistic, thematic and ideological conservatism, especially when set against alternative expressive potentialities represented by the avante-garde, by Japanese cinema, and so forth. *Auteur*-study lost favour.

Insofar as it had appealed to an interest in themes rather than the quality of perceptions, and had thus legitimated an enthusiasm for mediocre film-makers as well as good ones, it had anyway contained a self-destructive element, the element apparently most suited to semiotics and structuralism. A concern with the codes and conventions of a discourse finds genres easier to classify than genius. A Marxist/materialist approach might proceed similarly, since although it can easily demonstrate that all art conforms to the dominant ideology of the society which produces it, the residual fact that great art remains rewarding in ways that mediocre art produced within the same conditions does not, stays unaccounted for. Applying to the medium rather than the art neatly evades the issue, and then it is a simple step to concentrate on the more obviously derivative forms of popular television.

At the moment, as far as education goes, film is dead — a leading light of the BFI Education department told me so recently, and an examination of the GCSE media studies and communication syllabuses, or the rapid expansion in the publication of materials for studying sitcoms, TV serials, news broadcasts etc. will provide ample confirmation. But film is only dead for those zealous ideologues at the BFI and elsewhere, whose politics encourage such peremptory diagnoses.

Advances in video technology now mean that for the first time in its brief history film could be studied in schools almost as easily as any other discipline. It is, of course, unfortunate that at just this propitious moment the two organizations founded to promote film studies (BFI Education and SEFT) should be so heavily committed to a socio-historical approach to other media, but they may become more flexible again in time. Meanwhile, I shall offer a few practical suggestions.

Teaching Film

We must believe in human creativity as the force which generates and recognizes meaning, the discovery of the self and its complex relationships, and we must face the implications and be prepared to combat those strategies which will divert attention from the central educational goal of fostering creativity. The value of the GCSE syllabuses is that they extend 'learning by doing' across the ability range, instead of restricting practical work to the less academic children. The drawback, in media studies at any rate, is that the greater proportion of aims and objectives is related to the understanding of market forces, the structures of organizations and the manipulative capacities of the media. In dealing with mass media it is, of course, necessary to inculcate some awareness of these factors, and the overt and covert ways in which they shape what is produced — clearly all art could be studied in such terms, and the loss would be incalculable, the gain minimal. Art study need not be reductive in this way. The student who appreciates, say, Goya, Lawrence and Bresson will not necessarily be incapable of enjoying a popular soap opera, but nor will he be incapable of forming judgments relating politics and commerce to entertainment.

The cost of a film is no indication of its worth as light or serious entertainment, though in some cases one would want to make allowances for the constrictions of a small budget or the interference often implied by a big budget. What matters most, both for the study and the making of films, is the understanding of fundamental principles of film construction: screenplay, image, sound, editing. By 'teaching film', then, I do not mean teaching the secondary characteristics of the film industry, but providing sufficient materials for students to respond intelligently to a particular kind of art experience — in short, to enter the aesthetic field. The suggested exercises that follow presuppose that making and presenting will run alongside regular viewing and discussion sessions, and be supplemented by appropriate background materials. Response and evaluation will inform both the practical work and the viewings, returning with ever-increasing pertinacity in a controlled cycle of challenges, choices, decisions and meaningful understanding.

Storyboard

These exercises in visual storytelling introduce terms for camera placement (low angle, high angle) and camera/subject relationship (long shot, medium shot, close up). They are relatively ineffective for demonstrating in-camera or optical devices such as zoom, soft focus, fade, wipe, dissolve, and for indicating camera movement (pan, tilt, tracking shot, crane shot); nevertheless they do show the importance of composition and changes of viewpoint in the construction of a dramatic visual narrative, and thus enable students to ask relevant questions when watching film sequences, not to see the film as a mechanical recording of a dramatic event but to look for the dramatic purpose of each set-up, each change of set-up. Camera consciousness is a fundamental requirement for film appreciation.

There are numerous approaches to, and refinements of, these exercises. If suitable film extracts are shown on video they can be reshown immediately and paused at will to demonstrate angle, composition, effects of lighting etc. Other conventions such as the 180 degree rule or eyeline matching may also be introduced, their efficacy noted along with the possibilities for flouting them. Small rectangular masks can be used to select details from large still photographs; these details can then be cut out and arranged as storyboards. Narrative projects using still cameras — diary, market day, walking the dog — again develop skills in composition and sequencing, whichever method is used to display the photographs. Taped monologues or interviews may form part of a presentation, and then the creative possibilities of sound can be introduced: rhythmic sound patterns through repetition, montage or collage effects in sound or image.[22]

The storyboard may also carry verbal information, from instructions for camera movements and location details to sound effects and dialogue.

Screenplay

Shooting scripts are numbered in terms of each sequence and each shot within each sequence, and a full shot description is given. Dialogue is one element within this description, not necessarily the most significant. Thus the structure of the script follows the principle of film as an *edited* form functioning quite differently from a play. Film has affinities with performance arts, as it does with visual arts and the novel. George Bluestone (1957) tried to define specifically filmic qualities by painstaking comparisons between six films and the novels from which they were adapted.[23] This idea has been developed usefully by Christopher Williams (1981) as part of a degree course in which students take a short story or a reasonably self-contained section from a novel and convert it into a shooting script.[24] This exercise demands the closest possible reading of the story, with attention to narrative flow, syntax and imagery, the ways characters and incidents are presented, and authorial intention; it also raises questions of re-presentation: is the film bound to be different? What sort of detail has to be omitted, or will become ambiguous, or too concrete, or superficial? What may be given greater attention than the author has given? What visual hints may develop as legitimate analogies to non-visual information?

Scripting exercises could also lead to comparative studies of shooting scripts, cutting continuities and release scripts, all to be compared with the complete experience of the film itself. Both story boarding and scripting exercises tend to raise questions about the nature of the collaborative process of film-making, and these questions need to be extended into exercises in film-making and more detailed study of key films.

Film-making

Studio exercise

This should be scripted, whether or not it will have synchronized sound, with all students writing scripts, then groups working on those selected. As well as the most basic crew of director and cameraman there should also be an art director. Set designs, both practicable and ideal, should be drawn and discussed, as with costumes and props — as far as possible, everything that may appear on screen should be evaluated for its significance. For an exercise of this type natural light should be excluded if it is possible to construct and light the set artificially. The intention is to involve everyone in the discussion and creation of a film whose every detail is the result of a conscious decision — problems should continue to arise throughout shooting. With action confined to a single set it would be possible, especially with video, to experiment with various filming procedures and learn from the results, i.e. a 'staged' version with an immobile camera compared to an elaborate single take with the camera tracking throughout on movement or to select significant detail, or the conventional master shot intercut later with two-shots, shot-reverse-shots, etc. Alternatively the physical implications of editing could be conveyed by using part-sets, filming segments accordingly and only in the editing creating the illusion of continuities of time and space.

These exercises help to provide a standard of accepted procedures against which to appreciate departures from the commercial norm; they also provide a context for testing theories in practice and relating problems encountered in practice to the theoretical debate. Sequences shot on location might well be interpolated, but these basic exercises are worthwhile in themselves and as a substantial contribution to an arts training.

Documentary exercise

If the studio exercise is about creating a plausible reality with the art of artifice, the documentary confronts the student with protean reality as his raw material, and its value is in the way it highlights the difficulties of distinguishing between objective and subjective treatments, truth, reality and fiction, art and propaganda, information and persuasion. It can be set in the context of Grierson and the documentary movement, and the uses of the form on television, taking in both the 'fly on the wall' intrusions into public and private lives, and the dramatised documentaries of Ken Loach, as well as their influence in turn on writer/directors like Mike Leigh or Les Blair.

It could be argued that a similar acquisition of learning skills could proceed from other media studies — the practical work is often comparable. The three areas I have touched on are more rewarding only because they have an immediate and lasting connection with a major art whose importance, however, remains to some extent conjectural. Part of the reason for making a case for film studies now is precisely to take advantage of this unprecedented opportunity.

It was easy to acknowledge the importance of film in the 1960s, but virtually impossible to subject any films to close analysis. The new films of Godard, Bergman, Antonioni, Resnais and the others certainly seemed important, in that they communicated what felt like the spirit of the age with a directness that made one continually aware of the form of expression — the fragmentation of narrative, abrupt changes in sound, etc., seemed to demonstrate the film was as acute an instrument as, say, TS Eliot's language had been for accounting for the crisis in civilization. But even several viewings in ideal circumstances were not enough to establish with any precision the resonance or potential depth of the work. One gained a record of impressions, sensations and an apparent experience of thought, but its quality could only be tested by the recollected impact of the already retreating experience. Other arts rely on the immediacy of performance too, but a play is never confined to any one production. In its written form it has an existence which both precedes and succeeds performance, and which can be studied freely. The lack of this facility has probably been the most crucial factor in retarding the progress of film studies on the curriculum. Substantial critical literature is available, but not the films themselves — at least, not in a form as accessible or as amenable to individual study as the novel or play, painting in reproduction, or recorded music.

There are important differences of scale and atmosphere between watching a film on television and in the cinema: it is a distorted and inferior experience. At the same time the reduction in physical scale, combined with the accessibility of video, makes close study practicable. The disadvantages can at least be explained and taken into account and key films made available in this way for repeated viewing. This means that film need no longer be the privileged preserve of academics whose interpretations have previously had to be taken on trust, signs of sincerity or plausibility, and one's own memory.

How important an art is film? How great are its major works? How much attention will they bear? It seems to me that we can now begin to find out. No other art is so essentially unexplored as film, as far as the equivalent of the common reader is concerned. Of no other art has so much been written by so few, whose critical and theoretical positions have been, consequently, unassailable. Some of the most influential contributions to the debate have centred on the work of John Ford, but, however meticulous the arguments, nothing written so far can be given greater weight than an unsubstantiated opinion until one can participate by having access to the films oneself. I have some familiarity with about thirty-three of Ford's films, enough to feel that Lindsay Anderson is right to call him 'one of the great poets of humanity in our time',[25] and enough to feel, therefore, that there is something radically wrong with an arts/humanities curriculum which provides no adequate means of experiencing his work and determining the weight to give to that assertion.

Over twenty years ago, in 1964, Ivor Montagu acknowledged that the history of the cinema was, 'From one point of view, a tale of mortality', its decline from enormous popularity hastened by television:

> But from another point of view it is quite a different story. The cinema was, and is, a new invention, an extension of man's powers. It has given him a new means of studying, and assimilating to his knowledge, reality — new means of moving, influencing, communicating with his fellow men. Are films finished? In this sense they cannot be, and the apparent rise and fall are merely incidents of the interaction between this novel discovery and ephemeral factors of social habit together with the local availability of other inventions.[26]

The local availability of video gives everyone access to this new and living art. It seems to me at the least probable that the best work of Ford, Hitchcock, Renoir, Bresson, Bunuel, Bergman, Kurosawa and perhaps a dozen more is as challenging and rewarding as any art produced in the last half century. Not to take the initiative now that films can be made available cheaply and in sufficient quantity for widespread study — and given that creative work in photography, film and video is also relatively easy to organize — would be irresponsible of anyone who aspires to nourish rather than neglect the creative spirit.

Notes

1 RICHARDS, IA (1924) *Principles of Literary Criticism*, Routledge and Kegan Paul, p 231.
2 COLLINGWOOD, RG (1938) *The Principles of Art*, Oxford University Press, p 323.
3 MAYER, JP (1948) *British Cinemas and Their Audiences*, Dennis Dobson, pp 245–9.
4 MONTAGU, I (1975) 'Old man's mumble', *Sight and Sound*, autumn.
5 Quoted in LOW, R (1971) *The History of the British Film 1918–1929*, George Allen and Unwin, p 54.
6 Quoted in BUTLER, I (1971) *To Encourage the Art of the Film*, Robert Hale, p 17.
7 LAMBERT, RS (1937) 'The film in education', in DAVEY, C (Ed) *Footnotes to the Film*, Lovat Dickson, pp 279–305.
8 BUTLER, T (1971) *op cit.*
9 *Ibid.*
10 *Ibid.*
11 GARNHAM, N (1981) 'Film and media studies: Reconstructing the subject', in GLEDHILL, C (Ed) *Film and Media Studies in Higher Education*, BFI Education, pp 3–4.
12 GLEDHILL, C (1981) 'Introduction', in Gledhill, C (Ed) *op cit.*
13 SIMPSON, P (1981) 'Institutions and course structures', in GLEDHILL, C (Ed) *op cit*, p 66.
14 ROUD, R (1980) 'Introduction' to ROUD, R (Ed) *Cinema: A Critical Dictionary*, Martin Secker and Warburg.
15 ANDERSON, L (1981) *About John Ford*, Plexus, p 11.
16 BUNUEL, L (1984) *My Last Breath*, Jonathan Cape.
17 BAUDELAIRE, C (1965) 'The salon of 1859', in *Art in Paris 1845–1862*, Phaidon.
18 See METZ, C (1974) *Film Language, A Semiotics of the Cinema*, Oxford University Press, esp. pp 6–15.
19 ARNHEIM, R (1958) *Film As Art*, Faber and Faber (revised edition).
20 SPOTTISWOODE, B (1935) *A Grammar of the Film*, Faber and Faber; LINDGREN, E (1948) *The Art of the Film*, George Allen and Unwin; MANVELL, R (1944) *Film*, Penguin; MANVELL, R (Ed) (1977) *The Penguin Film Review 1946–1949*, Scolar. MANVELL, R (1955) *The Film and the Public*, Penguin;

STEPHENSON, R and DEBRIX, JR (1965) *The Cinema as Art*, Penguin.

21 BAZIN, A (1966) 'On the politique des auteurs', trans. in *Cahiers du Cinema in English*, January.

22 For many more practical teaching ideas, see LOWNDES, D (1968) *Film Making in Schools*, BT Batsford.

23 BLUESTONE, G (1957) *Novels into Film*, University of California.

24 WILLIAMS, C (1981) 'Film-making and film theory', in GLEDHILL, C (Ed) *op cit.*

25 ANDERSON, L (1981) *op cit.*

26 MONTAGU, I (1964) *Film World*, Penguin.

5   *The Dynamic Image: Changing Perspectives in Dance Education*

Anna Haynes

Introduction

Dance suffers from being a relative newcomer to the curriculum. Although its origins are to be found in the context of physical education at the turn of this century, the major thrust to establish its place in education did not occur until the 1940s and its position in the secondary school was not secured until the 1960s. Of all the arts in education, only film has been more neglected and misunderstood. Yet over the last two decades, there has been an extraordinary ferment of activity in the dance education world. In particular, there has been an attempt to define a theoretical framework for dance; an attempt to expand its frame of reference; an attempt to extricate it from its traditional location in physical education and to envisage it in an arts context. The general shift has been away from psychological justifications of dance as a means of emotional development, towards a conception of dance as an art form. This movement, still very much alive, has not been without bitter controversy and divisiveness. Yet in spite of all the argument, dance remains highly precarious in the curriculum of our schools and is likely to remain so unless a coherent aesthetic can be forged.

There is, however, an underlying set of difficulties which, until recently, has made any comprehensive teaching of dance problematic. These difficulties can be located both within the recent and constricted history of dance (which I will examine in this chapter) and in the essentially transitory nature of the medium itself.

Dance functions primarily on the dynamics of change. Its nature is elusive and mercurial; its non-verbal imagery resistant to fixity. At the heart of the dance lies what might be called *the principle of dissolution*. This ephemeral feature, together with the lack, until relatively recently, of adequate systems of dance notation or means of recording, has made dance historically inaccessible. There are, for instance, no equivalents in dance of a Bach, a Rembrandt or a Shakespeare, for there are no existing scores, artefacts or texts to bear witness to the works of past choreographers. As a consequence, there is no substantial body of literature on the dance, no tradition of scholarly research, no complex and varied schools of analysis and criticism — no common literate discourse. Compared to the abundant literature on all other art forms, dance is in a state of critical and historic impoverishment.

It is hardly surprising, then, that dance education has developed without a strong sense of heritage — its evolution largely influenced and structured by developments in dance which have occurred during this century alone.

The absence of a recorded history, the lack of developed critical discourse, coupled with the fact that dance was not recognised as a major art form until our own century, and in education was placed within the confines of physical education, has created a caucus of problems for dance educators. These features largely explain the low status of dance in the schools, the uneducated attitudes towards the medium and the widespread lack of interest in its place in an arts education. In turn, they illuminate the difficulties dance teachers *themselves* find in formulating a fitting and comprehensive aesthetic for their own discipline — for without a coherent tradition, they have still to forge the tools and concepts needed to make it possible.

Dance at the moment is in urgent need of such a comprehensive philosophy. Perhaps, for the first time, all the necessary elements for such a construction are available. At the end of this chapter I will return to this pressing issue. It is important first, however, to place dance education in its historic context, for its history reveals those very difficulties that have yet to be resolved. It is indeed significant that a concise history of dance in education has still to be written. What follows is an attempt to delineate the changing patterns of its development in order to understand its position and its problems today.

The Development of Dance in Education: 1900–1965

In many respects, the history of dance education during this period, 1900–1965, unfolds like a dramatic narrative. The major innovators appear as single individuals, as great characters in its early evolution.

During the first half of the twentieth century, the main sources of influence came predominantly from abroad. With the exception of Cecil Sharp, the small number of early pioneers were inspired by notable American, Scandinavian and European reformers from the fields of theatre dance, physical culture and education. Although the work of Isadora Duncan, Ling, Jacques-Dalcroze and Rudolf Laban appears to be diverse in approach, it will be seen that the central principles of their philosophical aims place a common emphasis on the 'holistic' nature of dance and rhythmic movement. It was this paradigm which emerged to form the foundation of dance in education until the late 1960s.

Until the turn of the century, the only official brief which embraced the notion of physical education of *any* kind was a short code[1] in the 1890s to the effect that 'drill' was to form part of the curriculum of elementary schooling. There is little evidence to record the exact nature of this activity but it would appear that 'music and drill' (or 'musical-drill') became the established form of physical exercise until it was gradually replaced by the moderately freer mode of 'Swedish gymnastics'. Although this method of gymnastics had no close connection with dance, the introduction of Ling's ideas, principally through the Swedish educationalist, Martina Bergman Osterberg, initiated a significant change in attitude towards movement education. It was during this turn-of-the-century period that the link between physical training and dance was forged and the precedent set for the subsequent restricting assumption that dance be subsumed under the aegis of physical education. Osterberg's training in 'Swedish gymnastics' — which included the waltz and national dancing — was to have a powerful influence on the direction of physical education for several decades to come. Her work inspired the establishment of the first women's pioneer colleges in physical training[2] and provided the foundation on which future developments in physical education evolved.

During this same early period, however, the vigorous efforts of Cecil Sharp had effected a strong interest in the revival and popularization of folk dancing. It was this form of dance which the 1909 Board of Education syllabus[3] saw fit to recognize as an appropriate physical training activity. It is difficult to ascertain how widespread the teaching of folk dance actually was. There is evidence to suggest that it enjoyed a flourish of activity during the war years (1914–18) only to decline into '. . . an indoor substitute for games on wet days'. There is also evidence to support the claim that folk, national and character dancing retained an active role in the timetable

Anna Haynes

Plate 15 Music and drill in the elementary school.
Source: Ministry of Education (1952), Moving and Growing, HMSO.

of many schools and physical training colleges for a much longer period. Nevertheless, it would seem that Sharp's insistence that folk dancing be taught seriously like all other subjects and that it held *artistic* as well as physical value contributed towards a gradual change in attitudes, preparing the way for the influence of a further number of pioneers inspired by the dance of Isadora Duncan.

Isadora Duncan (1878–1927) is generally seen to be the originator of a totally new concept of the dance — a conception which rejected the highly stylized conventions of the classical ballet and celebrated the spontaneous expression of 'natural' movement. Duncan's source of inspiration was rooted in her interpretation of the dances and artistic philosophy of ancient Greece. She sought to develop a form of dancing which was essentially expressive of what she described as her 'inmost soul' — its physical manifestation emanating in waves of energy from the centre of her being. The trajectory of her career as a solo dancer swept from America, across the European continent and into Russia. The powerful impact of her personal artistry has been well recorded. Furthermore, the philosophical theories upon which she founded a number of schools were to reverberate within the wider cultural climate of a tremendous 'fin de siecle' vogue for physical culture, sport and gymnastics.

Rather like the early progressives, Duncan believed that the educative value of dance lay in its powers to develop 'self-expression' and 'creativity'. She did not deny the need for systematic exercise but rejected the notion of technique as an end in itself. Pupils were not allowed to imitate her own style; she insisted they discover and

144

Plate 16   The Influence of Swedish Gymnastics.

develop movements which were their own. At the core of her work was an emotional drive towards self-realization. She states that she strove '. . . to express the truth of my being in gestures and movement.'[4] Her aim was to facilitate the same kind of direct expression in the children she taught. It was these principles which anticipated the tenets upon which the development of dance in the English educational system came to be later based.

Between the period 1910–1920, the three most notable English pioneers of Duncan's style of dance all established private dancing schools with an initial emphasis on theatre dance. Margaret Morris, Madge Atkinson and Ruby Ginner were professional dancers seeking to evolve contemporary techniques based on the forms of dance and movement illustrated on ancient Greek pottery, painting and sculpture. Within each individual style, there was a parallel stress on the sensitive use and interpretation of music, on natural rhythms, on 'nature' as a source of inspiration; on the expression of the emotions. In addition, there were strong similarities with regard to the physical dimension of their work: correct posture, breathing, suppleness and strength.

Within a relatively short time, the educational bias of their work had attracted interest from the state system. By 1925, Atkinson's form of 'natural movement' had been incorporated into the curricula of some schools in the Manchester area. By 1930, both 'natural movement' and Ginner's system of 'the revived Greek dance', had become included in the physical training programmes of schools and colleges over a more widespread area of the country. It is difficult to pinpoint the reasons why there was a more restrained response to

Margaret Morris' work. It was not until 1938 that her system of the 'new Greek dance technique' entered education, albeit briefly. The success of an experimental project with the British Army in Aldershot led to the foundation of a School for Basic Physical Training in Loughborough — later to become one of the leading men's physical education colleges in England.

Concurrent with this gradual growth of new dance forms entering the curriculum was the rise in popularity of Jacques-Dalcroze's system of 'eurythmics'. By 1929, over 2000 pupils had taken courses in the Dalcroze method.[5] 'The eurythmic movement' initially entered the curriculum of progressive private schools but in Manchester, again, the authority encouraged the inclusion of Dalcroze classes into the physical training programme of their schools. In the early 1930s, Ann Driver's 'music and movement' programmes (still broadcast in an adapted form today) gave a further impetus to the popularization of the work. For the next two decades, Driver's book, *Music and Movement*[6] continued in demand. Her exposition of the Dalcroze system delineated three significant issues which both re-echoed Isadora Duncan's philosophy *and* foreshadowed some of the principles which were to be emphasized by the nucleus of pioneers who introduced Rudolf Laban's work into education. Driver stressed the value of music and rhythmic movement in the education of the whole being: the psychological and therapeutic value of dance and finally, the then revolutionary concept of the place of dance in the education of boys.

An overview of the physical education syllabi (1909, 1919, 1933) and the Report of the Physical Education Committee: *Physical Education in Public and Secondary Schools* (1937)[7] indicates that the influence of 'eurythmics' and the various forms of the 'revived Greek dance' did effect changes in the growing movement consciousness of the physical training world. The 1933 syllabus, for example, recommended that *one* period of the physical training timeable be given over to dance! However, it was to be the achievement of the 'central European dance' pioneers to open the gates for the next major change in dance education.

In 1939, Leslie Burrows, Louise Soelberg, Joan Goodrich and Diana Jordan founded a dance centre in Chelsea. Their aim was to promote the techniques and philosophy of 'Ausdruckstanz' — a form of 'modern' dance which had already become popular within the fertile climate of the German expressionist movement.

Each one of these women was in a position to initiate the spread of modern dance over a wide field. As theatre dancers, Soelberg and Burrows worked within the professional field. As a physical edu-

Plates 17 and 18   The Influence of Isadora Duncan — 'Natural Movement' and 'The Revived Greek Dance'.

cationalist, Goodrich introduced 'central European dance' into the curriculum of the Bedford College of Physical Training (although it was initially met with suspicion). Within the sphere of the general teacher training colleges, which were already encouraging free expression in art, Jordan's work met with relative success. Together, they augmented the drive with the publication of papers and booklets. In 1938, Jordan produced the first English textbook on dance in education.[8]

The outbreak of the Second World War saw the closure of their London centre, the closure or evacuation of schools for the 'revived Greek dance', and the resiting of a number of the major women's physical training colleges. At this critical point in dance education there arrived in England a group of refugees from Germany. In 1938, Rudolf Laban joined Lisa Ullmann and the company of the 'Ballets Jooss' at Dartington Hall in Devon. It was from this centre — the heart of the progressive movement in English education — that a growing interest in the application of Laban's work to education was first generated.

Rudolf Laban (1879–1958) was 59 when he arrived in England. He left behind him a distinguished career in the theatre and the imprint of his innovatory concepts of the dance throughout central Europe. It is generally agreed that he was one of the most powerful influences on the evolution of the new form of 'modern' or German expressionist 'Ausdruckstanz'. In 1928, the publication of his system of dance notation, known today as 'kinetography', or 'Labanotation', marked then '. . . the first major step towards the elimination of illiteracy in the dance'.[9]

Laban's overriding interest was in the formulation of a systematic analysis of human movement and its meaning and application to dance and dramatic art. During the course of his career, however, the development of his work broadened in orientation to encompass the fields of recreation, industry, education and therapy. At the heart of his research lay a desire to generate a new 'movement consciousness'; to secure a wider recognition of the central role of movement as an activating force at both the universal and particular levels of life.

In 1938 there was little outlet for Laban's work here in the theatre. The dominant form of English theatre dance was the classical ballet. (The revolutionary new forms of 'contemporary' and 'modern' dance which were evolving in America and Central Europe were not to exert an influence here until some thirty years later.) Laban's arrival in England did, however, coincide with an era in which progressive philosophies and practices (described in the first chapter) were manifesting themselves in education, particularly, of course, at Dartington Hall. There was thus a pressure on educationalists, and therefore physical educationalists, to introduce a more free and creative approach to their work in schools. A number of important aspects of Laban's work related well to the progressive philosophy. (In retrospect, however, it is possible that the influence of the progressive movement partially recast Laban's work and in the process neglected some of its formal artistic qualities.)

Laban conceived of the dance as symbolic action; an expression of the 'life of feeling'; a manifestation of an inner drive to articulate '... intangible and often indescribable values'.[10] Although he was working to devise a system of technical training, which he termed 'Eukinetics' and 'Choreutics', he viewed the dancer as creator as well as interpreter. He placed a strong emphasis on personal expression; on spontaneous improvization and experimentation; on creative activity as a means of evolving a style of dance which was 'true' to the individual personality. One of the fundamental aims of his work was embodied in the belief that a training in the 'art of movement' facilitated harmonization of the individual and helped lead towards self-realization (towards what Jung called the process of individuation). He considered that the study of movement (seen as the raw material of dance), *coexistent* with creative practice, brought about the growth of intelligent activity in the medium and fostered integration of the whole personality. Thus, not only did Laban's work attune to the 'holistic' paradigm set down by the early pioneers of dance education, it also immediately connected with the progressive education approach. In addition, it appeared to provide what was lacking in the previous dance forms, namely, an analysis and classification of movement which was later seen to be applicable to physical education.

In 1941, in response to a growing demand, the Physical Education Association hosted a conference to investigate the educational potential of 'Central European Dance'. The success of the symposium — attributed mainly to the contribution made by Laban and Lisa Ullmann — effected a move which was to influence the course of dance education *for the next thirty years*. The Association made an official request to the Board of Education to promote 'modern' dance in schools. The event marked the beginning of an era in which dance was to gain a stronger hold in education: a period in which Laban's ideas formed the basis of what came to be known as 'modern educational dance'.

At the time that Laban was working to forge a coherent framework for dance in education, he was offered the opportunity to

Plate 19   Rudolf Laban — The German Expressionist Period.
Copyright: Ballett-Buhnen-Verlag Rolk Garske,Cologne 1985.

develop the application of his theories to the field of industry. It was his assistant, Lisa Ullmann (1909–1985) who was the major activating force and the pivotal influence for the translation and development of his ideas into education.

During the early 1940s, Ullmann lectured in schools and colleges across the country, instigated a series of intensive study course for physical educators and pioneered the introduction of 'movement' and 'modern dance' into a small number of schools in the Lancashire and Yorkshire area. At around the same time, the 1944 Education Act was passed. This lifted the level of physical education to the status of other subjects and gave teachers the freedom to devise the framework and content of their lessons. Here was a vital opening for physical

Plate 20   Kurt Jooss — dance training in Ascona, 1926.
Copyright: Ballett-Buhnen-Verlay Rolk Garske, Cologne 1985.

educators who were already fired by the new concepts of 'modern' dance. With the publication of Laban's handbook, *Modern Educational Dance* (1948),[11] with the Ministry backing for teacher training courses for serving teachers at the 'Art of Movement Studio' in Manchester, and with a drive from other parts of the country, dance in education began to spread on a wider scale.

1953 saw the reestablishment of the Manchester Studio in larger premises near Weybridge in Surrey. By the end of the decade, with sustained support from Her Majesty's Inspectorate, the influence of Laban's ideas manifested themselves in changing attitudes towards many aspects of physical education. In 1960, with the implementation of a DES approved course for the training of specialist dance teachers at secondary level, the 'Art of Movement Studio' had established itself as the major source of influence on the development of dance education since the war years.

There is no official research to reveal to what extent 'modern

educational dance' had become an established part of the physical education curriculum at this stage. The spate of books, published
throughout the sixties relating to the teaching of dance, gymnastics,
physical education and drama — at both primary and secondary level
— gives evidence of the spread and popularity of Laban's work. An
increase in the number of dance specialist teacher training courses also
points to the fact that a growing number of dance teachers were
entering the secondary schools. The Gulbenkian Report (1980) *Dance,
Education and Training in Great Britain* indicates, however, that dance
took hold in only a limited number of schools where individual heads
and local authorities offered a consistency of support. (Lancashire and
Yorkshire were an outstanding example in this respect.) It would
seem, however, that wherever dance posts were created, it was
ultimately the job of the individual teachers to carve an acceptable
place for the subject within their own schools. With no tradition
behind them, with the onerous task of formulating their own syllabi,
with little organized support, their work can be viewed as a
continuation of the line of pioneering efforts which had its root in
Swedish gymnastics at the turn of the century.

Throughout the sixties, though, with the encouragement of a
favourable government backing for the arts in general, the climate
for 'modern educational dance' seemed conducive to further
growth. By the end of the decade, however, the philosophical tenets
of Laban's foundation for dance education were to undergo rigorous
criticism and by the mid-seventies, the dance profession was in a state
of confusion and fierce debate.

The Changing Climate: 1965–1980

The radical challenges came from two different directions. There was
a gradual shift in perspective from within education itself and there
was a significant change within the wider context of theatre dance in
England.

The movement towards change was related to the introduction of
examination in dance at secondary level. It became an issue of serious
debate when the BEd degree was established and the first moves
towards postgraduate courses in physical education with a dance
component, took a tentative hold in the early 1970s.

The foundation for 'modern educational dance' was built on an
understanding of Laban's theories in direct relationship to a practical
and experiential knowledge of his system. The instigation of degree

Plate 21   Movement: Physical education in the primary years.

courses and the ensuing pressure from validating bodies on dance and physical educators to produce a coherent body of knowledge — examinable in traditional academic manner — precipitated a crisis. There was a pressing need to clarify the aims and objectives of physical education and dance. In the search for greater conceptual rigour, theoreticians from other disciplines were brought into the debate. For the first time, philosophers and sociologists were helping to define the nature of dance in education. As a result, towards the end of the sixties, Laban's seminal work was subjected to a prolonged critical reappraisal.

In a series of articles by the aesthetician, Gordon Curl,[12] it was argued that the theoretical basis of Laban's work was rooted in mystic

Plate 22   Moving and growing physical education in the primary school.

philosophy, that the practical application of his theories defied analysis and that the claims made for the justification of educational dance were 'grossly exaggerated'. In brief, Laban's approach was seen to be inadequate for the purposes of education. In the wake of the dramatic implications of this conclusion, there followed the publication of further investigations into Laban's work.[13] By the early seventies, a number of influential writers had begun to argue that dance education should shift its attention from its psychological/therapeutic orientation towards the more formal and aesthetic conception of dance as an art form. In addition, it was proposed that dance education should concern itself with the development of three major strands: *choreography, performance and appreciation* and that it should be placed within the context of the arts departments in schools and colleges. This general movement was further influenced and augmented by the appearance in England of a style of contemporary theatre dance based on the work of the distinguished American pioneer, Martha Graham.

Aside from the brief impact of the German dance company, 'Ballets Jooss', which toured Britain during the war years and the gradual move towards a 'modern' approach by the 'Ballet Rambert', the dominant form of theatre dance in England until the late 1960s had been the classical ballet. The formation of the London Contemporary Dance Trust in 1965 and the appearance a few years later of the

Plate 23   Dance and dance drama in education.

'London Contemporary Dance Theatre', was to initiate a *major* change in professional, public and educational assumptions with regard to the nature of dance.

The introduction of American 'contemporary' dance offered a new model of dance which was to exert a significant influence on the future of dance education. It is impossible in such a short history to delineate a detailed account of the numerous events which relate to the influence of 'contemporary' dance during this period of change. However, any thorough account would have to document at least the following: the setting up in 1968 of the first course in American contemporary dance at Dartington Hall: the 1974 Calouste Gulbenkian Foundation 'Action Conference in Dance Education', headed by Peter Brinson to determine the need for a national enquiry into dance education and training: the inauguration in 1976 of the first series of contemporary dance residencies which initiated the formulation of 'Dance Artists in Education' policies; and finally, a few years later, the establishment of dance courses unrelated to teacher training programmes in a number of further education institutions across the country.

It was towards the end of the decade that the relatively linear development of the history of dance education began to change course and diversify. All these activities and changes broke the Laban-centred unity of educational dance, placing more emphasis on professional dance, on theory and on the study of aesthetics. It was thus symptomatic that the Laban Centre[14] itself widened the parameters of the field of study to offer a variety of courses. Dance education became one of a number of options which included movement analysis, choreography, notation and recording, performance and production, dance history, criticism, aesthetics and philosophy. Dance was looking outward and discovering its own complexities.

None of these various movements to define a more formal aesthetics for dance went uncontested, however. Indeed, often dance teachers divided into seemingly irreconcilable groups. The division invariably took two related forms. There was a major contention over 'product' versus 'process'. Those committed to establishing a formal aesthetic stressed technique, expertise, performance —and for their model were drawn to the 'contemporary' dance theatre. Those committed to the individual development of their pupils, placed their emphasis on process, on feeling, on exploratory work, with the notion of performance in the background and often with no primary concern with aesthetic effects. The dispute is one that marks all of the arts, but in dance, the split between the two was often unnecessarily sharp. Then too, there was a major debate which revolved around a 'practical' versus 'theoretical' dichotomy. Many Laban-trained teachers saw dance as an essentially practical activity — a medium in which self-expression was of primary significance; while many others felt that, if dance was to develop, it required greater theory and scholarship. Here too, the divisions were often uncomfortable and extreme in nature. Yet in both cases, as I will try to show in the next section, the dichotomies are actually false to the field of dance. The innumerable disputes about Laban created a misleading opposition of terms. The divisions require a higher unity. A wider dialectical framework of reference is necessary, in which both process and product, both individual dance experience and good dance scholarship can be combined.

Towards a New Synthesis

These debates and dichotomies were to continue into the eighties and become ever more intricate but as the influence of Laban's ideas began to diminish — being commonly dubbed as old-fashioned — the dominant question facing dance educators was: what kind of dance should we teach? In a position of intellectual isolation and general insecurity, with a directive to embrace dance as an arts discipline, the profession had turned rather uncritically towards the current model of contemporary theatre dance. Here, at least, was an unambiguous field of skills and expertise! Furthermore, various educational policies promoted the connection by encouraging professional companies and dance artists to visit schools. At the same time, inspired by an unprecedented public interest, contemporary forms of dance began to flourish.

It is not easy to ascertain to what extent the *recommendations* of the Gulbenkian Report on 'Dance, education and training' — constituting a national plan of action to promote and popularize dance — have been instrumental in accounting for what amounts to a dance boom in England. At a general level, however, the extraordinary public interest in dance has been reflected in education by the growing number of pupils, including boys, opting for examination courses in dance. More specifically, at the level of higher education, the enquiry's urgent call for the creation of a chair in dance and for the funding of research projects to encourage a more scholarly and literate discourse for dance, either coincided with, or influenced the setting up of the first Faculty of Dance at the University of Surrey. In addition, the Report's recommendations to support ethnic dance, and to insist on the place of dance artists in education, can be related to the growth of a small number of black dance companies and the Arts' Council's recent brief to all dance companies applying for grant aid to submit an educational commitment.

At one level, then, the current situation appears to manifest a number of positive features. There has been a rise of standards in practical skill and expertise, an increased awareness and understanding of aspects of choreography. The recent introduction of an 'A' level in dance and the gradual growth of research has seen the emergence of a more literate and critical approach to dance as an art form. On the other hand, the ongoing preoccupation with contemporary forms of theatre dance has brought about a questionable situation whereby dance education has, to a great extent, become tied into a model of dance *whose tradition is confined to a period of no more than forty years.*

The only serious attempt to provide a critique of present practice in dance education, to address the pressing question of what kinds of dance should be taught and to tackle the difficult problem of formulating a coherent philosophical framework for the subject has been Janet Adshead's work, *The Study of Dance*[15] (first published in 1981).

This publication set down the potential for 'a coherent account of the totality of dance study' and the ways in which it could be trans-

Plates 24 and 25   The influence of contemporary dance in dance education.

lated into the curriculum. It amounted to a call for a redefinition and reconstruction of dance education — challenging the validity of the 'dance as art' orientation — on the grounds that its tendency to focus only on styles of contemporary theatre dance was highly restrictive. This orientation, she claimed, ignored the eclectic nature of dance and the variety of dance forms which exist outside the 'art' umbrella. Adshead suggested: 'It could be argued that not only is the art orientation a minute part of the relevance of dance to society, but also that it is of far less human significance than, for example, a socio/ historical study.'[16] Significantly, Adshead queries the predominant practical emphasis in dance education and argues the case for dance studies of a purely theoretical nature.

Wanting to widen the parameters of the field of study to encompass any kind of dance — wherever it has, or is occurring across

the map of the world — Adshead delineated three major areas which she claimed to be the central organizing structural principles underlying the study of dance: *Choreography, Dance Performance and Appreciation*. She further insisted that in order to give meaning to any such study, the work must be related to its time, location and context. She suggested that this model placed dance in a perspective which would be free of ethnocentricity and would thus serve to prevent either violent swings over what is taught in schools and colleges, or an emphasis on one form of dance to the exclusion of all others. In the light of our symposium, her work constitutes, in part, a critique of modernism. In their defence many school teachers would claim that they already follow or approximate to this model and it would appear that the concepts of choreography, performance and appreciation are beginning to emerge in the new proposals for the GCSE and 'A' level syllabuses. It could also be pointed out that some colleges of higher education do incorporate a wide variety of dance forms into curricula and extra-curricula activities. However, the implications with regard to the implementation of such a comprehensive and extensive programme of dance study as proposed by Adshead, do raise daunting questions in relation to the availability of teachers with the kind of qualifications to initiate such a radical set of proposals.

Adshead acknowledges that much of the research has still to be done — for what I named earlier as the *principle of dissolution* has worked against the establishment of dance traditions. Yet I believe Adshead is right to extend dance beyond the moment of modernisn, to expand its repertoire and reference and, in so doing, to indicate a way forward for dance.

What are the principles behind such a development?

Firstly, there is the principle of breadth and reconnection. This would entail an expansion of dance education to include *any* kind or style of dance and an understanding of its form and purpose. Such an expansion frees dance from the confines of the contemporary. Here it has the potential to discover a new set of relationships and expressive possibilities within an historic continuum. Dance reconnects with its past and becomes potentially richer for the encounter.

Secondly, such a conception of dance education suggests a closer alignment with the other major arts disciplines. The translation of this reconstruction into the curriculum invites, for example, parallels with the practice of literature or music. This kind of alignment demands that dance becomes reflexive; that it builds up a critical and interpretive literature; that it becomes, in this sense, intellectually and culturally engaged. And in doing this, it breaks the still dominant assumption that dance is merely a matter of technical skill and physical expertise.

Thirdly, Adshead's conception of the central organizing principles of dance: making, performing and appreciating, provide a comprehensive and coherent framework for the development of dance education. It can be no accident that Adshead's conception is very close to that of Keith Swannick's for music (outlined earlier by Marian Metcalfe in her chapter to this book) or to that of the aesthetic field put forward in the first chapter. If Janet Adshead's third category of 'appreciation' is sub-divided into 'responding' and 'evaluating', we can see that her terms are identical to those of the aesthetic field. Here, it would seem, are the central unifying categories for the reconstruction of dance within the community of the arts, the elements of a new synthesis — already available, if not yet brought fully together or widely acknowledged.

Such a philosophical reconstruction of dance throws an interesting light on its history. It provides a means of critically interpreting the evolution I have outlined in this chapter. For example, the work of the early dance pioneers and the movement powerfully promoted by Laban's 'modern educational dance' with its emphasis on 'process' and 'self-expression', worked almost exclusively within two parts of the aesthetic field — namely that of making and responding. Here the work in dance education was strongly influenced by the progressive movement, and in spite of the difficulties which adhered to its fusion with physical education, tended to follow a very similar pattern to that of drama, as described by Chris Havell in his chapter. Dance, like drama under Peter Slade, was geared towards emotional and social development. The recent shifts in perspective, in part a reaction against the progressive trend in the arts, can be seen as a movement towards 'performing' as a key feature. Thus, the great interest in theatre dance, in skill and technique — often dislocated from personal or expressive needs. While, more recently still, the developments at the two most influential centres of higher education — the University of Surrey[17] and the Laban Centre — in beginning to establish reputations for research and scholarship, indicate a powerful turn towards the hitherto neglected 'evaluative' element of the aesthetic field.

It can be seen, then, how the four elements of the aesthetic field have become available in the recent evolution of dance education. It is a question now of bringing them together into a balanced configuration, a broader synthesis for dance education. Perhaps this means that dance education must now draw equally on the distinctive contribution of Laban *and* the important proposals of Janet Adshead. It is vital that good expressive practice and scholarship function in a cohesive relationship. One without the other is bound to lead eventually to some kind of distortion.

It is impossible to conclude this chapter on too optimishic a note. Given the present lack of support for the arts in education and, more specifically, given the welter of problems facing dance educators, it seems unlikely that the kind of synthesis proposed here will be easily attainable. Yet, dance *does* hold a position in education, however minimal, and there is now a groundswell of public interest and support. The struggle to formulate a coherent aesthetic for dance must be sustained.

Notes

1 BOARD OF EDUCATION (1931) *The Year Book of Education*, Evans Brothers.
2 In 1885 the Bergman Osterberg College transferred to Dartford, Kent, where fifty years later it became the Dartford College of Education. This was followed in 1896 by the establishment of Anstey Physical Training College. Bedford College was founded at the turn of the century.
3 BOARD OF EDUCATION SYLLABUS (1909) *The Syllabus of Physical Exercises for Public Elementary Schools*, HMSO.
4 Quoted in SORELL, W (1981) *Dance in Its Time: The Emergence of an Art Form*, Anchor Press/Doubleday, p 328.

Anna Haynes

5 FOSTER, J (1977) *The Influences of Rudolf Laban*, Part Three, Laban and English Education, Lepus Books.
6 DRIVER, A (1936) *Music and Movement*, Henderson Spalding.
7 BOARD OF EDUCATION (1919/1933/1937) *Syllabuses of Physical Training*, HMSO.
8 JORDAN, D (1938) *The Dance as Education*, Oxford University Press.
9 SORELL, W (1981) *op cit*, p. 385.
10 LABAN, R (1960) *The Mastery of Movement*, ed. ULLMANN, L, 2nd ed, Macdonald & Evans Ltd, p 4.
11 LABAN, R (1948) *Modern Educational Dance,* Macdonald & Evans Ltd.
12 CURL, G (1966, 1967a, 1967b, 1968a, 1968b, 1969), *Philosophical Foundations*, Laban Art of Movement Guild Magazine, nos. 37–41 and 43.
13 REDFERN, B (1972) *Dance as Art, Dance as Education*, in ATCDE Dance Section, Conference Papers in Dance; REDFERN, B (1973) *Concepts in Modern Educational Dance*, Henry Kimpton; LAYSON, J (1970) *The Contribution of Modern Dance to Education*, unpublished M.Ed. thesis, University of Manchester
14 In the early 1970s, The Laban Centre moved from Surrey to the campus of University of London, Goldsmiths College.
15 ADSHEAD, J (1981) *The Study of Dance*, Dance Books Ltd.
16 *Ibid*, p 112.
17 The University of Surrey now has an extensive library of dance books, journals, microfilms and videos. It also houses the National Resource Centre for Dance.

References

Reference has been made throughout this chapter to:
CALOUSTE GULBENKIAN FOUNDATION (1980) *Dance Education and Training in Britain*, appendix B, outline history of dance education in the maintained sector.
COLE, A (1977) *The Development of Dance in England and The United States of America During the Twentieth Century*, unpublished MA dissertation, University of London.

6   *Rifts and Reunions — A Reconstruction of the Development of Drama in Education*

Christopher Havell

Introduction

It is not surprising, in the present political and economic climate, that drama teachers feel the need to reappraise the influences that have shaped drama in education. It is time for taking stock of what has been achieved and what might have been achieved. The future shape of drama will depend heavily on how well we cut out irrelevancies and heal rifts because very soon the full impact of the new instrumental government-imposed initiatives will be felt and drama teachers will be under more pressure than ever before to defend what they value. This essay is written to clarify the present state of drama. I will offer a brief historical account of its development and then move forward to offer an essentially symbolic and aesthetic conception of drama, of drama as an arts discipline working, with other arts disciplines, the aesthetic field.

The developments in drama in education in this century have been dominated by an overwhelming reaction against the traditions of play reading and play acting by children, and the struggle for recognition of the educational potential of drama that goes beyond the skills of interpreting a script and performing to an audience, and, beyond its use as a social function for the community. Of course, this reaction has been associated with the wider movement towards the 'new' or 'progressive' principles of education and the alternative views of drama have always upheld child-centredness, have rooted the methodology in activity based learning, have placed greater value on process than product, and on experience rather than performance. By placing process, not product, at the centre of drama in education drama teachers have found themselves, inevitably, promoting a form of learning that rejects the view of the learner as 'a vessel' into which knowledge is poured and the teacher as the 'one who knows'. However, for me, this alternative view should not involve rejection of performances by pupils. I value last week's College production for all sorts of reasons but I consider that it represents only one element in a complex aesthetic field. Furthermore, the division between drama and theatre which the progressive view inaugurated has created false arguments and false divisions in the drama community. In this chapter I will be analyzing the different alternative views of drama in education that have emerged during the last few decades. A condensed history of these developments is bound to produce some distortions but, even so, I think the risk is worth taking in order to place the present concerns of drama teachers in some context. In the following historical reconstruction of drama in education I have drawn heavily on Gavin Bolton's lucid book *Drama as Education* (1984), a book to which I am deeply indebted and to which readers should refer for further detail and illustration.

Drama in the Early Decades of this Century

It is difficult to precisely date when, early this century, the progressive movement began to influence teachers' thinking about the value of drama. Drama should seem to be the ideal vehicle for 'learning by doing' and to Caldwell Cook's 'play way' approach to child development. Significantly, in Edmund Holmes's Utopian vision of education described in *What Is and What Might Be* drama has an important role. In 1911 he wrote: 'In Utopia, acting is a vital part of the school life of every class, and every subject that admits dramatic treatment is systematically dramatized'.[1] Research into the early developments of drama in education has not yet produced a clear indication of the extent to which acting *was* a 'vital part of school life'. There are, though, isolated examples of an alternative view of drama being practised, such as in the work of Harriet Finlay-Johnson, as described in her book *The Dramatic method of Teaching*[22]. She was a Sussex village school headmistress who used drama as an approach to learning in many areas of the curriculum. An insight into her dramatic method comes from an account in 1908 of one of her classes journeying to the North Pole across their playground. Bolton has analyzed the beliefs and assumptions underlying her work.[3] These include: that both scripted and unscripted work has value, that the child possesses a natural dramatic instinct, that the process of dramatizing is more important than the product, that an audience is irrelevant, that children can take responsbility for structuring their own drama and, that, the happiness of children is a priority. This list suggests that her ideas belong very much with Rousseau and the progressive movement. Indeed they would still fit in with much of the thinking underlying drama practice today. It would, however, be misleading to see the work of such pioneers as having had a widespread influence, or, that they represented a movement that was speedily gathering momentum.

The 1919 Board of Education's Report on *The Teaching of English* gave its official backing to drama but the notion of drama that it presented doesn't represent the kind of work Mrs. Finlay-Johnson was doing. The authors of the Report concentrated solely on traditional drama and wrote:

> The pupils who take part in the performance of plays learn to speak well and to express emotion becomingly; to be expressive yet restrained; to subordinate the individual to the whole; to play the game; to be resourceful and self-possessed and mitigate personal disabilities.[4]

Later reports notably *Hadow* (1926–1931) and *Primary School* (1931) show the growing official support for the progressive movement and for drama as an appropriate way of implementing the new ideals. By the 1930s the Association of Teachers of Speech and Drama had been established and soon attracted a large membership. This provided a focus for the growing interest in drama as a means of self expression and learning by doing. However, a glance at the typical agenda of one of the conferences run by the Association reveals the membership's central concern to be not self-realization so much as an improvement in spoken English. The assumption was that a basic training in action, gesture and articulation was a prerequisite to the enjoyment of and skill in a wide range of speech activities from choral speaking to improvized dialogue in small groups. We can understand the experience being offered to children by looking briefly at what these teachers were examined in for their qualifying examinations. To become a Licentiate of either the Royal Academy of Music or of the Guildhall School a teacher was required to demonstrate a knowledge of the main developments in the history of the theatre and in the history of dramatic literature; a knowledge of the functions of the vocal organs and their relationship to the production of speech and the ability to diagnose various speech problems; and finally, to demonstrate the value of speech training in education. The study of dramatic literature was included, presumably, to ensure that the teacher had a suitable

range of material for the spoken English lessons. The history of
theatre was included in acknowledgement that dramatic literature
must always be studied in conjunction with the contemporary styles
of theatre, and this academic study still influences many CSE courses.
As a young primary school teacher I took the LRAM exam as, at the
time, it was the only nationally recognized qualification in the
teaching of drama. But the importance of these qualifications
diminished during the 60s as more teachers left colleges with BEd
degrees in drama and the Drama Board began its own more relevant
brand of in-service qualification.

Peter Slade — The 1940s and 50s

During the 1940s and 50s new developments in drama in education
were dominated by the thinking and teaching of one man — Peter
Slade. He was the first individual in this field to become a national
and international figure of attention and the representative of a new
movement. His influence spread with the publication of his book
Child Drama (1954) which was based on his work with children in
and out of school and in his drama centre that he set up when he
became Drama Advisor to the City of Birmingham. Like Marion
Richardson's *Art and the Child* (1948), a revolutionary work in the
visual arts, so Slade's book reveals a deeply held child-centred
philosophy of education and a deep respect for children's needs. There
is, interestingly, no reference in the book to the opposition he faced as
his ideas gained popularity.

   The essence of Slade's argument was that the children's natural
ability to express themselves through play had been stifled by their
early exposure to the demands of performance and the technical training of the 'speech and drama brigade'. Slade roared that drama was
rooted in play and that it was a natural medium for creative adven-
ture, not a watered down adult art form. As there was child art, so
there was child drama, an art form in its own right. Slade focussed
attention on children as they engaged in spontaneous dramatic play
and saw this as a natural way of discovery. He saw the adolescent
emerging from regular experience of drama possessed with 'cleanli-
ness, tidiness, gracefulness, politeness, cheerfulness, confidence,
ability to mix, thoughtfulness for others, discrimination, moral
discernment, honesty and loyalty, ability to lead companions,
reliability, and a readiness to remain steadfast under difficulties',[5]
Slade represents the paradigm of child-centredness. As in Rousseau's

Emile the child is seen as the seed that will grow upright and strong with the right care and attention. In this well-known metaphor of progressive education the teacher becomes the gardener tending the plants.

The teacher's responsibility was to create the right environment for child drama to flourish and, it should be added, to then keep out of the way. In a sense, Slade was applying Montessori's pedagogy to the field of drama. Yet it is easy to misinterpret Slade on the role of the teacher. He never actually denied the importance of the teacher in structuring the lesson and developing the quality of the work, but he insisted that the teacher's intervention should be carefully timed so as not to interfere with the children's creativity. Slade was a purist and most probably many of his followers applied selected aspects of his methodology so that children experienced a mixture of free dramatic play with doses of basic training in actions, gestures and speech.

There were purists in the speech and drama movement who were fiercely opposed to informal drama on the grounds that children weren't stretched enough and that Slade was anti-theatre. The division between the two movements deepened and Slade's followers, though not Slade himself, cut all their connections from anything to do with theatre. Bolton has pointed out that both movements were reacting against the traditional drama and that both sides were championing the development of the individual through the new drama, but in what they meant by the new drama they differed fundamentally. Slade's views may have been misinterpreted but there is no doubting the extent of his influence. The nature of his contribution to the development of drama in education has recently been reappraised and we need to examine his legacy as it now appears.

Slade's Legacy

An examination of Slade's claim that child drama is an art form reveals that he looked for symbolism within children's play and found it in the natural rhythms and movement of children using space. He saw, for example, the powerful image of the circle that children generally created, unconsciously, in periods of free flowing movements. The circle that each individual created became a symbol of self. By placing the child at the centre of the process, and not the thing the child made, Slade distracted attention *from the potential of the content of dramatic play to take on a symbolic significance for the participants.* Slade was absorbed by the *psychological nature*, and not the *aesthetic content* of a child's expression — one of the key fallacies, one might say, of any arts teaching which makes self-expression absolute. Yet Slade did look for form in child drama and instructed teachers on the importance of dramatic space by using contrasts of levels and groupings. Conflict was injected into the drama to create excitement, for example, a drama about a market place was made more interesting when a thief stole from a stall and was chased by the crowd. It seems that Slade thought that drama needed open, but controlled, confrontation to release the participants into high drama. Slade may have been aware of these aesthetic elements of the form, but his followers weren't. They mistakenly rejected all those theatre elements that we now see as being so crucial to the structuring of any dramatic activity.

One of the dilemmas Slade faced, but never resolved, was the relationship between process and product. He recognized quite distinct phases of the drama process. There was the stimulus of the story phase, then the enactment of the story, followed by refinements and reenactments. Gavin Bolton has pointed out that in the first place when children are either listening to, or telling the story they are likely to be experiencing the personal meaning of the story. He suggests that in the second phase, which involved a spontaneous acting out of the whole story, the child was required to demonstrate to himself and others *his initial personal response*, so that the orientation of the work shifted away from experiencing *the structural meaning* of the story. When the acting was finished the teacher, who had been observing discreetly from the sidelines, initiated a discussion about the dramatic playing that was at the level of 'how did it go?'; reference would be made, for example, to the effectiveness of the spacing or the appropriateness of the dialogue. The question to be raised is; effectiveness *to whom?* The teacher's view of the process is not much different from an audience's and it was the storyline and individual actions that were discussed rather than *the meaning of the work*. We have to conclude that the teacher's intervention is based upon two underlying notions: (a) that the drama process develops towards an end product; (b) that the plot in drama is tied to a narrative sequencing of events. The tension between creating an environment for the free expression of the individual and developing a collective dramatic experience was never resolved by Slade or his followers. The dependence on a sense of final product discouraged the teacher from entering the process to develop the significance of the events beyond the initial response to the story as it was created. Of course, the individual may have sensed the deeper meaning of the story as it was acted out; but there was no active intervention by the teacher to ensure this was happening. The emphasis upon the individual pupil and his personal response inhibited the function of the teacher to create opportunities for new levels of personal and universal meanings which could only be reached through the development of the drama itself. Slade's preoccupation with the child, with *child*-drama, tended to oust both traditional and aesthetic elements.

Slade's legacy is likely to undergo many re-examinations but he will remain a formidable example of the first in a long line of drama teachers who were willing and able to provide a model of practice for others and to articulate how that practice could be based upon play. Slade was the first to demand that dramatic play be viewed from the child's perspective and to show teachers ways of signalling to children the legitimacy of that perspective. When I first read *Child Drama* I remember being struck that I would have to be working within the children's logic and that was an exciting and frightening prospect.

The 1960s — 'A Young and Growing Subject'[6]

The climate in the 1960s was more sympathetic to innovation than in the period when Slade had first launched his ideas. Drama in the 1960s was seen to be relevant to the kind of progressive education that was eventually celebrated in the 1967 *Plowden Report*. In the same year as that Report a comprehensive survey of the nature and extent of drama in the school curriculum was completed by John Allen and his HMI colleagues. The facts that, for example, eighty-one drama advisers were employed and that many schools included drama on the time-table, led Allen to conclude that drama was a young and growing subject. But it appeared that by 1967 drama had grown too quickly and the main complaint in his Report is that too many different activities were claimed by teachers to be drama. 'It has been surprising to find how much time is being devoted in schools and colleges to a subject whose real identity there is no general agreement',[7] ... and, later, ... 'does there exist in the middle of this range of artistic expression a discipline that can be defined or identified as drama?'[8] In the Report there are many descriptions of the work that had been observed during the survey. From them a popular lesson structure emerges. Children were given a stimulus to excite their imaginations and then given opportunities to express their responses through improvization (as dramatic playing was termed) through mime or movement. Such a practice placed, at the outset, tight boundaries around the child's expression yet the function of the teacher, during the process of recreation, was limited to controlling the improvizations from *the outside*. The teacher, for example, would bang tambours to create a sense of climax or play some carefully chosen music. While the teacher initiated the work, he or she yet remained outside the actual dynamic of making. The teacher was exiled from the drama process. The HMI's witnessed a great deal of preparatory work for drama which usually led, much to the team's confusion into dance-drama, film, choral speaking, in fact everywhere, except *into the continuing drama*. The team couldn't find a coherent rationale behind this muddle of activities. Nor could they find a consistency in the quality of practice that matched the high claims that were made for the work. If they had seen a copy of the manuscript of Brian Way's book *Development Through Drama* (1967), then they would have found a highly developed and systematic methodology.

Though Brian Way's career had begun in children's theatre, this book, which was to be extremely influential, represented the work he had been exploring since his early association with Peter Slade. His company of actors toured schools presenting a combination of theatre and audience participation. Way saw that his actors and the children needed to develop their expressive resources and so he devised an elaborate series of exercises designed to help the individual to become more self-aware. The essential purpose of these exercises was to promote an awareness of self; the drama in the classroom existed to develop the whole personality — hence the title *Development through Drama*. In other words, *the individual* rather than *the drama* is found at the centre of the teacher's concern. Once again the concern is with self-expression rather than any sustained initiation into aesthetic or symbolic activity within a cultural continuum. Drama amounted to a psychological preparation for 'the real world'. Thus at this time drama spaces were designed to help the teacher create an atmosphere in which children, in the privacy of a darkened room and to the sound of soft music, could begin the process of self-discovery. Way's systematic series of exercises were popular because they gave a strong sense of direction — that feeling of progression that accompanies any skills-training. The method was straightforward but I remember having difficulty in determining when the process was complete. The fact that very few well balanced children resulted from my drama lessons was puzzling! So, like many others, I extended my drama work by introducing the theatre arts.

In retrospect one can see clearly that, under the influence of Brian Way who was, in turn, under the influence of the progressive paradigm in education, teachers were placing a great emphasis on *doing*, but that the doing was more like a continuous preparation for drama than drama in its own right. Brian Way insisted that no work with the whole class acting as a single group should be attempted until the exercises in cooperation and concentration had been completed. The paradoxes and limitations of Way's methods can best be seen by placing them against the work and thinking of another great drama teacher: Dorothy Heathcote.

Dorothy Heathcote — Developments in the 1970s

In the same year as I first read *Development Through Drama* and received my LRAM I saw a programme in the Sunday night *Omnibus* series on the work of Dorothy Heathcote, who was a lecturer in drama at the University of Newcastle. The programme had a profound affect on drama teachers. Here was a drama teacher who didn't do endless warm-ups with her class of boys in a remand home, but instead moved them quickly into the drama they had chosen on the theme of British soldiers escaping from a German POW camp in the Second World War. Mrs. Heathcote began by pointing out to them that if they wanted to be prisoners then they would first have to be captured and she proceeded to disarm them. She did this by actively *taking a role within the drama as a German officer*.

There are many ways in which Heathcote's drama lesson came to exemplify the major preoccupations of drama teachers throughout the 1970s. Two crucial changes in method and understanding are demonstrated in the very first moments of the POW drama.

The first point of interest is that under Heathcote all that was required of the participants was their agreement to enter a make-believe world. Like Way, Heathcote saw a willing suspension of disbelief as a natural human ability but unlike Way, instead of indirectly cultivating it, she used it immediately and consciously as the fundamental premise of drama-making. Throughout the 1970s, teachers were to refine their understanding of what enabled children to enter the fiction of drama. They discovered that when children took on a role they did not need to be labelled a character, did not need to invent an age or a name. All that was required for drama to start was the *adoption of an attitude*. This attitude could be close to or distant from the actual participant. Heathcote claimed: 'There is never any acting involved. It is more a matter of taking up an attitude, a way of looking at a situation and being involved with it.'[9]

The second point about the lesson is that the initial task drew upon the existing experience of the participants. This meant that they could all bring their own emotional integrity to the work. In the POW drama Heathcote, at first, questioned the boys about soldiering. She soon discovered that the 'kicks' were that soldiers carried guns. Heathcote, then, took them a step further into the drama by telling them to pick up their (imaginary) guns and to get used to the feel of them. She was *not* asking them to demonstrate *a convincing mime* of a soldier holding a gun. Her concern was to help the boys establish the significance of a weapon that 'is all that stands between you and the enemy'. The simple method allowed the boys to draw upon their own experience. They had all had some experience of handling tools. They all knew the feeling of power that comes from holding a weapon. So, without any previous experience of drama, without any trust exercises, without any preliminary mime work, the boys stepped into the drama with immediate interest and commitment. Here was a revolution in drama teaching!

The boys' commitment also related to what Dorothy Heathcote was later to term 'the big lie', namely the belief in fiction that is necessary for drama. An agreement to pretend, an agreement to live through the dramatic playing is part of a contract that has to be made between teachers and pupils. For Heathcote the implications of entering a drama is that the consequences of actions and decisions will have to be faced and that, as a result of facing them, values and attitudes will be challenged and new understanding reached. Yet these decisions are also structured by the form of the drama. And in drawing attention to *the drama* Heathcote also shifted the interest from self-expression to meaning and universality. In Heathcote the previous preoccupation with self realization changes to a preoccupation with *the meaning of the drama*. Indeed, this interest in 'what the drama is about' dominated drama teaching throughout 1970s.

When the whole class was working as a single group — after Heathcote's example it became a common practice — the task of the teacher was to sense the collective meaning that was emerging from the drama. Carefully structured through the intervention of the teacher the drama experience could thus contain both personal and universal levels of meaning. Heathcote concentrated on the collective meaning because her concern was to place the individual in relationship to the world so that, by understanding the commonality of experience, pupils could begin to understand how they related to the world *they* lived in. In a recent issue of 2D (autumn 1983) David Davis gives a clear analysis of the meanings Heathcote could have been touching upon in the POW lesson as she searched for the 'universal at the centre of the particular'. He writes that 'she is concerned through the particularization of the role to find the universal that belongs to all those who have been in this position, i.e. defeated but defiant'.[10]

Implicit in Heathcote's view of drama is that, at its most significant, the experience in drama can produce a growth or change in understanding. As O'Neill and Lambert state:

Where the drama teachers' primary aim is achieved the participants will grow in insight and understanding, they will make discoveries about attitudes and implications, and they will grasp truths to do with human behaviour and its consequences.[11]

If understandings of this kind are to emerge from the drama, it is essential for the teacher to develop their pupils' reflective power. Heathcote claimed:

The having of experience itself is not good, if you have not also brought about, through your understanding of it, some kind of digestive process so that you can perceive what it is about ... we have to bring about reflective processes.[12]

To engender reflection Heathcote used the strategy of the teacher taking, at times, an active part in the drama. This came to be known as 'going into role'. As a 'teacher in role' her aim was to switch on the watcher in the participant. This represents a fundamental change in teacher intervention, even Mrs. Finlay-Johnson stayed at the side of the playground. By taking a role the teacher is in a position to support, challenge and clarify the pupils' responses as the drama progresses. Heathcote was to show how this strategy could be used to help pupils reflect upon the action of the drama. On board ship, for example, as one of the crew she might draw at one moment attention to the bird flying above the mast and wonder how it viewed the ship and the men waiting for their rations, and, at the next moment, she might use the same role to focus attention on some particular aspect of the sailor's lives. By entering the evolving drama in role the teacher is able to work the actual medium from inside. In role the teacher is able to bring out a *certain attitude*, to draw awareness to the *context* or to pose a number of *dilemmas inherent in the dramatic narrative*. Going into role can also raise the involvement of the pupils for it can bring out the dependence of 'the teacher' on 'the pupils'. Heathcote has coined the phrase 'the mantle of the expert' to denote that moment when the teacher deliberately reverses the usual teacher/pupil relationship and bestows expertise on the children.

The powerful innovation of the teacher entering 'in role' has brought with it a new interest in the dramatic medium. Once the drama has begun the teacher must constantly bring structure to the emerging ideas. This means that the teacher must be highly aware of the fundamental elements of the medium. In a direct way, in action, the teacher has to draw on all those structural elements that all dramatists in the great tradition of drama-making have used.

In 1978 a conference was held at the Riverside Studios to explore the relationship between theatre and drama as there was growing interest in what the two media shared rather than on how they differed. In characteristic style, Bolton clarified the issue for many of us in his opening speech.

> As the playwright focusses the meaning for the audience, so the teacher helps to focus meaning for the children; as the playwright builds tension for the audience, the teacher builds tension for the children; as the playwright and director and actors highlight meaning for the audience by the use of contrast in sound, light and movement, so does the teacher for the children; as the playwright chooses with great care the symbolic actions and objects that will operate at many levels of meaning for the audience, so will the teacher help children find symbols in their work.[13]

It is these common elements of theatre and drama that form an important set of underlying organizing principles of the teacher's structuring of dramatic work in the classroom.

It is useful here to return to Davis's analysis of the POW lesson in which he identifies the structural elements in operation. The plot involved the prisoners in stealing a key from one of the guards as part of their escape plan. Their plans were, however, foiled because the Germans had planted a stool pigeon who revealed where the keys were hidden. Although the boys knew of the stool pigeon they didn't know when or how he would betray them. The teacher had ensured that the keys had been invested with symbolic significance to do with freedom so that the handing over of the keys became a moment of heightened tension and an outstanding example of a simple action resonating universal meanings 'to do with betrayal of trust, the way illusions are shattered, the denial of freedom. It stands as a moment for all those people in history who have been betrayed, seen their vision at least temporarily shattered'.[14] It must also have carried personal significance for the boys — for they were in a remand home. Davis continues his analysis by identifying how tension was created. There was, he sugggests, *a sense of time* (will we succeed or not?); *a focus* (will the stool pigeon reveal the keys or not?) and *surprise* (the moment of betrayal had not been anticipated). Furthermore *contrast* was created through the Commandant's (one of the boys) change in approach to the stool pigeon — he became quiet and controlled, whereas he had previously shouted and bullied the prisoners. In all of these elements we see the play and development of artistic, symbolic and aesthetic energies; a development not only of the child but of the drama medium itself.

During the same years there had been a remarkable growth of drama as a general means of learning, also inspired by Heathcote. Drama was envisaged as a learning medium — it could contribute to factual understanding, to the development of skills, to many kinds of social learning. Drama it was argued enables:

> Individuals to see their ideas and suggestions accepted and used by the group. They can learn how to influence others, how to marshall effective arguments and present them appropriately. They can try out roles and receive feedback. The group can become a powerful source of creative ideas and effective criticism. [15]

Because it can create such a dynamic sense of engagement and of involved learning, drama is now used extensively across the curriculum. It is used for 'problem-solving' as much as 'linguistic enrichment'. This expansion of drama in our times has been an exciting development. However, as I will try to show in the next section, it could lead to the impoverishment of drama as an arts medium. It could be that we need to cultivate two related conceptions of drama, one as a general learning medium, the other as an arts discipline. Because of the utilitarian pressures on education there is a danger that the former could eclipse the latter. There is a need now to develop drama in the aesthetic dimension, not at the expense of but alongside the more general and well established notion of drama as a learning medium.

I have presented in some detail the developments in drama during the 1970s and early 1980s because it was a time when drama teachers rigorously examined a number of related issues: of how children learn through drama; how drama can operate as an integrating force across the curriculum; of how in drama the teacher can give responsibility for the direction of the learning to the learner; and, how the experiential nature of the activity enables the teacher to respond immediately to the needs of the group and individuals. Moreover, in the strategy of teacher in role, drama teachers developed a precise teaching tool that can be employed right across the curriculum. In brief, drama teaching during the 1970s was in a fertile and excited state, though somewhat confined to the dominant theories of two closely related practitioners, Dorothy Heathcote and Gavin Bolton. In neither of them do we find a consistent emphasis on the aesthetic medium of drama in an arts context, but we do find a great shift from self-expression to structural meaning, from individual to communal significance, from symptomatic action to symbolic form. We also find an emergent interest in theatre, in all those links between drama and theatre which had been largely severed under the influence of the progressives. This shift takes us directly into the ground of the aesthetic.

In Search of the Aesthetic

Our historical analysis shows that a theoretical framework for drama had been built upon the model of play linking the make-believe activities of children with the activities they engage with in the drama process. As a model it has provided a rationale for regarding experience in drama as having important educational potential. Recently, this potential has been presented as the acquisition and practise of skills, as an influence on levels of social awareness, as the creation of new demands on children's language development, as as a way of challenging and developing thinking. By comparison, *less attention has been given to the examination of participation in drama as an aesthetic experience.* Malcolm Ross recently accused drama teachers of avoiding this issue and argued:

> In my view, the aesthetic is the only necessary term as it is an entirely sufficient objective for any form of arts education, drama included, and if drama has traditionally been unable or unwilling to admit this overriding obligation, then that might be one reason behind the persistent problems of drama education.[16]

In fact, drama teachers have begun to acknowledge this obligation and some attempts have been made to identify the nature of the aesthetic experience in the drama process. I consider that this search for aesthetic factors in the drama experience constitutes an important new development in the theoretical thinking about drama as education. This search has been led by Gavin Bolton, who has argued that for too long we have offered children the chance to develop skills for drama, shown them how certain elements of dramatic form operate, but have denied them access to the experience of the medium itself. Before we examine the implications of this trend we need to look briefly at what this search has so far produced.

Keith Swanwick, an influential writer on music education, (see Marian Metcalf's chapter) and Gavin Bolton are interested in how aesthetic behaviours exist *within the experience of arts education* and focus their attention primarily on process. They refer to a set of psychological processes which, when applied to experience, introduce an aesthetic dimension. A fundamental aspect of these processes is that the experience is viewed as having *intrinsic aesthetic significance*. The experience is seen to stand in its own right, its other functions, theoretical and practical, are seen to be largely extraneous. The experi- ence has been defined as a 'special attitude or stance on the part of the experiencing individual'.[17] With this special stance comes a set of inner states that Bolton has suggested 'might be characterized as aesthetic intention, aesthetic attention and an overall aesthetic concep- tion by the teachers'.[18]

Aesthetic *intention* involves the attitude that *significance* will be found in the actions of the developing drama and that *the meanings* that emerge will have *universal implications* for the participants. Our expectations of drama, whether we are observers or participants, are that the actions, events, and objects will take on symbolic signi- ficance. Members of an audience are content to observe 'the immedi- ate, visible responses of human beings'[19] knowing that a level of meaning beyond the literal will be revealed. Drama, like all art, appeals to our need to explore further meanings that the action repre- sents. As Harding points out: 'the interest of the people and events in their own right comes first', but that we are prepared for 'incidents that hint at a further meaning beyond themselves'.[20] Over a period of several lessons in drama the significance of the actions, events and objects may often take on a symbolic character to the participants. It is this concern with symbolic significance which is central to aesthetic intention. This happens in drama when characters and events become invested with a meaning that is somehow greater than their obvious representation, when they become resonant with a cluster of meanings and feelings which not only unify the action but also universalize it. When this preoccupation for symbolic significance is present we could say that then the aesthetic intention is also at work.

In *attending* aesthetically to the drama process the participant becomes aware of how the meanings — and their artistic forms — are developing through the degree to which this awareness governs the developing form of the work, at a conscious or at an intuitive level, is highly problematical. Redfern argues that there must always be some critical appreciation of the process. The artist, she states: 'looks or listens reflectively, discriminately, and proceeds in the light of this assessment.'[21] There is here a sense of conscious control being exercised upon the experience — control, that is, over the way 'coherent constructions'[22] are being worked from the media. Ehrenzweig, in his work on the intuitive factor in art-making, stresses the importance of the artist tolerating unconscious perceptions. He claims that the conflict between conscious and spontaneous control over 'rational thought and image-making'[23] creates in art-making a productive tension. This demand that the artist must be capable of switching from conscious to unconscious modes of control. The art-maker, for Ehrenzweig, must be able to work with processes that 'proceed in steps and stages, each of them represents an interim result that cannot be connected with the final solution'.[24] The artist in the act of creative making is seen as maintaining a delicate balance between attending to and submitting to the emerging aesthetic form. There are rich clues here for the drama teacher, both in the way he acts in the drama workshop and in the way he conceives the activity he is out to engender.

An indication of the way children respond to form came recently from a group who wanted the 'Dr. Barnado' figure they had invented to succumb to a terrible disease he had caught from the street urchins. The children wanted to reverse the roles so that they (the urchins) could care for the doctor (their teacher). In discussion about this development one boy said that: 'It seemed to give the drama a good shape'. Perhaps, it is a reflection like this that helps us to understand how aesthetic attention to structural form is a sensed/felt response to the experience.

So far I have mentioned only the subjective psychological nature of aesthetic attention, but there are aesthetic factors to be accounted for in the *object* of attention. The object, writes LA Reid, 'must be sufficiently interesting to hold our attention'.[25] He suggests we need to recognize that there must be a satisfaction in the process of creating an object or event and that that satisfaction stems from the insights the artist experiences during the act of art-making, 'art for the artist is the discovery of what was not there before'.[26]

Children's attention in drama is held by an overriding interest and concern for the people and events. Their satisfaction, as participants, stems primarily from ordering a sequence of events, i.e. developing and resolving a plot line. Developing a plot will rarely be the main objective for a drama teacher who recognizes that the quality of the drama experience rests upon the exploration of what lies behind the decisions and relationships of the protagonists at a particular moment of time, and of how present actions will affect the future. To achieve his objective the teacher has to sensitively introduce *structures that enable the children to reflect upon the fictional situation*. He must accept their primary source of interest, but if the children are to achieve the insights Reid refers to, then the teacher must also help them to reflect as protagonists and as participants i.e. in and out of role, on the experience of the drama proceeds. Through sensitive intervention, inside the aesthetic process, the teacher can see that what may have been unconsciously apprehended can become articulated and shared, and so a language of drama is built up.

In this way, the teacher's role becomes crucial in developing the aesthetic consciousness of the participants. In effect *the teacher offers himself as the model of the artist* who is willing to work in 'steps and stages' without predetermining final outcomes, who attends and submits to the emerging form, who intends that the plot will provide the means of encapsulating meaning in vital symbols. It is the teacher's task to provide an overall aesthetic conception of the drama experience. By bringing the dramatist's perspective to the work the teacher arouses the dramatist in the participants. He may be the one who first adopts a 'special attitude or stance' but in doing so he invites the children further and further into the aesthetic dimension.

It is, perhaps, too soon to assess the full impact of the current reflections on the aesthetic experience in drama, though they seem to provide a fresh impetus for looking at the problems of drama education. The most persistent of these problems remains the insecurity many drama teachers feel about their craft. The dominating influence of 'the playway' approach has left teachers unsure how to enrich children's ideas. To fully understand the nature of this insecurity we have to acknowledge the pervasive influence of the progressive movement which still forms the basis for much of the philosophy and practice of drama teaching today. The rift between drama and theatre has been so deep and the divorce from tradition so complete that it may take another decade before teachers can comfortably draw upon the past as a source of guidance about their craft. I am not arguing for a return to arid study of texts and meaningless performances of them but for *a placing of children's ideas in the context of an aesthetic tradition, a tradition that teachers can draw upon as they engage with children in the drama process.*

Perhaps the new interest in drama as an aesthetic dicipline will encourage a further reappraisal of the work and influence of Dorothy Heathcote. To many teachers she represents not only a great practical innovator but also the champion of drama as a learning medium. She herself so stressed this aspect that it may take a decade for teachers to see how she actually taught through the *art form of drama.*

Our analysis of the art of drama, though, may soon be undermined because of the increased bias of the curriculum, particularly in secondary and further education, towards vocational preparation. There is increasing pressure on drama teachers to use their teaching expertise purely for the development of social and life-skills training. This instrumental work may, at times, closely resemble the drama process, but the intentions will be confined to an experience that simulates or resembles those 'real life situations' that it is expected students will encounter. The aesthetic search for the 'universal at the centre of the particular'[27] will not be a relevant aim in any vocational training! One can only hope that the emerging interest in the aesthetic nature of drama and its place in a coherent arts education will encourage teachers and students to reflect on the final inadequacy of any instrumental view. If we don't attempt to place drama squarely in the aesthetic field then narrow and partial influences will determine its nature recasting it as a recreation or simulation activity for the young, and not as a potent artistic medium and as a great arts discipline. We can only hope drama teachers' interest in the aesthetic has not come too late.

Notes

1 Quoted in BOLTON, G (1984) *Drama as Education*, Longmans, p 7.
2 FINLAY-JOHNSON, H *The Dramatic Method of Teaching*, Nisbet.
3 BOLTON, G (1984) *op cit*, p 11.
4 BOARD OF EDUCATION (1919) *Report on the Teaching of English*, HMSO, p 316.
5 SLADE, P (1954) *Child Drama*. University of London Press, p 125; quoted by BOLTON, G (1984) *op cit*, p 35.
6 DES (1967) *Education Survey 2 : Drama*. HMSO.
7 *Ibid*, p 2.
8 *Ibid*, p 2.
9 HEATHCOTE, D (n.d.) *Drama in the Education of Teachers*, University of Newcastle.

10 DAVIS, D (1983). 'Drama for deference or drama for defiance?' *2D*, 3, 1, autumn, p 30.

11 O'NEILL, C and LAMBERT, A (1982) *Drama Structures*, Hutchinson, p 15.

12 HEATHCOTE, D (1976) *Drama as Education*, New Destinations, Greater London Arts Association.

13 BOLTON, G (1980) 'Theatre form in drama teaching' in ROBINSON, K (Ed) *Exploring Theatre and Education*, p 72.

14 DAVIS, D (1983) *op cit*, p 31.

15 O'NEILL, C and LAMBERT, A (1982) *op cit*, p 13.

16 ROSS, M (1982) *The Development of the Aesthetic Experience*, Pergamon. p 148.

17 REDFERN, B (1983) *Dance, Art and Aesthetics*, Dance Books Ltd, p 69.

18 BOLTON, G (1983) 'An attempt to define simulation, role play and drama' *2D*, 3, 1. p 26.

19 LANGER, S (1953) *Feeling and Form*, Routledge and Kegan Paul Ltd, p 316.

20 HARDING D (1963) *Experience into Words*, Penquin Books Ltd, p 73.

21 REDFERN, B (1983) *op cit*, p 40.

22 *Ibid*, p 12.

23 EHERENZWEIG, A (1967) *The Hidden Order of Art*, Weidenfeld and Nicholson, p 12.

24 *Ibid*, p 47.

25 REID, LA (1981) 'Assessment and aesthetic education', in ROSS, M (Ed). *The Aesthetic Imperative*, Pergamon Press, p 9.

26 *Ibid*, p 9.

27 HEATHCOTE, D (1980) *op cit*, p 32.

THE CASE OF THE VISUAL ARTS

7   *Towards a Shared Symbolic Order*

Robin Morris

Introduction

I would like to begin my analysis of the visual arts with a quotation from the work of Peter Fuller. Exploring the nature of the visual arts Fuller wrote:

> As for what painting can be: that is another story. But the roots of good painting remain in its traditions, its real skills, its accumulated knowledges, techniques and practices ... And, as for the absence of a shared symbolic order ... even if we have ceased to believe in God, nature can provide it for us: the answer lies not in the reproduction of appearances, but in an *imaginative perception* of natural form, in which its particularities are not denied, but grasped and transfigured.[1]

Here is a conception of painting pertinent to the terms of this chapter. While searching for a biological basis for the creation of all works of art, Fuller nevertheless locates these firmly within a cultural and historic context — within a 'shared symbolic order' — and secondly, he provides a direction, a practice even, by and through which such an order can be realized through 'imaginative perception' and, as he states earlier in the same article, the 'profound transformation through imaginative and physical working' of paint.

Fuller is in the forefront of a movement which seeks to re-establish values and criteria for painting that have been lost in much modernist and post-modernist practice. I suspect that what is happening amongst critics like Fuller is comparable with what is beginning to emerge in educational circles where the arts in general are seen as being in need of curricula realignment and of redefinition in content, form and practice. This, after all, is the function of this symposium. What links us all is the value we place on the aesthetic dimension of human experience and the way in which the life of feeling is inextricably bound up and expressed through the creation and reception of works of art, to the creative processes of expressive symbolism.

The question that has to be asked is whether the teaching of art in schools has ever reflected such a conception. My immediate response is that, for the most part, it has not. But that is too simplistic an answer and a brief examination of art education history is necessary.

In my account I will first concentrate on the practice of art education as it existed at the turn of the century and, then, on the two subsequent and major changes that have taken place since; the 'child art' movement led by Marion Richardson, and the 'basic design' movement initiatied, in this country, by the artist-educators Victor Pasmore, Harry Thubron, Tom Hudson and Richard Hamilton.

The Training of 'Hand and Eye'

Surprisingly, art has been part of the school curriculum since the advent of the elementary board schools in the nineteenth century.[2] But then there is art and there is art ...

> You should endeavour to disabuse persons of the notion that the kind of drawing which has been hitherto known as an accomplishment in schools for the rich, is that which would be taught under the present minutes in schools for the poor. The kind of drawing which it is proposed to teach, is, in the strictest sense, an education of the eye, and of the hand, such as may be the first step in the career of a great artist, but must at any rate enable the common workman to do his work more neatly and better.[3]

What we find, then, at the end of the nineteenth century is a wholly instrumental, utilitarian approach to the skills inherent in the practice of drawing, an activity devoid of any cultural or subjective elements and one aimed indirectly at producing a more effective workforce to meet the needs of industry. Such an instrumental class-based understanding still largely determines the location of art in the comprehensive-school curriculum, where it is invariably viewed as a marginal practical subject having no intellectual gravity and possessing virtually no value to anyone contemplating higher education.

A narrow training of 'hand and eye' was aimed solely at

developing the following: an ability to render in outline and tone the representation of objects and ornament with precision and accuracy; an ability to draw straight and curved lines and, above all, the ability to copy. All of these skills were developed through the process of copying. Pupils were asked to copy from the flat in the form of printed examples, from diagrams and drawings made by the teacher, or from life by the drawing of geometric solids. Indeed, the teaching of geometry was closely linked to the teaching of drawing. The only aesthetic element in such teaching would seem to lie in the pleasure given by making ornamental patterns (these were largely based on geometric structure, considered to be appropriate and representative of 'good' taste) and, possibly, in the artistic power of one or two antique casts which were, sometimes, made the subjects of drawing exercises. The materials used would be strictly limited and were frequently, at the elementary level, slate and slate pencil or chalk and blackboard. If pencil, brush and paint were used at a more advanced level then the emphasis remained on accuracy, on 'proper' technique and an objectivity indistinguishable from the notion of copying, regardless of subject matter, be that plants, still-life or the human figure.

It is not my intention to be totally dismissive of the 'academic' tradition of drawing. What has to be questioned, however, is a philosophy and practice that conceives the subject as no more than an objective perceptual discipline and a craft activity. It is a conception that denies any opportunity for creative expression, for engagement with the life of feeling, for that liberating experience which is dependent upon a personal encounter with the actual material processes of art-making and the shared symbolic order which it gives access to. It neither has room for the traditions and conventions of the aesthetic field of the visual arts, nor has it place for the spontaneous pictorial response of children on which the child-art movement of the 1930s was to put so much emphasis. In brief, the 'academic' tradition of drawing ignored all the major elements of the aesthetic field. The first challenge to its hegemony came in the 1930s with the progressive movement.

Child Art — The New Art Teaching

It was not until the 1930s that there was any real recognition of the educational and aesthetic value of children's art and of the importance that this could have to the child's overall development. This was

Plate 26 *A typical art class at the end of the nineteenth century.*

Plate 27 *Child-art in action.*

largely due to the influential work of Marion Richardson (1892–1946). When she was 19, Richardson began teaching at Dudley Girls High School and, while there, developed the technique of encouraging her students to paint pictures based on 'mental imagery' created through the stimulus of 'word pictures' given by herself. Such a technique was clearly different from the prevalent practice of the time, and of its effects Marion Richardson wrote:

> Whereas before it had been little more than the reproduction of something photographed by the physical eye, it now had an original and inner quality.[4]

The acceptance of this 'original and inner quality', the natural vitality and subjectivity of children's art and the way in which it operated under its own rules, not those of adult art, had been prepared for philosophically by the naturalism of Rousseau and scientifically through psychological research into child development.[5] As it has been shown in the first chapter a more 'progressive', 'natural' and 'evolutionary' approach to education had taken hold of the imagination of many teachers at the beginning of our century. In this country and in Europe, educationists such as Froebel, Viola and Cizek had celebrated the specific value of spontaneous 'child art'. Of these, Franz Cizek (1865–1946) was the most directly influential on Marion Richardson. Exhibitions of children's artwork, produced by Cizek in Vienna, had toured throughout Europe and North America between 1908 and 1935. Richardson had seen these and had also visited Cizek, in Vienna, in 1926. Cizek stressed both the importance of encouraging and developing creativity before the imposition of rules and strict technique and the essential difference of the child's world from that of adults. The movement towards a 'child-centered' approach to education was also reflected in a dramatic change of official attitudes. The Hadow Reports of 1926 (*Education and the Adolescent*) and 1931 (*The Primary School*) stressed the importance of 'learning through doing' and of the value, both educational and aesthetic, of the arts and handicrafts.

In his history of art education, Stuart Macdonald (1970) makes the point that the recognition of child art depended upon an increased interest in modern painting, primitive art and psychology. For Marion Richardson the most important influence was that of modern painting, particularly that of the Impressionist and post-Impressionist periods, and the influence of her friend and ally, the critic Roger Fry. Richardson felt supported in her teaching methods by the parallel she believed to exist between the Impressionist paintings and the work of her students, an affinity of kind rather than of quality — the presence of a 'vital something':

> a common denominator was evident between the children's infinitely humble imitations of artistic experience and the mighty statements of these great modern masters.[6]

It is worth noting that this affinity also had formal roots. One of the principal challenges made by modernist painting, from the post-Impressionists onwards, was to the academic tradition of perspectival (linear and aerial) realism and, in some instances, a shift from representation towards a greater expression of subjectivity — with an emphasis on sensation.

In 1930 Marion Richardson was appointed District Art Inspector for the LCC and her influence became more widespread. For the first time in the state education system, it became common for children to be encouraged to draw and paint on their own terms, and for the aesthetic and educational value of such activity to be widely recognized. This indicated a dramatic change of concern from the reality of the empirical world to the reality of the child's inner life. This led, in turn, to further changes of practice within the art room. Copying increasingly became replaced by more imaginative work. The act of painting became centered around the child's own experience. Often the teacher stimulated mental rather than observed images by suggesting what Marion Richardson called 'word pictures'. The teacher allowed freedom of composition and encouraged the use of colour in the form of liberal quantities of powder paint. When drawing, in the academic sense, was taught it was done so with greater sensitivity to both media and subject matter. Art became essentially a matter of 'doing' — and of 'doing', as spontaneously and as freshly as possible, within a whole range of picture-making, pattern-making and related handicraft activities, using a wide range of both improvised and manufactured materials.

In 1938 Marion Richardson organized a major exhibition of artwork from London schools. This was opened by Sir Kenneth Clark. It was visited by 26,000 people. Its purposes were two fold:

> to tell the story of an ordinary child's natural artistic development, and to suggest the teacher's share in furthering it.[7]

Although this new form of art teaching *was* child-centered, Marion Richardson was at pains to deny that her approach was simply concerned with any notion of 'free expression'. For her this was not the case and the work[8] produced by her method demonstrates a

Plate 28   Painting from the 1938 Child Art Exhibition organized by Marion Richardson.

quality that can only be achieved through a structured and disciplined approach by both teacher and taught. Although Marion Richardson laid so great a stress on the idea of mental image, she was equally sensitive to material considerations. A sensitivity to colour, the expressive and technical demands of media and the wholeness of compositional structure were all elements to be considered and mastered by her students, although Kenneth Clark tempers his praise of her work by suggesting that:

> She sometimes underestimated the added richness which comes from the discipline of representation.[9]

Richardson was also aware of another factor, the importance of the children's physical, social and cultural environment to their artistic efforts. She wrote:

> We were members of a community with its own strong customs and conventions ... and the drawings were in the Dudley dialect, traditional, intimate, indigenous to the soil, and mysteriously revealing ... These, and a hundred seeming

trifles so slight that I can feel rather than describe them, united
to produce a native style, a painting idiom through which the
children became articulate; for it provided that framework or
form which is one of the necessities of art.[10]

What is evident in this work is the placing of equal value on both the
artifact produced and the process or experience that the child has
engaged in. In fact, Marion Richardson's work, rather like that of
Caldwell Cook at the Perse School in Cambridge, would seem to
insist on all the main elements of the aesthetic field, the place of
making and performing of responding and interpreting within a
context defined by a reciprocal movement between the individual and
the community. At the same time, it has to be granted that the origins
of a wholly unstructured and permissive approch to the visual arts can
be found in the many excesses of the progressive movement and in
the general elevation of the child's self-expression above all other
aesthetic and artistic elements. Like the English teacher Caldwell
Cook, Marion Richardson seemed to be of the progressive movement
and yet, in her general practice and advocacy, largely transcended its
weaknesses and philosophical fallacies.

The Basic Course — Art as Process and
the Formalist Aesthetic

While the 'child art' movement continued to evolve and undergo
modifications in secondary and primary schools throughout the 1940s
and 1950s, another revolution was taking place among professional
artists and in the art colleges of this country. The move towards
abstraction and formalism in the visual arts, interrupted by the war,
became firmly established in the two decades that followed. The
conception of art as evolutionary, organic and psychological became
one of the cornerstones of modernism for both artists and critics. Of
the latter, Herbert Read (1893–1968) deserves a position of special
importance for two particular reasons; firstly for his association with
the ICA which became the forum for so much critical debate in the
1950s and 1960s; and, secondly, for his integration of psychology,
particularly that of Jung, into an organic, scientifically-based formal
aesthetic. D Thistlewood describes Read as being able to distinguish
between:

an art of Romanticism, responding to 'projected' feeling or
emotion, exploiting unconscious leaps of aspiration, and an art

of classic precision, apprehending the forms and proportions of universal beauty.[11]

Each of these were seen as the opposite poles of a continuous axis, allowing for varying proportions of each to be present in any one artist. The value Read conferred upon both intuitive and scientific forms of knowledge was of immense importance to those seeking new educational strategies in the visual arts.

A 'new art for a new age' — with all its attendant and problematic historicism — was called for. In the colleges of art a new form of visual education was developed principally through the work of Victor Pasmore, Harry Thubron, Tom Hudson and Richard Hamilton and inspired, to a great extent, by the pedagogic innovations of the Bauhaus of pre-war Germany. This movement centered on a few colleges. But it was given a wider audience through exhibitions held at the ICA, 'Growth and Form' in 1951, 'Man, Machine and Motion' in 1955 and 'The Developing Process' in 1959. Its dissemination was further accelerated by the *Coldstream Report* (1961) and the establishment of pre-diploma and DipAD courses.

A number of different approaches and terminologies have developed around this concept of art education; 'basic design' and 'foundation studies' being the most common and the most revealing. The titles clearly denote what was, indeed, advocated, an abstract and formal language common to both art and design, to both two- and three-dimensional work, and a shift of emphasis from a personal aesthetic concept of 'fine art' orientated education to a more widely applicable notion of 'visual language'. The term language was used to denote a similarity to verbal languages, i.e., that images and objects are constructed from a vocabulary of formal elements (line, shape, tone, texture, etc.) and a grammar, a group of rules and conventions that govern and structure the process. But these were not seen as the conventions and traditions of representational painting that were handed down through the exercise and teaching of skills, but, rather, rules that had to be discovered by each individual student, by use of intellect and intuition, through a confrontation with specific problems and exercises.

A number of principles and assumptions lie behind the development of a basic course of this kind, and some of these are particularly relevant to the way in which art education has developed in schools. The first of these reminiscent, in a way, of Rousseau's pedagogy, was that it was necessary to dispense with all past preconceptions of art and to start afresh with a 'clean slate'. Secondly, it was considered that by open-ended research and enquiry (con-

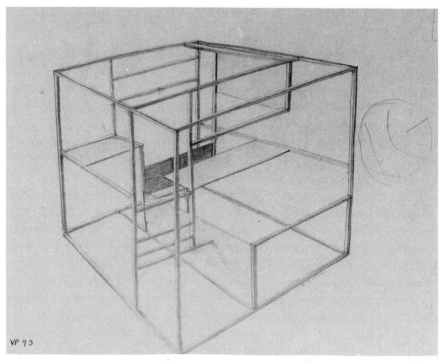

VP 93

Plate 29   From a folder of students' work collected by Victor Pasmore.

sidered by some to be akin to the procedures of science) a natural and individual visual language would be free to develop, a kind of formal language which was seen to develop through the dual faculties of intuition and intellect. Thirdly, it was thought that all art and design activities were interrelated and could be developed progressively and sequentially:

> The production of art is a developing process which originates in the first dimension, the making of a single point. By an expansion into the second dimension, drawing and painting, and into the third, sculpture and architecture, it is possible to achieve a developmental association between, at one extreme, the simple mark and, at the other, free-standing constructions in space.[12]

Fourthly, and particularly under the influence of Hamilton, it was argued that the sources and references for use by students should be widened to include 'popular culture', the images and forms of advertising, cinema and the media. Finally, it was the process that was emphasized and not the artifact. Students did not set out to make art,

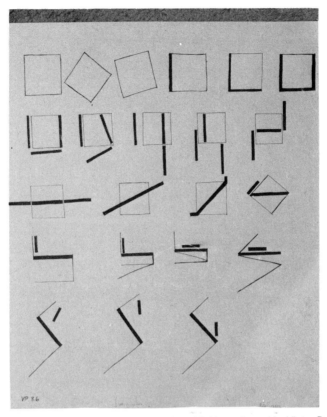

Plate 30   A progressive exercise from students' folder collected by Victor Pasmore.

but to analyze, enquire or to conduct research into specific problems or formal qualities. It can be seen how the movement towards a general visual education incorporated both the scientific element of modernism and the free enquiry methods of the progressive school. This approach, where being an artist was considered to be more a question of attitude than of specific and productive skill, applied as much to work related to the figure or the environment as it did to totally formal or material-based exercises.

It did not take long for this new approach to dominate pre-diploma and foundation courses in art schools or for it to be adapted and presented in suitable form for use in the secondary sector. Kurt Rowlands' *Learning to See* is one of the best known programmes of this type, in which a basic design course is closely related to the child's experience of the natural and man-made environment. Nor did it take long for the aims of *visual*, as opposed to *art education* to become the objectives of many secondary art departments. For a

Plate 31   Objective drawing.

time the result was the virtual rejection of the complex aesthetic field in the teaching of art. Stuart Macdonald quotes Edward Jenkins, a tutor at Cardiff School of Art, as saying:

> Art education can and does suffer from a limited interpretation of ART as being the dominant factor ... We should be establishing a non–art situation not a process of self-conscious art-making, not endowing the artefact with the 'mystique' of esoteric significance.[13]

This rejection of the fine art tradition, paradoxically, opened yet another door into 'child centered', non-interventionist teaching by claiming that:

> The teacher can afford no longer to teach from his own, or anyone else's propositions, formal understanding, systems,

and/or personal dominance of style ... we should aim not so much at giving our students ideas but perhaps more towards giving students' ideas a chance.

Such a position, demonstrating a curious fusion between modernism in art and progressivism in education, was extreme but not untypical. Also it marks a distinct turning from aesthetic to propositional concerns. It is of interest that Edward Jenkins does not refer either to *artistic* materials or to the *inherited traditions of art* but to 'ideas' and the giving of 'ideas a chance'. Many students at this time were urged, in effect, to construct *ideas* in modern materials and not to create sculpture and paintings embodying aesthetic experience and aesthetic value. The approach was arid and extreme but it nevertheless had a strong influence on secondary education throughout the 1970s, albeit less dramatically and less comprehensively than in the art colleges.

The State of the Art: Current Practice in Schools

The current practice of thinking in secondary art departments reflects, in varying quantities, a combination of the practices and conceptions outlined so far; art as the development of skill, art as a means to child development, art as visual literacy. This, of course, is not to say that artistic and intellectual movements were the only factors to have influenced change in art, or any other aspect of education. We are all aware of the social, ideological, political and economic pressures to which education is subject, and we should also remember that it has been the nature of the British educational system to allow considerable diversity of structure and variation of practice from region to region, and from school to school in any one area — although, through the impact of the forthcoming GCSE and increasing central control, this may not be the case in the future.

If there has been a common trend in the teaching of art in the last twenty years, it has been a desire to broaden and extend the nature and 'relevance' of the subject, to include all aspects of art, craft and design, and an attempt to teach these in a coherent and structured way. Three specific forces have helped bring this about. In the first place the reorganization of secondary schooling into the comprehensive system, created larger and often purpose-built departments which were often staffed with specialist teachers of different art, craft or design disciplines. In the second place the introduction of the CSE examination, through its mode-three format, allowed teachers an

Chapter

2

Or we can arrange the boxes even more freely as in the picture above. In the next picture the boxes have been covered and lined with coloured paper. The pattern of light and shade adds still more variety. Which of these patterns do you prefer?

Let us make more patterns from matchboxes, but this time let us use the insides of the boxes. We could make them into a pattern like the one above. To make it more interesting we can turn some of the boxes back to front as shown below. This breaks the sameness of the pattern.

So far we have arranged the boxes as a flat wall. Now let us join them at angles to each other. Let us make a composition; not a flat composition such as those we made in the first book, but one which can be looked at from all sides. As we turn our composition, or walk round it, or look

16

Plate 32   A formal exercise.

unprecedented level of control and responsibility for marking and the kind of work that could be submitted for examination. And thirdly, the raising of the school leaving age to 16 brought into the examination arena a huge number of pupils not catered for previously. The DES estimates (Art in Secondary Education 11–16, 1983) that in

at it from high up, we get different pictures of it. Each one of these views is really a composition by itself. The whole arrangement is many compositions all in one.

The picture above shows a composition of shapes over the entrance to a building. Compare it with the one at the bottom of page 14. Do you like them both equally?

17

1982 some 300,000 fifth-form pupils were entered for art and art related examinations, and that almost 40 per cent of all senior secondary pupils studied art or art-related subjects. Examinations are clearly an important factor, but this is not the point at which to discuss their virtues and failings. What I *do* want to point out is the importance they have for most art teachers, not just as a real pressure and responsibility, but as a force on the content and method of teaching. Without set books and without externally set syllabuses, art teachers have considerable autonomy over how their subject is conceived and taught. Even at advanced level, syllabuses are remarkably vague and often offer little more than a description of the examination structure:

> The syllabus provides for candidates who have made a special study of Painting.
> Candidates will be required to take both papers and to submit Coursework.
> Paper 1 is designed to test creative ability, skill and craftsmanship.
> Paper 2 provides a test of the candidate's knowledge of the history and technique of the subject.
> Candidates are also required to submit Coursework.[14]

As the exam boards have been unwilling, or perhaps even unable, to provide clear marking criteria, it has left teachers dependent upon past examination experience or vague assumptions as to what is required.

Traditionally, the GCE examination is essentially a performance test, a limited amount of time is given in which candidates must demonstrate their skill by producing a finished piece of work. This may or may not have been prepared for before the examination. Inveitably, any examination of this kind is going to stress the importance of teaching skills and techniques within a limited range of subject matter and media. On the other hand, the CSE examination has tended to mark coursework and this has often led to an emphasis being placed on a broad experience of the subject, which in practice has meant the use of a variety of media and processes.

The question of 'breadth' versus 'depth' appears to be one that dogs art education continually and, in my own examination and teaching experience, is ever present. A common solution seems to lie in an approach that sees the early years of art education as being 'foundational'. The foundation years are then seen as offering a breadth of experience, a range of materials and an introduction to the formal elements of visual language. This structure, in turn, allows for greater specialization and the development of individual aptitudes and skills in the final two years of the course. In some instances, this has led to a 'circus' strategy in the early years, a system whereby pupils rotate through a whole range of different art, craft and design disciplines and, very often, a whole range of different teachers. In others, a variety of work is undertaken by a single teacher, a situation which has the advantage of continuity in staff-pupil relationships, but which tends to stretch to the limit the skills that any one teacher can be expected to possess. But, however structured, any broad-based course is expensive to operate and with the economic cuts of recent years, it has become increasingly difficult to teach effectively in this way.

However, this is not just a question of economics but also of philosophy. Under the influence of the basic design movement, the prior concept of art education as aesthetic and expressive, as essentially a matter of doing and enjoying has been seriously eroded. The dominant conception now sees the subject as constituting a clear body of knowledge, made up of conceptual, material and technical skills, which can be taught to pupils of all abilities and which are 'relevant' to a much wider social context that that of the child's subjective experience. This view, as we have seen, dismisses the distinction between high and popular culture and dissolves the classification of separate functions implict in the terms 'art', 'craft' and 'design'. *Art education* thus becomes *visual education* and, while it *is* seen as a way of knowing, the particular kind of knowledge is often seen as being *more transactional than aesthetic* in nature. Learning about design has more to do with the outer objective world than the inner and personal one. Such an approach, in the end, must stress the utilitarian rather than the symbolic, the functional rather than the aesthetic, the objective rather than the personal. At their best, such visual language courses have been highly effective, combining an extensive and carefully balanced content with sensitive teaching. At their worst, they have led to a negation of art as personal, aesthetic and symbolic experience, and to a philosophy and practice of art that is entirely instrumental.

A Shared Symbolic Order

It is clear that art education is today seen in terms that are both instrumental and expressive, and that this problematic duality of purpose has a general acceptance and approval. The Gulbenkian Report, *The Arts in Schools*, stated that

> The uses of the arts as ways of approaching a variety of work
> in cultural studies across the curriculum were highlighted and
> we concluded by arguing that children can thus be enabled

both to use the processes of the arts for their own ends and to produce works of art in their own right.[15]

While the 1983 DES Report *Art in Secondary Education* declared that:

There is no doubt however that there is evidence of a change in thinking about the balance of the art curriculum. Many of the schools described here, while producing artifacts of great quality, also lay stress on the need to educate their pupils to know about the work of other artists and designers both past and present and to be articulate in the judgements they make about them. They encourage their pupils to be critical of the visual qualities of film, television and other contemporary media, and to relate their developing sensibilities to the world outside the art room. These extensions of the art curriculum are not necessarily brought about by abandoning or limiting practical work but may result from projects that look for outcomes which are both instrumental *and* expressive.[16]

Yet there is nothing particularly new in this, for Marion Richardson in 1948 had suggested:

Through their own painting ... these girls had an internal test, a diviner's rod by which to discover the common denominator of art.[17]

That aesthetic, creative work can and does promote conceptions of excellence, autonomy and judgment, applicable beyond their immediate spheres, is one of the important claims for arts education[18], and forms a strong argument for the general value of such experience. It is not my intention to take issue with the idea that education should have an instrumental dimension, or that it should enable children to understand and make critical judgments about their culture — of course, it should and must. My position is that the instrumental and critical should be seen to arise naturally and logically from creative and expressive art work — for they are parts of a larger aesthetic practice, elements of the aesthetic field not self-justifying totalities. The danger is that the expressive and symbolic essence of art will become lost in a narrow and misconceived instrumentality, will become isolated from both inherited culture and from living and subjective response.

To try to understand more clearly just what I mean by the 'expressive and symbolic essence' I want now to return to where I began, to Peter Fuller's concepts of a 'shared symbolic order', to 'imaginative perception' and the capacity of paint to allow 'profound transformation', a capacity for transcendence and the embodiment of meaning and feeling. Both the reception and the creation of all art forms depend upon a leap of imaginative perception, a state of mind different and separate from normal objective or transactional conditions. And clearly, the work of art is credited with a value and meaning not attributable to its literal material condition. The purpose of the work of art is to mediate between the perceived, exterior world and the subjective self. As such, its function is symbolic rather than instrumental and its accessibility to others must depend upon a common language — a shared symbolic order.

Such an order is determined by a number of factors, cultural, biological, environmental, ideological, social, formal and technical. To understand that order is, in effect, to understand how the arts embody and communicate meaning. In *Education through Art*, Herbert Read suggested a formal classification of arts disciplines and their related forms of mental activity and expression. Thus, poetry and drama were seen to correspond to feeling; music and dance to intuition; crafts (constructive education) to thought, and design (visual and plastic education) to sensation. Few arts teachers would now be willing to accept so rigid a classification and would want to argue that each of these modes of mental activity play a vital role in any arts discipline. In the visual arts, they do so through three definable forms of discourse.

Firstly, they do so through *representational subject matter* — in painting this is the closest element to semantic meaning, working through the direct and indirect associations of resemblance. There is a close correlation here between pictorial and literary forms in as much as this discourse may be narrative, descriptive, autobiographical etc. Secondly, they work through *formal elements* — of genre, composition, conventional systems such as perspective and the elements of line, tone, colour, etc. And thirdly, they work through *the physical engagement with plastic media* — the very substance of paint, clay, etc., and the traces of thought and feeling imprinted in these as marks; the record of process and performance; an individual, subjective quality of technique that can be discerned in both child and adult work.

These three — subject matter, form and media — constitute the special experience of the visual arts, and if we are to teach them well *then due consideration must be given to each, at all stages of development, in all sectors of education.* They can also serve as a structural link to other arts disciplines. In this way, literature can be seen as possessing form and subject matter; music, form and media; and dance and drama as

Plate 33   *Self portrait: Gwyneth Williamson, sixth-form, South Hunsley School, North Humberside.*

having all three. Thus, within the common framework set by the aesthetic field of making, presenting, responding and evaluating all the arts disciplines can be seen to share common constituents. Educationally and culturally, a 'shared symbolic order' cannot be realized through isolated experience in any one discipline. A full aesthetic education depends upon a common framework of understanding, each school having the six major arts disciplines, each differentiated in form and by practice, but related in common purpose. At present, neither our schools nor our culture provide such a context and for many children and adults the arts remain inaccessible and irrelevant. If the arts are to be taught with meaning and sensitivity, then their teachers need both clarity of purpose and an understanding of each other's concerns. They also need the means by which to teach. In a system currently under so much pressure and so

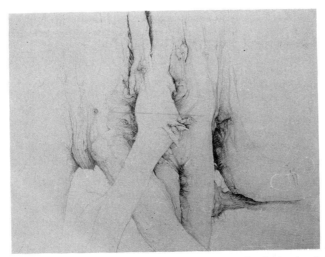

Plate 34 A study of tree roots, *Rosalind Newby, sixth-form, South Hunsley School, North Humberside.*

clearly focussed towards the instrumental, it is hard to believe that more curriculum time and resources will be provided, or that due recognition will be given to the value of aesthetic and creative education.

And yet, as an arts teacher, I believe it essential that means be found by which the level of productive discourse enjoyed by many teachers of art, through CSE, 16+ and other forums, be extended across all the arts disciplines. At present few schools or teachers generate a significant level of interdisciplinary discourse, yet is is only through mutual understanding that the expressive arts as a whole can consolidate and develop their position in the curriculum. Teaching, in many respects, is an isolated activity and this isolation is further increased by the failure of arts disciplines and arts teachers to recognize their common concerns. The failure is not so much one of a questionable integration but more that of a failure to share, to understand and to collectively create the conditions necessary for a comprehensive aesthetic education. This remains the task for the future.

Notes

1 FULLER, P (1985) *Images of God*, Chatto and Windus, p 16.
2 1870 Elementary Education Act; 1888 Cross Report — recommending the introduction of linear drawing for all boys in elementary schools.

3 Minutes of the Committee of Council on Education, 1856–57, p 25, in MACDONALD, S (1970) *The History and Philosophy of Art Education*, University of London Press Ltd, p 168.
4 RICHARDSON, M (1948) *Art and the Child*, University of London Press Ltd, p 13.
5 SULLY, J (1842–1923) *Studies of Childhood* (1895) — First analysis and classification of developmental stages in children's drawings.
6 RICHARDSON, M (1948) *op cit*, p 14.
7 *Ibid*, p 78.
8 Much of this work is now part of the NAE Archive at Bretton Hall College, nr Wakefield, Yorkshire.
9 CLARK, K (1948) 'Introduction' to RICHARDSON, M *Art and the Child*, University of London Press Ltd, p 8.
10 RICHARDSON, M (1948) *op cit*, pp 40–1.
11 THISTLEWOOD, D (1984) *Herbert Read — Formlessness and Form* Routledge and Kegan Paul, p 2.
12 PASMORE, V as quoted in THUSTLEWOOD, D, *The New Creativity in British Art Education*.
13 JENKINS, E, Lecture to Art Conference of the Colleges of Education of Manchester University, October, 1967, in MACDONALD, S (1970) *History and Philosophy of Art Education*, University of London Press Ltd, p 376.
14 AEB (1986) *Syllabuses*, Section 1, p 22, Art-Painting-603.
15 CALOUSTE GULBENKIAN FOUNDATION (1982) *The Arts in Schools*, p 47.
16 DES (1983) *Art in Secondary Education 11–16*, HMSO, p 65.
17 RICHARDSON, M (1948) *op cit*, pp 34–5.
18 CALOUSTE GULBENKIAN FOUNDATION (1982) *op cit*, p 27.

Part III
Into the Future

Peter Abbs

We have looked backwards largely with the intention of moving forwards with a greater sense of understanding and of possibility.

The historical reconstructions of the arts, studied together, should provide the necessary pragmatic elements for a new synthesis while the notion of the aesthetic field may well provide the necessary conceptual terms for unity. It is clear that applied to the different arts disciplines the aesthetic field model reveals different needs and different strengths. It would seem just to conclude that English does not stress sufficiently 'making' and 'presenting'; drama does not stress sufficiently 'presenting' (in its more formal aspects) and 'evaluating'; that dance and the visual arts still do not sufficiently stress 'evaluating'; that music, until recently, has not stressed 'making' and that film has not stressed any of the aesthetic elements being misconstrued as a kind of illustrated sociology. The model allows us to perceive, at an instant, the strong and weak elements and invites us to envisage ways of creating a better and more dynamic balance. In the tight confines of space we have tried to outline what that balance might look like in each arts discipline.

It remains to draw together the essential argument of the book. I would like to do so by putting forward two sets of closely related propositions. Put together they offer a manifesto for a coherent aesthetic education and make clear, I hope, the major challenge of our book.

Some Philosophical Propositions Concerning the Relationship of the Arts to the Curriculum

It is proposed that:

    (i)   The six major art disciplines, art, drama, music, dance, film and literature, belong together under the aesthetic category.

   (ii)   Any comprehensive aesthetic education must include these six art disciplines.

  (iii)   As aesthetic activities, working through the intelligence of feeling and sensibility, the arts explore and symbolically represent the complex forms of sentience and consciousness.

  (iv)   As symbolic re-presentations of experience they are, therefore inherently concerned with meaning and knowing.

   (v)   This form of knowing is non-propositional or rather sensuous, imaginal and aesthetic in nature.

  (vi)   Such aesthetic knowing is intrinsically valuable and need serve no instrumental end for its educational justification.

 (vii)   The arts must, therefore, be conceived as a major part of any curriculum concerned to develop and extend human understanding.

Concerning the Nature of Art and its Relationship to Teaching

It is proposed that:

    (i)   The arts, like the sciences, provide communal symbols. While sometimes being distinctive and individual they yet belong both to the continuum of cultural time and to the life of the community.

   (ii)   Innovation and tradition, individual and community are not antithetical but complementary terms.

  (iii)   A good arts education should, therefore, encourage an aesthetic awareness of the cultural past-present continuum and also of the relationship between the individual and the community, between, for example, the solitary making of the poem and its communal performance or publication.

  (iv)   A proper aesthetic education at secondary level must include, at different times, in different degrees and combinations, all four elements of the aesthetic field.

Some Practical Propositions

The implications of these connected philosophical propositions for the comprehensive school curriculum are many and complex. Certainly, in our view, they should include the following:

(i)   That each school develop a coherent aesthetic policy.

(ii)   That this policy includes all the six art disciplines in some kind of strong organisational relationship.

(iii) That in each school about one third of the timetable is allocated to the arts.

(iv)   That the timetable in each school is blocked for the arts thus securing both spans of time for sustained work in the aesthetic field and providing opportunities for collaborative work across the arts.

(v)   That each school has at least one yearly arts festival in which a representative selection of aesthetic work is formally and informally presented to the community.

(vi)   That teachers of the arts ensure that the new GCSE exams in the arts refer to all four elements of the aesthetic field.

The implications and ramifications of these six proposals call for another book. Here it must suffice to say they seem to follow from the philosophy of art-making developed in the previous chapters and outlined in the previous propositions.

Many readers will feel (as we have felt writing this book) an uncomfortable gap between the philosophical conception and the actual reality of our schools. How, a sceptic might ask, can one possibly realize a programme of aesthetic education in the school described in the introduction? How can one develop the aesthetic field in six related art forms in an allocation of a little over three hours? Of course, it is not possible. And it is the seeming impossibility that has led to many fine art teachers resigning from the comprehensive school system. The difficulty, perhaps even the impossibility, of realizing an aesthetic education for our children must be squarely faced. We have to decide, as a nation, what we believe education is for. The signs, at the moment, are that we believe it to be about training for the materialist society. On such a premise, the arts in schools have no choice but to wither and die.

And yet there are other signs in our divided and contradictory decade. There are signs of a growing concern for a renewal of the aesthetic dimension. This is not only manifest, for example, in the influential writings of Peter Fuller and Roger Scruton, but also in, say, a marked and broad-based enthusiasm for dance as an art form, for a new commitment to vernacular architecture, for an emerging interest in figurative painting, for a growing preoccupation with the writing and reading and performing of poetry. Cultural ecology, perhaps dialectically related to the dominant technological imperialism, seems to be also of our decade, part of a deep shift in sensibility away from the brutalities of the wilfully mega-technic and the purely in-strumental. In the educational context we know against all the odds that good and sensitive work in the arts continues to be done. We know that thousands of arts teachers found support and hope in *The Gulbenkian Report: The Arts in Schools,* a report — with its emphasis on heritage, repertoire of skills, aesthetic meaning and the human community — which belongs to the same ecological cultural shift.

Here, then, are some of the signs which prefigure a better future for the arts. Our task is to see them, to draw them together, to clarify them and to take them forward into the aesthetic practice of our schools. In this book we hope, in some small measure, looking backwards and forwards, to have done precisely that.

Bibliographies

Arts and Education

ABBS, P (1975) *Reclamations: Essays on Culture, Mass Culture and the Curriculum* Gryphon Press.

ASPIN, D (1984) *Objectivity and Assessment in the Arts: The Problem of Aesthetic Education,* NAEA.

BANTOCK, GM (1967) *Education, Culture and the Emotions,* Faber and Faber.

BERLEANT, A (1970) *The Aesthetic Field,* Charles C. Thomas.

BEST, D (1985) *Feeling and Reason in the Arts,* Allen and Unwin.

BLOOMFIELD, A (Ed) *Creative and Aesthetic Education Aspects,* 34, University of Hull.

BROUDY, H (1972) *Enlightened Cherishing: An Essay in Aesthetic Education,* University of Illinois Press.

CASSIRER, E (1944) *An Essay on Man,* Bantam Books.

CASSIRER, E (1955–8) *The Philosophy of Symbolic Forms* (in three volumes), Yale University Press.

COLLINGWOOD, RG (1958) *The Principles of Art,* Oxford University Press.

DEWEY, J (1934) *Art as Experience,* Minton Balch and Company.

DONOGHUE, D (1985) *The Arts Without Mystery,* BBC.

EAGLETON, T (1983) *Literary Theory,* Basil Blackwell.

ELIOT, TS (1975) *Selected Prose of TS Eliot,* edited Frank Kermode. Faber and Faber.

FREUD, S (1973) *Introductory Lectures on Psychoanalysis,* Penguin.

FREUD, S (1973) *New Introductory Lectures on Psychoanalysis,* Penguin.

FRYE, N (1957) *The Anatomy of Criticism,* Princeton University Press.

FULLER, P (1980) *Art and Psycho-Analysis,* Writers and Readers.

FULLER, P (1980) *Beyond the Crisis in Art,* Writers and Readers.

FULLER, P (1982) *Aesthetics after Modernism,* Writers and Readers.

FULLER, P (1985) *Images of God,* Chatto and Windus.

GOMBRICH, E (1960) *Art and Illusion,* Phaidon.

GULBENKIAN FOUNDATION (1982) *The Arts in Schools,* Gulbenkian Foundation.

HARGREAVES D (1982) *The Challenge of the Comprehensive School,* Routledge and Kegan Paul.

HOSPERS, J (1969) *Introductory Readings in Aesthetics*, Collier MacMillan.
JONES, D (1973) *Epoch and Artist*, Faber and Faber.
JUNG, C *et al* (1964) *Man and his Symbols*, Aldus Books.
JUNG, C (1967) *The Spirit in Man, Art and Literature*, Routledge and Kegan Paul.
KANT, I (1952) *Critique of Pure Reason*, Oxford University Press.
KANT, I (1952) *Critique of Judgement*, Oxford University Press.
KOESTLER, A (1975) *The Act of Creation*, Picador.
LANGER, S (1953) *Feeling and Form*, Routledge and Kegan Paul.
LANGER, S (1957) *Philosophy in a New Key*, Havard.
LANGER, S (1957) *Problems of Art*, Routledge and Kegan Paul.
LANGER, S (1974) *Mind: An Essay on Human Feeling*, Johns Hopkins University Press.
LIPMAN, M (Ed.) (1973) *Contemporary Aesthetics*, Allyn and Bacon.
LODGE, D (1981) *Working with Structuralism*, Routledge and Kegan Paul.
MARCUSE, H (1978) *The Aesthetic Dimension*, Macmillan.
MUMFORD, L (1971) *The Myth of the Machine*, Secker and Warburg.
PHENIX, P (1964) *Realms of Meaning*, McGraw Hill.
POLANYI, M (1973) *Personal Knowledge*, Routledge and Kegan Paul.
READ, H (1943) *Education through Art*, Faber and Faber.
READ, H (1955) *Ikon and Idea*, Faber and Faber.
REDFERN, HB (1986) *Questions in Aesthetic Education*, Allen and Unwin.
REID, LA (1961) *Ways of Knowledge and Experience*, Allen and Unwin.
REID, LA (1970) *Meaning in the Arts*, Allen and Unwin.
REID, LA (1986) *Ways of Understanding and Education*, Heinemann Educational Books.
ROBERTSON, S (1982) *Rosegarden and Labyrinth: Art in Education*, Gryphon Press.
ROSS, M (1975) *Arts and the Adolescent*, Schools Council, Evans.
ROSS, M (1978) *The Creative Arts*, Heinemann Educational Books.
ROSS, M (1984) *The Aesthetic Impulse*, Pergamon.
ROSS, M (Ed) (1983) *The Arts in Education*, Falmer Press.
SCHILLER (1974) *On the Aesthetic Education of Man*, Clarendon Press.
SCRUTON, R (1974) *Art and Imagination*, Methuen.
SCRUTON, R (1979) *The Aesthetics of Architecture*, Methuen.
SCRUTON, R (1983) *The Aesthetic Understanding*, Methuen.
STEINER, G (1967) *Language and Silence*, Penguin.
STEINER, G (1986) *Real Presences*, Cambridge University Press.
STOKES, A (1965) *The Invitation in Art*, Tavistock.
STORR, A (1972) *Dynamics of Creation*, Penguin.
TIPPETT, M (1974) *Moving Into Aquarius*, Picador.
VALERY, P (1964) *Aesthetics*, Routledge and Kegan Paul.
WARNOCK, M (1980) *Imagination*, Faber and Faber.
WHALLEY, G (1953) *Poetic Process*, Greenwood Press.
WINNICOT, DW (1971) *Playing and Reality*, Tavistock.
WITKIN, R (1974) *The Intelligence of Feeling*, Heinemann Educational Books.
WITTGENSTEIN, L (1966) *Lectures and Conversations on Aesthetics, Psychology and Religious Belief*, Oxford University Press.

WOLLHEIM, R (1970) *Art and its Objects: An Introduction to Aesthetics*, Harper and Row.

English

ABBS, P (1982) *English Within the Arts*, Hodder and Stoughton.
ABBS, P (1985) *English as an Arts Discipline*, Take up No 2, Nationational Association for Education in the Arts.
ALLEN, D (1980) *English Teaching Since 1965*, Heinemann Educational Books.
BARNES, D (1969) *From Communication to Curriculum*, Penguin.
BARNES, D and TODD (1969) *Language the Learner and the School*, Penguin.
BRITTON, J (1972) *Language and Learning*, Penguin.
COOK, C (1917) *The Play Way*, Heinemann.
CREBER, J (1965) *Sense and Sensitivity*, University of London Press.
DIXON, J (1975) *Growth through English*, Oxford University Press.
HARRISON, B (1982) *An Arts-based Approach to English*, Hodder and Stoughton.
HOLBROOK, D *English for Maturity*, Cambridge University Press.
HOLBROOK, D (1979) *English for Meaning*, NFER.
HOURD, M (1949) *The Education of the Poetic Spirit*, Heinemann Educational Books.
ROSENBLATT, L (1970) *Literature as Exploration*, Heinemann Educational Books.
SAMPSON, G (1975) *English for the English*, Cambridge University Press.
SCHAYER, D (1972) *The Teaching of English in Schools 1900–1970*, Routledge and Kegan Paul.
WHITEHEAD, F (1971) *The Disappearing Dais*, Chatto and Windus.
WILKINSON, A (1971) *The Foundations of Language*, Oxford University Press.

Music

BROCKLEHURST, B (1971) *Response to Music: Principles of Music Education*, Routledge and Kegan Paul.
FLETCHER, RD (1985) 'New forms of examination in music: The assessment of listening: A discussion paper', unpublished paper generally available from the Secondary Examinations Council, Newcombe House, 45 Notting Hill Gate, London, W11 3JB, or from the author at 8 Olivers Battery Gardens, Winchester, Hants. SO22 4HF.
DES (1985) *General Certificate of Secondary Education: The National Criteria: Music*, HMSO.
DES (1985) *Music from 5–16*, Curriculum Matters 4, an HMI Series, HMSO.
HALE, NV (1947), *Education for Music: A Skeleton Plan of Research into the Development of the Study of Music as part of the Organized Plan of General Education*, Oxford University Press.
LONG, N (1959) *Music in English Education*, Faber and Faber.
NETTEL, R (1952) *The Englishman Makes Music*, Dennis Dobson.

PAYNTER, J (1972) *Hear and Now: An Introduction to Modern Music in Schools,* Universal Edition.

PAYNTER, J (1982) *Music in the Secondary School Curriculum: Trends and Developments in Class Music Teaching,* Cambridge University Press.

PAYNTER, J and ASTON, P (1970) *Sound and Silence: Classroom Projects in Creative Music,* Cambridge University Press.

PLUMMERIDGE, C et al (1981) *Issues in Music Education,* University of London Institute of Education Bedford Way Papers 3.

PRESTON, GHH (1986) 'A new approach to music examinations', *International Journal of Music Education,* May.

REIMER, B (1970) *A Philosophy of Music Education,* Prentice-Hall Inc.

SMALL, C (1977) *Music, Society, Education,* (2nd edn) John Calder.

SWANWICK, K (1979) *A Basis for Music Education,* NFER, Nelson Publishing.

SWANWICK, K and TAYLOR, D (1982) *Discovering Music: Developing the Music Curriculum in Secondary Schools,* Batsford Academic and Educational.

TAYLOR, D (1979) *Music Now: A Guide to Recent Developments and Current Opportunities in Music Education,* Open University Press.

Film (with notes)

Almost every aspect of film has its own immense bibliography. The following suggestions are simply introductions to a few relevant areas.

Courses Combining Theory and Practice

HERBERT, F MARGOLIS, 'The American scene and the problems of film education', *The Penguin Film Review,* January 1947.

WILLIAMS, C (1981) *Film-making and Film Theory,* This paper gives a detailed outline of a degree course and is the most persuasive short account of film teaching I have found, especially taken in its context.
See also:
ALVARADO, M 'Practical work in television studies', (BFI pamphlet).

BOBKER, LR (1969) *Elements of Film,* Harcourt, Brace.

DICKINSON, T (1921) *A Discovery of Cinema,* Oxford University Press.

HORNSBY, J 'The case for practical studies in media education', BFI pamphlet.

LINDGREN, E (1948) *The Art of the Film,* Allen and Unwin.

Practical Teaching Ideas

LOWNDES, D (1968) *Film Making in Schools,* Batsford — highly recommended.

WALL, I and KRUGER, S (1986) *Reading a Film.* This pack of materials is available free, as part of British Film Year, from Film Education, 12 St. George's Avenue, London W5.

Literary Adaptations, Screenplays etc.

BLUESTONE, G (1957) *Novels into Film*, Johns Hopkins Press — American cinema.

CORLISS, R (1975) *Talking Pictures*, David and Charles.

COULOURIS and HERRMANN (1972) 'The Citizen Kane book', *Sight and Sound*, spring.

KAEL, P (1971) *The Citizen Kane Book*, Secker and Warburg.

MCFARLANE, B (1984) *Words and Images*, Secker and Warburg — Australian cinema.

Auteurism, Structuralism etc.

BRITTON, A 'The Ideology of Screen', *Movie* 26, winter 78/79 — fairly impenetrable but effective critique of theories derived from Althusser, Lacan and Barthes.

CAUGHIE, J (Ed) (1981) *Theories of Authorship*, RKP recommended.

COOK, P (Ed) (1985) *The Cinema Book*, BFI thorough summaries, but written in the deadly style of the new academicism.

NICHOLS, B (Ed) (1976) *Movies and Methods*, University of California Press highly recommended.

WOLLEN, P (1969) *Signs and Meaning in the Cinema*, Secker and Warburg.

Critical Studies of Directors

ANDERSON, L (1981) *About John Ford Plexus* — this is the most intelligent study of any body of work in films. Anyone more interested in theory than film should perhaps consult the sections on Ford in *Theories of Authorship* and *Movies and Methods*.

ARANDA, F (1975) *Luis Buñuel: A Critical Biography*, Secker and Warburg.

BAZIN, A (1974) *Jean Renoir*, W.H. Allen.

BJÖRKMAN, MANNS, SIMA (1973) *Bergman on Bergman*, Secker and Warburg — Interviews.

BOGDANOVITCH, P (1978) *John Ford*, University of California Press — Interviews.

DURGNAT, R (1973) *Jean Renoir*, University of California Press.

MCBRIDE, W (1974) *John Ford*, Secker and Warburg.

PLACE, JA (1974) *The Western Films of John Ford*, Citadel Press.

PLACE, JA (1979) *The Non-Western Films of John Ford*, Citadel Press.

RENOIR, J (1974) *My Life and My Films*, Collins.

ROUD, R (Ed) (1980) *Cinema, A Critical Dictionary*, Secker and Warburg.

SALLES GOMES, PE (1972) *Jean Vigo*, Secker and Warburg — recommended.

SARRIS, A (1976) *The John Ford Movie Mystery*, Secker and Warburg.

SESONSKE, A (1980) *Jean Renoir, the French Films, 1924–1939*, Harvard University Press — highly recommended.

SIMON, J (1973) *Ingmar Bergman Directs*, Davis-Poynter.

TRUFFAUT, F (1968) *Hitchcock*, Secker and Warburg — Interviews.
WOOD, R (1965) *Hitchcock's Films*, Zwemmer — highly recommended.
WOOD, R (1968) *Howard Hawks*, Secker and Warburg — recommended.

Historical Development of Film

BROWNLOW, K (1968) *The Parade's Gone By...*, Secker and Warburg.
CERAM, CW (1965) *Archaeology of the Cinema*, Thames and Hudson.
COE, B (1981) *The History of Movie Photography*, Ash and Grant.
DICKINSON, T (1971) *A Discovery of Cinema*, Oxford University Press.
MONTAGU, I (1964) *Film World*, Penguin.
SALT, B (1983) *Film Style and Technology: History and Analysis* — highly recommended.
WENDEN, DJ (1975) *The Birth of the Movies*, Macdonald and Jane's.

Dance

ADSHEAD, J (1981) *The Study of Dance*, Dance Books Ltd.
ADSHEAD, J and LAYSON, J (Eds) (1984) *Dance History*, Dance Books Ltd.
BANES, S (1980) *Terpsichore in Sneakers: Post Modern Dance*, Houghton Mifflin.
BEST, D (1974) *Expression in Movement and the Arts*, Lepus Books.
BEST, D (1978) *Philosophy and Human Movement*, Unwin Educational Books.
GULBENKIAN FOUNDATION (1980) *Dance Education and Training in Britain*, Oyez Press.
MYERS, G and FANCHER, G (Eds) (1981) *Philosophical Essays on Dance*, Dance Horizons.
HUMPHREY, D (1959) *The Art of Making Dances*, Dance Books Ltd.
KRAUS, R (1969) *History of the Dance*, Prentice Hall.
LABAN, R (1960) *The Mastery of Movement*, Macdonald and Evans.
LANGER, SK (1953) *Feeling and Form*, chapters 11 and 12, Routledge and Kegan Paul Ltd.
PRESTON-DUNLOP, V (1980) *A Handbook for Dance in Education*, MacDonald and Evans.
REDFERN, B (1982) *Concepts in Modern Educational Dance*, Dance Books Ltd.
REDFERN, B (1983) *Dance, Art and Aesthetics*, Dance Books Ltd.
SMITH, JM (1976) *Dance Composition*, Lepus Books.
SORELL, W (1981) *Dance in its Time: The Emergence of an Art Form*, Anchor Press.
ULLMANN, L (1984) *A Vision of Dynamic Space*, Falmer Press.

Drama

ALLEN, J (1979) *Drama in Schools: Its Theory and Practice*, Heinemann.

BOLTON, G (1979) *Towards a Theory of Drama in Education*, Longman.

BOLTON, G (1983) *Bolton at the Barbican*, National Association for Teachers of Drama.

BOLTON, G (1984) *Drama as Education*, Longman.

DAY, C (1975) *Drama for Middle and Upper Schools*, Batsford.

HEATHCOTE, D (1980) *Drama as Context*, NATE.

HEATHCOTE, D (1982) 'Signs and portents?', *SCYPT Journal*, 9, April.

JOHNSON, L and O'NEILL, C (Eds) (1983) *Selected Writings of Dorothy Heathcote*, Hutchinson.

LINNELL, R (1982) *Approaching Classroom Drama*, Edward Arnold.

McGREGOR, L TATE, M and ROBINSON, K (1977) *Learning through Drama*, Schools Council Drama Teaching Project (10–11), Heinemann.

O'NEILL, C and LAMBERT, A (1982) *Drama Structures*, Hutchinson.

ROBINSON, K (1980) *Exploring Theatre and Education*, Heinemann.

SLADE, P (1954) *Child Drama*, University of London Press.

WAGNER, BJ (1978) *Dorothy Heathcote: Drama as a Learning Medium*, National Education Association.

WATKINS, B (1981) *Drama and Education*, Batsford Academic and Educational.

WAY, B (1967) *Development Through Drama*, Longman.

Visual Arts

ADAMS, E (1982) *Art & the Built Environment* Schools Council, Longman.

ART ADVISERS ASSOCIATION (1978) *Learning Through Drawing*, Art Advisors Association, North East Region.

BARRATT, M (1979) *Art Education: A Strategy for Course Design*, Heinemann Educational Books.

BAYNES, K (1976) *About Design*, Heinemann Educational Books.

BERGER, J (1972) *Ways of Seeing*, Penguin.

EISNER, E (1972) *Educating Artistic Vision*, Macmillan.

FRY, R (1920) *Vision and Design*, Chatto and Windus.

GENTLE, K (1985) *Children and Art Teaching*, Croom Helm.

GREEN, P (1974) *Design Education: Problem Solving and Visual Experience*, Batsford.

LOWENFIELD, V (1947) *Creative and Mental Growth*, Collier Macmillan.

READ, H (1943) *Education Through Art*, Faber.

RICHARDSON, M (1948) *Art and the Child*, University of London Press.

ROBERTSON, S (1982) *Rosegarden and Labyrinth* Gryphon Press.

ROWLAND, K (1968) *Learning to See*, Ginn and Co.

De SAUSMAREZ, M (1964) *Basic Design: The Dynamics of Visual Form*.

VIOLA, W (1936) *Child Art*, Simpkin Marshall.

Notes on Contributors

PETER ABBS is Lecturer in Education at the University of Sussex where he directs, with Trevor Pateman, the Master of Arts course *Language, the Arts and Education*, as well as running the PGCE English curriculum group. He is author of a number of works on education and culture, including *Autobiography in Education* (Gryphon Press); *Reclamations: Essays on Culture, Mass-Culture and the Curriculum* (Gryphon Press); and *English Within the Arts* (Hodder and Stoughton). He has published two volumes of poetry: *For Man and Islands* (Gryphon Press) and *Songs of a New Taliesin* (Gryphon Press). Currently he is working on a study of the autobiographical impulse in Western culture, parts of which have been published in *The Pelican Guide to English Literature, Vol. 8* and as the introduction to the recent Penguin English Library Edition of Edmund Gosse's *Father and Son*.

PETER FULLER is one of our most influential art critics. He has written extensively for *New Society, Art Monthly* and *Design*. His books include: *Art and Psychoanalysis, Beyond the Crisis in Art, Aesthetics after Modernism* and *Images of God*. His most recent contribution has been an experimental autobiography *Marches Past* published in the spring of 1986.

ANNA HAYNES is a freelance, Laban trained teacher of modern dance, currently lecturing at the City Literary Institute, London. She also runs open classes and workshops in the south of England; is involved in 'in-service' teacher-training courses, and weekend workshops and summer schools in England, Scandinavia and Europe. Trained in classical ballet, mime and contemporary dance, she is a graduate of the Laban Art of Movement Centre. Previous teaching posts include a girls' comprehensive in the East end, primary school work in the West Country and a lectureship in dance at the University of London, Goldsmiths' College. Her interest and commitment to the concept of a unified arts curriculum stems from active involvement in the experimental arts-based 'Looking Glass School' in Somerset and the University of Exeter 'Curriculum Issues in Arts Education' project. Present MA studies in *Language, the Arts and Education* at the University of Sussex have increased this commitment. She is editor of the Southern Dance Teachers' Association biannual magazine.

CHRISTOPHER HAVELL was trained as a primary school teacher at King Alfred's College of Education, Winchester. He taught in junior and secondary schools before being appointed as one of the first ILEA drama advisory teachers. He now tutors teachers on in-service courses that lead to advanced drama teaching qualifications. He is an external examiner for the Royal Society of Arts Diploma and Advanced Diploma examinations for drama teachers and is also a member of the RSA's Drama Committee and various sub-committees that were responsible for drawing up new syllabus. He is currently interested in exploring the aesthetic nature of the experience in drama process, an interest that stems from the *Language, the Arts and Education* course at the University of Sussex.

MARION METCALFE was born in New Zealand and came to England in 1972 where she is currently Head of Music at the Grove School, St. Leonards-on-sea, Sussex. As well as running a lively music department in her own school, she is also a member of the South East Regional Examining Board Music Panel, the Southern Examining Group Subject Working Party for Music, and the Secondary Examinations Council GCSE Committee for Music. She has an honours degree in music, a licentiate of the Royal School of Music, and has recently completed an MA in *Language, the Arts and Education* at the University of Sussex.

ROBIN MORRIS has had wide experience of teaching and examining the visual arts since doing his fine art training at Brighton Polytechnic. For seven years he acted as a moderator in the 16+ art and design examinations. He has recently completed his MA in *Language, the Arts and Education* at the University of Sussex and even more recently moved from being Head of Art at South Hunsley School in North Humberside to becoming Head of Art at Brighton, Hove and Sussex Sixth Form College in Sussex.

ROBERT WATSON was educated at the London School of Film Technique, (1967–69) and later at Brighton College of Education and the University of Sussex. Since 1976 he has taught English and some film studies in comprehensive schools in Dorset, West Glamorgan and Suffolk. In 1982 he became Fiction Reviews Editor of the quarterly journal *The Gadfly*. Publications include contributions to *Tract, Poetry Wales, The Use of English, Planet* and the novels *Events Beyond the Heartlands* (1980), and *Rumours of Fulfilment* (1982) (both Heinemann). He has recently been appointed as lecturer in English at Bretton Hall College, Yorkshire.

EDWIN WEBB has taught in secondary schools and a technical college; is currently senior lecturer in English at a London college of education. He has also been a guest lecturer and speaker for a variety of organizations and institutions. His literary and critical articles, educational writings and poetry have been widely published in UK, Commonwealth and American journals. His most recent publication is *Notes on Spontaneous Cases* (Platform Poets, 84). He has also produced with Edward Lee *The Sounds of Poetry* (Sussex Tapes 1985) a cassette to encourage a direct awareness of the power of poetry.

Index

Pages in **bold** refer to plates, and in *italics* refer to figures. An 'n' represents a note.